The Politics of Intersectionality

The Politics of Intersectionality series builds on the longstanding insights of intersectionality theory from a vast variety of disciplinary perspectives. The books in this series represent an interrogation of intersectionality at various levels of analysis. They unabashedly foreground the politics of intersectionality in a way that is designed to both honor the legacy of earlier scholarship and push the boundaries of intersectionality's value to the academy and most importantly to the world. We interpret the series title, "The Politics of Intersectionality," in two general ways:

First, we emphasize the politics of intersectionality, broadly conceived; that is to say we include debates among scholars regarding the proper conceptualization and application of the term "intersectionality" as part and parcel of the series' intellectual project. What this means pragmatically is that rather than dictatorially denote an extant definition of intersectionality and impose it on every author's manuscript, as series editors our task has been to push each author to grapple with their own conceptualization of intersectionality and facilitate their interaction with an ever-growing body of global scholarship, policy, and advocacy work as they render such a conceptualization *transparent* to readers, *reflexive* as befits the best feminist work, and *committed* to rigorous standards of quality no matter the subject, the method, or the conclusions. As editors we have taken such an active role precisely because grappling with the politics of intersectionality demands our adherence to the normative standards of transparency, reflexivity, and speaking to multiple and mutually constituting sites of power for which intersectionality is not only known but lauded as the gold standard. It is our honor to build this area of scholarship across false boundaries of theory and praxis, artificially distinct academic disciplines, and the semipermeable line between scholarship and activism. No less importantly we emphasize politics to mean, well, *politics*, whether everyday senses of justice; so-called formal politics of social movements, campaigns, elections, policy, and government institutions; or personal politics of identity, community, and activism across a broad swath of the world. While this general conceptualization of politics lends itself to the social sciences, we define social sciences in a broad way that again seeks to unite theoretical concerns (whether normative or positive) with interpretive and empirical approaches across an array of topics far too numerous to list in their entirety.

The second way we interpret the series title is with an emphasis on the word intersectionality. That is, the books in this series do not depend solely on 20-year old articulations of intersectionality; they are steeped in a rich literature of both substantive and analytical depth that in the twenty-first century reaches around the world. This is not your professor's "women of color" or "race-class-gender" series of the late twentieth century. As series editors we seek to develop manuscripts that aspire to engagement with the best and brightest global thinking on intersectionality as a body of research that is in fact worthy of the intellectual, political, and personal risks taken by so many of its earliest interlocutors in voicing and naming this work. We thus relate to intersectionality as both methodological and analytical tools that are firmly rooted in the epistemological tradition of the feminist-situated gaze but do not necessarily prioritize discussion of gender relations over other crosscutting social, economic, and political power relations.

Series Editors:

Ange-Marie Hancock, University of Southern California
Nira Yuval-Davis, University of East London

Also in the series:

Solidarity Politics for Millennials
Ange-Marie Hancock

Social Change and Intersectional Activism: The Spirit of Social Movement
Sharon Doetsch-Kidder

Urban Black Women and the Politics of Resistance
Zenzele Isoke

Gender Equality, Intersectionality, and Diversity in Europe
Lise Rolandsen Agustín

Gender Equality, Intersectionality, and Diversity in Europe

Lise Rolandsen Agustín

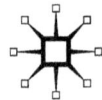

GENDER EQUALITY, INTERSECTIONALITY, AND DIVERSITY IN EUROPE
Copyright © Lise Rolandsen Agustín, 2013.

Softcover reprint of the hardcover 1st edition 2013 978-1-137-02808-2

All rights reserved.

First published in 2013 by
PALGRAVE MACMILLAN®
in the United States—a division of St. Martin's Press LLC,
175 Fifth Avenue, New York, NY 10010.

Where this book is distributed in the UK, Europe and the rest of the world, this is by Palgrave Macmillan, a division of Macmillan Publishers Limited, registered in England, company number 785998, of Houndmills, Basingstoke, Hampshire RG21 6XS.

Palgrave Macmillan is the global academic imprint of the above companies and has companies and representatives throughout the world.

Palgrave® and Macmillan® are registered trademarks in the United States, the United Kingdom, Europe and other countries.

ISBN 978-1-349-43990-4   ISBN 978-1-137-02810-5 (eBook)

DOI 10.1057/9781137028105

Library of Congress Cataloging-in-Publication Data is available from the Library of Congress.

A catalogue record of the book is available from the British Library.

Design by Newgen Imaging Systems (P) Ltd., Chennai, India.

First edition: July 2013

10 9 8 7 6 5 4 3 2 1

*To Óscar and Kira
Linus and Marcos*

Contents

Series Introduction: The Politics of Intersectionality — ix
Acknowledgments — xi

Introduction: Challenges to European Union Gender Equality Policies — 1

1. Policy making, Institutionalization, and Collective Mobilization: A Model for Transnational Intersectional Analysis — 25

2. Gender and Other Inequalities in the Institutionalization of Multiple Discrimination Policies — 49

3. Minority Intersectional Constituencies and Women's Collective Mobilization at the European Level — 67

4. Gender-Based Violence and the Framing of Equality Policies — 89

5. Transnational Policy Framings: (De)Gendering in the Context of Institutionalization — 117

6. Problematizing the "Gendered Other": Integration, Violence, and Culturalization — 141

Conclusions: Interrelating Gender Equality, Intersectionality, and Diversity at the Transnational Level — 157

Appendix   List of Empirical Documents: European Union Policies on Multiple Discrimination and on Gender-Based Violence — 171
Notes — 187
Bibliography — 201
Index — 215

Series Introduction: The Politics of Intersectionality

Currently intersectionality scholarship lacks a meaningful clearinghouse of work that speaks across (again false) boundaries of a particular identity community under study (e.g., Black lesbians, women of color, environmental activists), academic disciplines or the geographical location from which the author writes (e.g., Europe, North America, Southeast Asia). For that reason we expect that the bibliographies of the manuscripts will be almost as helpful as the manuscripts themselves, particularly for senior professors who train graduate students and graduate students seeking to immerse themselves broadly and deeply in contemporary approaches to intersectionality. We are less sanguine, however, about the plethora of modifiers that have emerged to somehow modulate intersectionality—whether it be intersectional stigma, intersectional political consciousness, intersectional praxis, post-intersectionality, paradigm intersectionality or even Crenshaw's original modes of structural and political intersectionality. Our emphasis has been on building the subfield rather than consciously expanding the lexicon of modes and specialities for intersectionality.

In this fifth book in the series, we are expanding our focus from social movements and theoretical debates to study also the ways politics of intersectionality operate in the arena of public policies. Rolandsen Agustín studies the complex ways in which the EU has been tackling issues of diversity and intersectionality. In particular she differentiates but also examines the relationships between questions of mobilization and issues of institutionalization of policies in the EU. Focusing on the EU also facilitates the examination of the methodological question of how to study politics and policies of intersectionality in the supra-, if not transnational space.

One of the major contributions of this book is serving as a cautionary tale for policy makers from other regions of the world who seek to implement such policies at the national or transnational level as well as for feminist and other activists who seek to intervene in this domain.

While on the one hand this tale is disappointing to strong advocates of intersectionality, to ignore these risks might just enhance them in other parts of the world. Part of the issue, of course, is that just advocating politics and policies of intersectionality is a necessary but not a sufficient step and the analysis offered in this book is important when we aspire to refine and constitute case-sensitive approaches to tackle these issues. To do so, Rolandsen Agustín suggests we differentiate analytically, when studying these issues, between the dimensions of ideas, agency, and context that interact with each other as strategic policy frames are set forward in a context of particular political and discursive opportunity structures, which create dynamics of inclusion and exclusion within the European transnational framework of multilevel politics.

The Politics of Intersectionality series therefore includes theoretical, empirical, and policy considerations of the ways questions of equality, diversity, and marginalizations are being tackled in different geographical, social, and political spaces. We welcome further proposals from any scholar or activist who can offer us and the readership of the series further insights of these complex issues in either a monograph or an edited volume.

Acknowledgments

Thanks are due to a lot of people who helped and encouraged me through the long research process leading up to the writing of this book, which builds on my PhD dissertation, submitted and defended in early 2011. First of all I would like to thank Birte Siim and Anette Borchorst, my supervisors during the PhD studies. Whereas Birte has always enthusiastically encouraged me to take up any challenge, big or small, that presented itself along the way, Anette has constantly reminded me not to get lost or lose sight of the road ahead. Together they have made a tremendous effort to guide me with their insights, knowledge, and constructive comments. I want to extend this acknowledgment to my other colleagues at the Feminist and Gender Research Centre (FREIA) and at the Center for Equality, Diversity, and Gender (EDGE), both at Aalborg University (Denmark). I want to thank every single member of FREIA and EDGE for making my day-to-day working life so positive and enjoyable. Particular thanks are due to Christina Fiig, Lotte Bloksgaard, Helene Pristed Nielsen, Pauline Stoltz, and Diana Højlund Madsen for common research endeavors and debates, and for commenting on individual chapters of this book. I am grateful to Ruth Emerek for inviting me into the Expert Group on Gender, Social Inclusion and Employment (EGGSIE) and for introducing me in this way to the "Brussels machinery." Thanks are also due to staff members and colleagues of the Department of Culture and Global Studies at Aalborg University.

The kindness and hospitality that I met during my research stay with the QUING team at Complutense University in Madrid in 2007 is incomparable, and I want to thank María Bustelo and Emanuela Lombardo in particular for taking me in and for contributing to my research. I also want to thank Ana Fernández de Vega for being an amazing teammate in our common work on the EU, and the entire QUING network, headed by Mieke Verloo, for sharing work, thoughts, debates, and meals at the Vienna seminars.

In the last couple of years, I have worked closely with a number of researchers on common articles and book chapters, which have inspired the research developed and presented in this book. Thanks are due to Emanuela Lombardo, for her inclusiveness and generosity; to Silke Roth, for a constructive and efficient cooperation; and to Celeste Montoya, for the hard work and inspiring conversations. It has been a great privilege and a pleasure working with all of you, and I look forward to continuing the collaborations.

Others have commented on drafts and papers, showed an interest in my research and encouraged me, allowed me to participate in interesting seminars and conferences, given me the opportunity to publish my work, and/or shared their work and experiences with me: thanks to Petra Ahrens, Carol Bacchi, Jean-Michel Bonvin, Cristina Borderías, Thomas Bredgaard, Maria Carbin, Camilla Elg, Karen Celis, Sarah Childs, Sara Clavero, Yvonne Galligan, Jane Freedman, Bernard Harris, Anne Maria Holli, Johanna Kantola, Andrea Krizsán, Ann Phoenix, Raluca Popa, Sune Qvotrup Jensen, Merce Renom, Hilda Rømer Christensen, Birgit Sauer, Judith Squires, Sofia Strid, Pat Thane, Mieke Verloo, Sylvia Walby, Fiona Williams, and Alison Woodward.

In Brussels and beyond, I want to express my immense gratitude to the representatives from the EU institutions and European women's organizations who contributed, through interviews, to the realization of this book with their time, energy, and insights. Furthermore, I want to thank my dear friend Maria Zuber for hosting me and showing me the "ropes" of the European Commission through the eyes of an insider.

A number of people helped me in particular in terms of transforming the research material presented here from a PhD dissertation into a book. First I want to thank the members of the PhD evaluation committee, Henrik Halkier, Myra Marx Ferree, and Johanna Kantola. Not only did they make the experience of defending the dissertation an enjoyable one, with their constructive approach and interest in the academic debates, they also provided me with useful comments, insights, and ideas for further elaboration of the material and the arguments. This has helped me tremendously in the subsequent work with the book manuscript. Together with Birte Siim I elaborated on the theoretical ideas of the dissertation through a number of common articles and book chapters concerning transnational intersectionality. I would never have embarked on writing this book had it not been for her encouragement, practical help, and academic discussions. Decisive in the leap from dissertation to book were also Nira Yuval-Davis and

Ange-Marie Hancock, editors of the book series "The Politics of Intersectionality." Thank you so much for your generosity and for giving me this opportunity. Thanks are extended to Robyn Curtis, Matthew Kopel, Scarlet Neath, Ciara Vincent, and Desiree Browne at Palgrave Macmillan for all the help, support, and patience in the realization of the final manuscript, and to Cecilie Zhang for taking on the task of reading the whole piece with a keen eye.

Finally, I want to thank my parents, my sister and my brother, and the rest of our amazing family and friends. Kira, thank you for making it so easy to get the priorities right between work and family life and for making sure that intensive writing was combined with hours of fun and joy. Óscar, my greatest thank you goes to you for being a constant source of support, inspiration, and encouragement, and for always lending a ear, and your bright head, to my academic concerns.

LISE ROLANDSEN AGUSTÍN
Aalborg, August 2012

Introduction: Challenges to European Union Gender Equality Policies

Gender equality policies in the European Union (EU) have, from the adoption of the equal-pay principle in the 1957 Treaty of Rome up until the late 1980s, mainly focused on equal treatment in the employment field. In the 1980s and especially in the 1990s measures of positive action and equal opportunities were increasingly introduced in the soft law policies of the Union.[1] In this way a dual-track strategy emerged, combining formal equality before the law (equal treatment and women's rights) with substantive equality of outcome (positive action and gender equality) (Hoskyns 1996; Kantola 2010; Lombardo 2003; Lombardo and Meier 2007; Rees 1998; Stratigaki 2005).[2] However, in the mid- and late 1990s, the limited impact of both equal treatment and positive action led to the introduction of a third gender equality strategy, namely gender mainstreaming (Squires 2007). All policies at all levels should take into account gender equality concerns and the potentially gendered impact of their adoption. This was a way of directing attention toward structural and systemic dimensions of gender inequality, and at the same time the strategy broadened the scope of EU gender equality policies to areas outside employment (Kantola 2010; Lombardo 2003; Lombardo and Meier 2007; Stratigaki 2005).[3]

Nevertheless, the dominant discourse on gender equality, not least in the European Commission (EC) and the Council, has been marked by the main objective of increasing women's labor-market participation (Duncan 1996).[4] This is directly linked to aims of economic development and growth (COM[2000]335; COM[2006]92): Higher rates of women's labor-market participation are thought to strengthen economic competitiveness by enhancing the labor force as well as diversifying it. Thus, the Europe 2020 strategy for jobs and growth, adopted by the Council in March 2010, includes the aim of a 75 percent employment rate for both women and men, and the 2009

Council conclusions on gender equality: Strengthening growth and employment specifically state that

> gender equality is crucial for fulfilling the EU objectives of economic and social cohesion and of a high level of employment, as well as for ensuring sustainable growth and competitiveness, and for tackling the demographic challenge; all these aims can be furthered by reaching the target of higher employment rates for women and men. (15488/09)

This book focuses on how specific gender equality policies in the EU have come about by analyzing policy-making processes and negotiations over policy meanings, which include both EU institutional actors and civil society organizations operating at the transnational level. The empirical analyses of the different chapters illustrate the ways in which the dominant discourses and practices of the EU gender equality policy framework influence what can be done and proposed through current policy-making structures and mechanisms, as well as vice versa. As an example, gender equality demands that are phrased and formulated in such a way as to resonate with the dominant EU discourse of economic growth will have a better chance of impacting policies, even if this means reducing the meaning of gender equality to cover mainly women's labor-market participation. Inspired by the methodological perspective of frame analysis, I consider frames, such as the articulation of gender equality as women's labor-market participation, to relate to discourses, such as the one on economic growth, in the sense that frames draw on discourses as general ideational frameworks. Framing can be considered a possibility of enacting agency within the limits and constraints of a particular discourse.

Shedding light on these processes of policy making, throughout the book I focus particularly on the institutionalization of intersectionality in the EU and the ways in which intersectionality concerns have developed at the transnational level. This is linked to the Amsterdam Treaty (1997), which introduced one of the major novelties of EU equality policies in the last decades, namely article 13 on antidiscrimination.[5] This article has become a common point of reference for European policy makers[6] and academic scholars alike (Kantola 2010; Lombardo et al. 2009a; Squires 2007; 2010; Van der Vleuten 2007). It envisages EU actions to combat the six grounds of discrimination: sex, racial or ethnic origin, religion or belief, disability, age, or sexual orientation.[7] The EU works with a multiple discrimination perspective on these grounds, meaning that there is a focus on addressing several grounds together when pertinent (see the 2007 EC report "Tackling Multiple Discrimination. Practices, Policies and Laws"). Together with the introduction of article 13 of the Amsterdam Treaty and multiple discrimination policies on the EU policy agenda, I argue that the enlargement process, the right-wing turn in member-state policies as well as in the composition of the Council and the European Parliament (EP), the struggle over competences, and the increased focus on migratory processes and minority groups, as well as economic growth and employment have impacted the discourses of the three key EU institutions (Commission, Parliament, and Council) and influenced the understanding of gender equality within the EU.

However, it does not follow from this interpretation of recent events in EU policy making within the social field that developments are linear. Rather, I dispute the idea of an evolutionary policy constantly increasing and improving the gender equality content of EU policies. On the contrary, I find developments to be marked by conjunctures or waves through which strong gender equality substance is replaced by weaker notions and vice versa. Similarly, strong notions in one area coexist with weak notions in other areas. I thus contest the suggestion made by Ruzza (2004) that "bureaucratic incrementalist logics" may take over once a policy issue is introduced on the EU agenda; I do not find this to be necessarily the case in the field of gender equality policies. Usually, elements of policies articulated in the context of EU gender equality policies in recent years have references or more elaborated antecedents in the early years of the EP.

The political scope for action is always contested as gender equality policies beyond the labor market is placed in a limbo between the impossibility of advancing policies due to legal constraints, the division of competences between the EU and the member states, as well as member states' reluctance, and the apparently strong political will demonstrated by specific actors across the institutional spectrum.[8] Gender equality policies are a particularly interesting policy field in this sense; it is a contested area of policy development and this strengthens the research interest in the negotiation of the policy content and the lessons that can be drawn from its analyses. One Council representative interviewed in relation to this research endeavor particularly argues that gender equality policies are understood to be a sensitive political area due to its value-laden characteristics:

> We have actually had some quite hard battles in order to agree on some of the texts in [the gender equality] field precisely, harder than I have

experienced with any of the other fields because there are such cultural values behind this really... I think there is more of a struggle regarding gender equality... When we have had debates on gender equality, then they have been harder to finish, it has been more ferocious debates, they have reached a higher level [institutionally]... So I actually think, you could say that, that there is somehow more at stake because it is a matter of value communities. (Council official, permanent representation, interview June 2010)

In this sense, gender equality stands out as a policy field from which we can learn important lessons about policy-making processes. More importantly in a broader perspective, the role of the EU case can be used as a lens through which we can interpret and assess transnational politics in general. The EU case analyzed here is, in many senses, a forerunner of transnational policy making due to its relatively advanced multilevel structure. Even though the EU in these terms is rather unique on a global level, the case nevertheless potentially sheds light on transnational policy dynamics elsewhere, be that in other regions or at a universal level. This concerns, for instance, other contexts in which a multiplicity of states are involved in policy negotiations or where civil society actors make use of differentiated channels of institutional access, at different levels of decision making, in order to make an impact on policy outputs. Whereas the EU is an advanced case of both transnational policy dynamics and multilevel policy structures, the findings of this case study may shed light on similar yet less-developed trends elsewhere in the world and on a global level, for instance, through the institutions of the United Nations.

AIM OF THE BOOK

Empirically, the book analyses EU policy-making processes in the field of gender equality, up until 2010, with a particular focus on diversity and intersectionality. The focus is placed on gender as a ground of discrimination. The legal and institutional framework of multiple inequalities is a challenge for gender equality policies (Squires 2007) and, thus, the tension between different grounds of discrimination is one of the key dimensions of this book. Concerns have been voiced by civil society actors as to whether gender would be marginalized with the increased attention to multiple discrimination. This debate is central to the contents and analyses of the book, as it seeks to uncover the impact that the particular way of institutionalizing intersectionality in the EU has had on gender equality policies and whether or not processes of policy degendering has occurred as a consequence of this. At the same time the civil society landscape at the European, transnational level is becoming increasingly diversified as new groups begin to mobilize. Herein lies a potential for a second impact of the institutionalization of intersectionality in terms of gender concerns, in this case the ways in which women's interests are being represented in EU policies and policy-making processes through civil society participation and whether or not this interaction may have changed due to intersectional concerns, that is, how women's organizations and their demands are included or excluded from policy making.

Analyzing the developments that have characterized EU gender equality policies and women's mobilization at the European, transnational level since the introduction of multiple discrimination policies, two specific challenges are identified: (1) diversity of women's interests and (2) concerns regarding the degendering of policies. On the one hand, these two aspects are separate, in that the former focuses primarily on the civil society panorama and its actors and the latter on policy making. On the other hand, they are interrelated as they address some of the developments that have characterized the field of EU gender equality policies in recent years, especially after the introduction of the multiple discrimination approach.

The diversity challenge is intensively discussed in the literature, both on a theoretical and on an empirical level. Some attention has been directed toward the interaction (alliances or competitions) between different nongovernmental organizations (NGOs) combating discrimination and inequality (see for instance Woodward 2006). However, little focus has been placed on transnational organizations working with constituencies who are discriminated against in multiple ways.[9] I analyze the challenges faced by these organizations and their interaction with majority organizations focusing on one discrimination ground exclusively. I also seek to address the ways in which majority organizations themselves handle the challenges coming from the current panorama of European, transnational civil society that includes both organizations covering other discrimination grounds and minority organizations. The aim is to cover new empirical ground by identifying, analyzing, and discussing the diversity challenges faced by women's organizations in Europe. Furthermore, I analyze the interaction between the different transnational women's organizations and the EU institutions with a particular focus on processes of in/exclusion.

As regards degendering, this can be defined as the disappearance or inarticulation of gender dimensions in relevant policies of a given field or institution. Even though references to the concern regarding degendering recur in the relevant literature, few scholars have conducted detailed textual analyses of the phenomenon or looked into policy-making processes and immediate policy consequences.[10] I analyze whether or not tendencies of degendering can be detected and to what extent they might be problematic for gender equality objectives at the EU level. The increased focus on diversity and multiple discrimination in EU polices may lead to a diminished focus on gender and, subsequently, a degendering of policies. In this way, the two identified challenges are intimately related to each other.

Mobilization and Institutionalization

The book is structured around the two thematic challenges related to the development of intersectionality at the transnational level, as mentioned above, namely those of diversity (chapters 2 and 3) and degendering (chapters 4 and 5), as well as the interrelation between them (chapter 6). I argue that transnational intersectionality in practice concerns processes of institutionalization and mobilization (chapter 1). This means that both a top-down and a bottom-up perspective are included in the theoretical arguments and empirical analyses presented in the book. Processes of institutionalization and mobilization occur in relation to three different levels, each of them addressed in the individual chapters of the book: (1) the institutional setup (see especially chapter 2 on multiple discrimination and chapter 5 on transnational policy framings); (2) policies and policy making (see especially chapter 4 on policies combating gender-based violence and chapter 6 on the "gendered other"); and (3) civil society mobilization and interaction (see especially chapter 3 on minority intersectional constituencies). Attending to intersectionality at the transnational level through mobilization means that we must look at the diversity of (intersecting) voices present in civil society through the organizing of majority and minority women, their demands, and the ways in which they are in/excluded as policy interlocutors of the transnational institutions of the EU. The dimension of institutionalization is concerned with making room for diversity in policies (i.e., the content and the diverse interpretations of "women's interests" and "gender equality") as well as in policy making (i.e., the institutional processes of in/exclusion).

Thus, throughout the chapters and analyses of this book, I will argue that the development and practice of intersectionality at the European, transnational level are the result of the parallel and interrelated processes of mobilization, on the one hand, and institutionalization, on the other. Mobilization refers here to the claims-making efforts set forward by transnational women's organizations in their attempts to influence EU policies on gender equality as well as their representation of the diversity of women's voices, seen from a transnational perspective. Conceiving mobilization as a dual dynamic that covers both the representation of interests through civil society activism and the inclusion of these voices and interests in institutional policies and policy-making processes through participatory mechanisms, I analyze in-depth the ways in which mobilization, in particular of transnational women's organizations, has been conducive to the way in which intersectionality is developed and practiced transnationally through EU policies and institutional structures. Social movements can attempt to put pressure on decision-making institutions in order to achieve change, but they are often limited in their efforts by the discursive structures in which they are embedded:

> Movement actors and institutional actors often participate in the same discourse, framing specific ideas differently... Institutional discourses carry important assumptions that affect what even the challengers' discursive logic is able to "see." (Ferree and Merrill 2000, 459)

Thus, ideas are included and excluded through framing processes (Ferree 2003). In other words, I argue that while transnational mobilization of women's interests is constrained by the EU discourses and practices, it has nevertheless, at times, been decisive in terms of how, and which gender equality concerns were placed and maintained on the EU policy agenda and thus contributing to the institutionalization of intersectionality concerns.

Institutionalization, in turn, is conceptualized in this context as the ways in which policies and policy-making processes at the transnational level include and direct attention towards different inequalities. This concerns both policy contents and participatory processes, as mentioned above, that is, the potential inclusion of civil society organizations in policy-making processes or what can also be labeled as the institution/civil society interface of the EU gender machinery.[11] Thus, I analyze the ways in which intersectional concerns have been institutionalized at the transnational level by looking at the ways in which gender equality policies are formulated and framed, on the one hand, and at the institutional setup developed to include or exclude a diversity of (intersectional) voices, on the other. Concerning the latter, I argue that the transnational model developed by the EU over the years have proven not to be inclusive enough to reflect the diversity of demands set forward by civil society organizations operating at the European level. Whereas the transnational space of mobilization opens up possibilities of collective action not found at the national and local levels, the difficulties of initiating and maintaining mobilization transnationally may exclude minority groups that do not have the resources or the institutional know-how to work as efficient advocacy groups at the European level. Thus, the institutional channels of access and the practices surrounding them impact the concerns, which may or may not be reflected in transnational gender equality policies.

The dual processes of mobilization and institutionalization and the ways in which they work at the transnational, European level in the development and practice of intersectionality in the EU is the key contribution of this book. It entails a combined focus on policymaking processes, civil society activism, and interaction between EU institutions and transnational women's organizations, which requires attention towards both policy content and policy processes. In this vein, a key argument set forward here is that diversity at the transnational level concerns both collective mobilization, through civil society organizations, as well as contestation over policy meanings, as an expression of the diversity of women's interests.

Political Intersectionality

Combining discursive policy analysis with a focus on institutions and collective agents, this book explores interrelations between gender equality, diversity, and intersectionality at the European level as these are expressed through EU policy-making processes and women's transnational mobilization. The theoretical and empirical aim of the book is to integrate the concepts of difference, diversity, and gender equality into a coherent and contextualized model for analyzing intersectionality at the European transnational level. I argue that such a model must take into account gender and diversity in relation to women's organizing in the transnational sphere and EU policy-making processes. Furthermore the interrelation between the two—the EU/civil society interface—should be incorporated into the model as it highlights the dynamic aspects of the intersectionality model proposed and the way in which EU institutions and civil society organizations mutually influence each other (see chapter 1). Thus, a key integrating dimension of the book is the way in which intersectionality is institutionalized at the European level, bearing in mind that this institutionalization is dynamic and changing and occurs in an interaction between EU institutions and transnational civil society organizations.

Intersectionality is intimately linked with the dual dynamic of mobilization and institutionalization, the theoretization of which is a key concern of this book. I distinguish intersectionality, as a theoretical and methodological concept implying the interaction between different inequality creating categories, from multiple discrimination, which is the term used in EU policies, suggesting an approach where different inequalities are added to one another rather than necessarily interacting. I furthermore argue that in politics, intersectional concerns can be expressed both in an inclusionary and an exclusionary manner, depending on the ideology and political strategy of the articulating actors.

In terms of mobilization, intersectional concerns come to the fore in relation to the representation of minority groups and intersectional constituencies. In terms of institutionalization, the recognition of minority women as policy interlocutors and target groups and of their demands as legitimate policy concerns, are key indicators of the development and practice of intersectionality at the European, transnational level. Thus, here I address the political dimensions of intersectionality as a theoretical and methodological approach. This is operationalized through a dual focus on intersecting categories in policies, on the one hand, and minority intersectional constituencies, representing diverse interests and setting forward a plurality of claims in civil society, on the other. In other words, the intersectional analysis pursued here is divided into the intersectional categories articulated through policies; the way in which different categories are addressed in the institutional setup of the EU (i.e., how are intersectional categories reflected in the institutional division of responsibilities of the different units); and the channels of access offered to different constituencies through the EU/civil society interface.

Following Ferree (2009), I argue that analyzing political intersectionality requires attention to the contextualization of how inequalities have been institutionalized, in this case at the transnational level. This has several implications in the case of the EU: Contextualizing intersectionality implies taking into consideration the privileged position of gender in the history of EU equality policies, where gender has hitherto been the most significant inequality category, as well as the recent turn towards diversity and multiple inequalities, emphasizing other inequalities in new policy initiatives, with the risk of ignoring or downplaying gender. Furthermore through contextualization, attention is also directed towards the multilevel structure of EU policy making and the way in which the institutional setup has influenced the institutionalization of intersectionality, by facilitating different levels of policy making and channels of access to policy processes as well as the consequent possibilities of civil society mobilization and participation in policy-making processes. The latter also concerns conflicts and contestations between different actors; the increased emphasis on multiple discrimination in EU policies has lead both to competition between civil society organizations representing different inequality categories and to new alliances, facilitated and promoted by the new institutional framework that favors cooperation across inequality grounds and their respective transnational umbrella organizations.

Ideas, Agency, and Context

A key interest in this book is how frames (understood as configurations of ideas) are institutionalized in the development of gender equality policies in the EU. Building on the presumption that ideas and framing of ideas[12] matter in policy making, one of the objects of analysis is the particular frame articulations set forward in the policy processes and the development of EU policies in terms of change and continuity. As an interviewed Council official argues, "There is a wording. You really have to look at wording very carefully...The wording is very, very important because that is always negotiated in detail...It is important to look at exactly how these things are phrased" (Council official, General Secretariat, interview May 2010). Analyzing the "phrasing" or the framing of policies is a central aspect of my arguments here.

Discursive policy analysis and studies of policy making at the EU level are still developing, and research within these areas are not many. This book contributes to the methodological challenge of developing and qualifying policy frame analysis mainly by strengthening the attention directed at contextual dimensions, on the one hand, and frame nuances, on the other. The aim is to interpret framing strategies in policy-making processes as well as shifts and contestations in the ideational development of EU policies, both in terms of continuity and change. Particularly, I interpret the role of ideas in policy processes as well as their interrelation with dimensions of agency and context. The ideational elements include both frames and discourses, as articulated through policies; agency refers to particular institutions and organizations active in the field as well as their strategies and intentions; and context covers the institutional setup and structures, including the civil society interface, as well as political and discursive opportunity structures emanating from this context. The interrelation between the dimensions of ideas, agency, and context leads me to focus on the key actors' strategic framings of policy ideas as well as the specific opportunity structures of the institutional context of the policy-making processes. A key argument made throughout the book is that the identified dimensions interact with each other as strategic policy frames are set forward within a particular context, namely that created by the political and discursive opportunity structures of the EU as well as its civil society interface. This context is marked by processes of inclusion and exclusion, which means that certain actors have more and better access than others to policy-making processes within the transnational framework of multilevel politics. For example, at the transnational level, the agenda of women's organizations defending women's participation in the labor market as a primary goal of gender equality policies has resonated with dominant EU policies. According to an EC official interviewed, the Commission is open to listening to and receiving all organizations, but an organization such as the European Women's Lobby (EWL) adapts more adequately to the needs and interests of the EC than other organizations because they share the political goals and dominant discourse of the EU institution, namely those of increased female labor-market participation (EC official, DG Employment, interview December 2007). Thus, organizations whose demands resonate with the dominant discourses of the EU institutions are to a larger extent included in policy-making processes than those organizations who challenge the dominant discursive framework. Ideally the institutional inclusion of civil society voices would allow for the expression of a diversity of ideas and challenge dominant discourses; however, I argue that in practice efficiency is often prioritized over plurality, and resonance and dominant institutional discourses are given prevalence over challenging alternative discourses in the actual functioning of the transnational institutions of the EU.

The aim of the analysis presented throughout the chapters of the book is to interpret key actors' strategic framings of policy ideas within particular political and discursive opportunity structures, contextually related to the policy-making processes of the EU. Methodologically, I focus on discursive approaches to policy analysis[13] by highlighting the intersubjective construction of meaning in EU policy making as well as the discursive negotiations taking place in the interinstitutional dialogue and in the EU/civil society interaction. In relation to this, the distinction between frames and discourses is significant.

Analyzing Policy Problems

Analyzing policy problems from a constructivist perspective, with a focus on ideational dimensions, entails looking at the ways in which policies are framed vis-à-vis the institutional context and dominant discourses. The notion of policy frame depicts a particular configuration of ideas, which articulates a specific representation of a policy problem such as gender inequality, for example. Here I consider both the concept of discourse and that of frame by looking at the way in which the frames, employed strategically by political actors, draw on and relate to discourses embedded in an institutional context. Both discourses and frames are socially constructed, but, in my conceptualization of the terms, discourses are constructed by an anonymous collective, that is, the social structures and the origin of the agency is not immediately identifiable because they are a result of collective, subjective practices that are reproduced. Frames, on the other hand, are the "conscious shaping of political demands to negotiate desired political outcomes" (Bacchi 2005, 204) with a more or less clear agency, defined as social and political actors. It would, however, be too simple to state that frames relate exclusively to actors, and discourses relate to structures: Both concepts contain both dimensions, and the difference is rather a matter of the weight each dimension is given within the specific approach.

Based on political sociology, linguistics, and theories on social movements, frame analysis seeks to shed light on how social phenomena and relations are ascribed meaning and how political topics are problematized in different ways. The term frame comes from the sociological tradition and the work of Erving Goffman, who defines it as a

> [S]chemata of interpretation…rendering what would otherwise be a meaningless aspect of the scene into something that is meaningful…[It] allows its user to locate, perceive, identify, and label a seemingly infinite number of concrete occurrences defined in its terms. (1974, 21)

Thus, frames are structures that help us organize our experiences; they are basic frameworks of understanding that we can access socially in order to make sense of reality (situations, events, policies, practices, etc.) and to create and structure meaning (Squires 2006).

Here I focus particularly on policy frames as a particular kind of frames, defined as an "organising principle that transforms fragmentary or incidental information into a structured and meaningful problem, in which a solution is implicitly or explicitly included" (Verloo 2005b, 20). In accordance with this definition, I consider policy frames to be a kind of problem frames, that is, the problem representation is the core of the policy frame, which is articulated in policy processes. Without ignoring the dual character of the frames, which implies that they can be both intentional and unintentional, I focus particularly on the intentional dimensions since I analyze strategic framings as they play out in policy-making processes.

Methodologically and theoretically, the point of departure of this book is constructivist. I am inspired by the focus on discourse, gender, and politics developed in scholarly literature in recent years (see especially Bacchi 1999; 2009b; Kantola 2006; 2010; Lombardo et al. 2009b; Verloo 2007), operationalized elsewhere as feminist comparative discourse analysis (Kantola 2006), problem representation analysis (Bacchi 1999; 2009b), or Critical Frame Analysis (CFA) (Lombardo et al. 2009a; Verloo 2005b; 2007). In the theoretical fields of both International Relations (Christiansen et al. 1999; Keck and Sikkink 1998) and Social Movement Studies (Ferree and Merrill 2000), a constructivist turn has taken place during the 1990s, leading to an increased focus on ideational dimensions, in the case of policy-making processes. This concerns in particular interaction between actors, the intersubjective construction of meaning, shaping of understandings, and the negotiation of identities and interests. I draw on the theoretical perspective of discursive institutionalism, which seeks to explain institutional change and continuity by focusing on ideas and discourses as explanations to these processes while considering at the same time the institutional contexts in which they are embedded. My main interest concerns the role of ideas in transnational, European politics and their institutionalization as frames, taking into account the dimension of agency as well as the particular opportunity structures, which may be available in the immediate institutional context.

The book makes two key contributions to the methodological literature on frame analysis. On the one hand, through methodological choices it clearly conceptualizes the main difference between frames and discourses as one related to the underlying strategic nature of frames and the possibility of identifying specific agency behind the articulation of particular frames. On the other hand, arguing that contextualization is necessary in the identification of policy frames, following from this that analysis cannot be based solely on policy documents, it takes CFA one step further, potentially adding new explanatory power to the analysis undertaken by including more dimensions.

Frames and Discourses

Frames and discourses are often confused or defined in similar terms in the literature. Both concepts refer to a way of articulating ideas, which can limit and/or enhance the possibilities of action and thinking. I understand discourses as constructions of meaning created and enacted through social relations. The meaning is negotiated continuously in public space, and therefore discourses must be understood as open processes within which different ideologies and social and political struggles are enacted through a contested notion of the social reality (Laclau and Mouffe 1985). The overall discursive approach adopted here is what draws attention to the role and importance of political "meaning making."

The articulation of discourses relates to processes of inclusion and exclusion as the construction of a particular discourse favors certain interests and oppresses the discourses that are contrary to this one (Lazar 2000). Referring to a poststructuralist discursive approach, Kantola (2006) argues that power relations constitute the very subjects through mechanisms of empowerment (creating possibilities) and dominance (excluding possibilities). According to this approach, (hegemonic) discourses are constraining in the sense that they leave certain (legitimate) subject positions open for the actors to selectively choose between. The subject retains agency but only within the limits of possibility set by the dominant discourse; thus, agency is performed in constant interaction with the structures in which it finds itself (Kantola 2006, 32).

The discourse, thus, emerges through the interaction between actors and structures, that is, the actors can create change through language use, but they are, at the same time, limited by the discursive systems embedded in the institutional structures, for instance, which establish a certain margin of action (Bacchi 1999, 43). I argue that we must look not only at the textual level (policy documents) but also at the contextual level (institutional and sociopolitical frames as well as opinions of stakeholders) of the discursive practices in order to analyze meaning making in politics. In other words, the discourse is created in interaction with the context in which it appears (text on context) (Wodak and Weiss 2005), through "a dialectical relationship between a particular discursive event and the situation, institution and social structure that frame it: the discursive event is shaped by them, but it also shapes them" (Wodak 1997, 17).

Meanings do not originate in language as such but are constructed through the discursive articulation in institutional practices, power relations, and processes of in/exclusions as well as social positions. In this way, the discourse can be interpreted as structural but nevertheless socially constructed by an anonymous collective, that is, the structures are social, but their origin cannot be identified since they depend on collective subjective practices that enact, reproduce, and sustain them. The institutional realm is a site for reproduction of dominant discourses, and this makes it all the more relevant to look at the institutional context, on the one hand, and the articulation of discursive dimensions that succeed in influencing the institutional debates, on the other. The discursive approach may contribute to analyzing the tensions and negotiations going on in the policy-making processes of the EU, the actors involved and their capacity for agency within the constraints set by legitimizing, hegemonic discourses as well as the power relations underlying these discourses and their (in)articulation.

Returning to the key issue of discourses and frames, one important distinctions is that discourse analysis tends to focus more on power relations than frame analysis. Frame analysis theories usually do not include power perspectives but rather perceive frames as parts of a larger discourse (in some literature referred to as master frames; see Ferree et al. 2002; Snow et al. 1986). Discourses, on the macro level, can be perceived as the broad context within which frames are formulated. They limit the possibilities of frame articulation within a given context. In other words, frames are discursively contingent whereas discourses are the underlying logic upon which frames are built.

I find that two basic distinctions are crucial to the conceptualization of frames and discourses as well as the differences between them: structure/agency and intentionality/nonintentionality. Discourses can be defined as systems of dominance and subordination (Laclau and Mouffe 1985). They are ideational structures supporting specific understandings at the same time as they limit them (Bacchi 2005). Framing, on the other hand, can be conceptualized as a space for maneuvering within the discursive field: "'Frame bridging' allows actors to pursue diverse aims, whilst acknowledging that these frames are inevitably discursively constrained and therefore not freely chosen" (Squires 2006, 5). The frames are constrained by established interpretive repertoires (dominant or hegemonic discourses), but they can be selected strategically within these discursive limitations (ibid.).

The objective of using the frames is to change behavior. Framing, then, can be conceived as the "conscious strategic efforts by groups of people to fashion shared understandings of the world and of themselves that legitimate and motivate collective action" (McAdam et al. 1996, 6). In policy making this means persuading key political actors about the adequacy of a certain policy proposal, for example, through the strategic framing of its content. To be successful, there must be a high degree of frame resonance in the audience. In this regards, I argue that the framing should fit the institutional context with which it seeks to interact. The process of making frames resonate is an intentional and strategic endeavor carried out by norm entrepreneurs who wish to construct frames that are convincing for a targeted audience (Squires 2006). Ferree argues that resonance is the "mutually affirming interaction of a frame with a discursive opportunity structure supportive of the terms of its argument" (2003, 310).

Thus, frames can be seen as an intentional articulation of political demands within the space given by discourses, with the aim of achieving specific goals and results (Bacchi 2005). Bacchi proposes a dual-focus research agenda, which looks at the impact of discourses on reform proposals and the intentional use of language by political subjects to shape political demands. Discourses can both delimit action and be used by actors, powerless as well as powerful ones. Frame analysis is about "how social movement actors manoeuvre within discursive limits to shape issues in ways that advance their specific political projects" (ibid., 207). A dual focus on both actors (the active frames) and structures (the passive discourses) is highlighted here while frame analysis in the version of the social movement theories to a larger extent focuses on strategic dimensions and agency (i.e., the way in which political actors act within the discursive space).[14]

Discourses, on the other hand, are not chosen strategically in the same manner as frames: They are shaped through an interaction between structures and actors, and they constitute the subject and are constituted by it simultaneously. Verloo's (2001; 2005b; 2007) way of theorizing the political frame analysis supports this focus as the aim is to analyze strategic framings of political demands in situations where language and arguments are adapted to a specific political context and discourse.

The importance of distinguishing between frame and discourse is reflected in the key literature of the field of policy analysis. Two methodological approaches have been developed in the "cross fire" between discourse analysis and frame analysis: CFA (Verloo 2001; 2005b; 2007) and WPR (What's the Problem Represented to be) (Bacchi 1999; 2005; 2009b). The two approaches complement each other, and they also engage in interesting dialogues.

The WPR approach is based on the assumption that a political proposal for a solution of a social problem always contains a particular representation of the problem, which it seeks to solve. Similarly, CFA[15] focuses on the analysis of articulations of policy proposals and movement demands. One of its main purposes is to deconstruct the multiplicity of meanings of gender equality, which are articulated in policies. CFA analyses policy documents in relation to three main categories: diagnosis (representation of the problem), prognosis (proposal for a solution), and voice (who produces the frame, whom is given a role/attributed authority). In any kind of policy proposal a representation of a diagnosis can be found, and this is related to a specific prognosis (Verloo 2005b).

The WPR approach is not interested in strategic frames or cognitive processes. CFA, on the other hand, considers the use of frames to be fundamentally strategic. Frames can be used strategically on an intentional or unintentional basis, that is, they can develop a strategic significance even though an intentional purpose or an explicitly conscious, political decision on a specific frame articulation is not the starting point. This occurred for example in the case of the equal-pay provision of the Treaty of Rome, which was not originally intended to be a gender equality measure but rather a provision to correct market distortion between member states (Cichowski 2002; Hoskyns 1996). Among other things, this is a consequence of the fact that political actors cannot always think exclusively, strategically, or independently of the general discourses that they themselves are a part of.

The advantages of CFA, in terms of analyzing competing ideas, shifts over time, and contestations between different frames, are the focus on strategic dimensions and agency through the ways in which actors use the frames. WPR does not conceive these dimensions as it considers the subject to be an integral part of the discourse. I perceive the articulation of policies as closely interlinked with actor interrelations and contextual dimensions. I do not consider policies and policy making to be isolated from the institutional and discursive context in which they are embedded and to which they refer. Therefore I find it necessary to look closely at the interaction between text and context as well as the relation between structure and agency and, with this, the scope for action, which civil society actors, for instance, hold. The rejection of strategic agency as well as the focus on internal policy logics (as they are articulated in problem representations) without analyzing policy-making processes, actor interrelations, and movement dynamics make the WPR approach less adequate than CFA for these purposes.

Contextualization

The empirical data gathered for the analyses presented here consists of EU policy documents, civil society position papers and reports, and interviews with key actors within the three EU institutions (the Council, the European Commission and the European Parliament)[16] and representatives of a series of European women's organizations.[17] This empirical data is analyzed through CFA at the textual level of interaction (documents) and through a strengthened focus on the political institutional and discursive context in which the frames are articulated (interviews). The two sets of empirical material complement each other in the sense that the identification of frames is made through the analysis of policy documents, and these frames are then contextualized through the interviews in order to uncover strategies, conflicts, and silences. I consider this contextualization to be necessary in order to interpret the framing processes adequately: Frames are only articulated in interaction, that is, texts are framed in interplay with other texts, structures, processes, contexts, etc. In other words, framing processes are dynamic as they take place in the very interaction between a variety of actors: I argue that we cannot analyze ideas stemming from policy documents as detached from the institutional context (discourses, structures, power,[18] resources) in which they are produced, and the actors who produced or opposed them in the course of the policy-making process. Policies are created through negotiations over textual content as well as through the institutional context and history within which these take place.

Combining analysis of policy documents and interviews with key actors from EU institutions and civil society organizations allows me to analyze shifts over time as well as trace a single policy-making process in detail (i.e., the negotiation and adoption of the DAPHNE program, see chapters 4 and 5). The interview data highlights contestations between frames, political conflicts, as well as the strategic dimension of framing. Furthermore, by emphasizing the contextual dimensions, I find that nuances in framings in terms of their simultaneous articulation, their different strength and scope of institutionalization, as well as institutional differences are significant in the interpretation of policy developments within the EU. In other words, I emphasize the interrelation between frames as well as their contextualized institutionalization (see chapter 5). This gives a more faithful and diversified picture of the dynamics of institutionalization as it reflects a reality where policies are produced and articulated both through visible policy documents and less visible institutional and discursive practices beyond formal decision-making processes. In sum, by focusing on contextualized in-depth textual policy analysis in conjunction with an emphasis on agency, I am able to look into the dynamic framing processes in EU policy making as well as the differences between the institutionalization of frames in this particular transnational context.

Thus, the main question to address in a (critical) revision of CFA is how far this approach can take us if we wish to move beyond the analysis of the frames "at face value," that is, as they appear in the policy documents. CFA can uncover details of policy texts, problem perceptions, as well as the voice given to different actors in the policy process. However, its main shortcoming is the lack of scope: It deals with text-based analysis exclusively, but it does not tell us much about what is going on outside the text, in the political and institutional context. This translates, among other things, into a lack of focus on power relations. Ferree argues that CFA "becomes more dynamic when it is complemented by studies of the political processes through which [the policy] texts were created, interpreted and used as resources for mobilization" (2009, 90). Therefore I suggest combining CFA, based on analysis of policy documents, with the analysis of interview data. Interviews contribute to the contextualization of the analysis of the policy documents by shedding light on aspects such as the policy process, the institutional framework, the opportunity structures of the transnational space, agenda-setting mechanisms and the strategic reflections, and framings made by key actors in the development of the policies under scrutiny. Furthermore, through the contextualization of the policy processes, the interviews are expected to reveal patterns of (potential) conflicts and silences (i.e., unarticulated policy issues or frames) in the textual material by articulating issues such as intentions and actor relations.

By combining ideas, agency, and context as the three main dimensions, my approach differs from studies focusing explicitly on the policy level (such as the QUING project[19]; Lombardo et al. 2009a) as well as from the ones centered around advocacy coalitions (Keck and Sikkink 1998; Lang 2009; Locher 2007; Montoya 2008; 2013; Zippel 2004; 2006) or opportunity structures (Ferree 2003; Ferree et al. 2002; Hobson 2003; Locher 2007; Zippel 2004; 2006). I have chosen to place the main focus on an explicitly constructivist theoretical perspective, namely gendered discursive institutionalism, in order to grasp the ideational nuances in policies and policy making as well as variations over time. My interest lies in the detailed textual level of policies, the intersection between policy analysis and discourse analysis, and the way in which frames are articulated and determine the potential of policy action. The aim is to feed into the methodological and theoretical developments by shedding empirical light on framing processes in the transnational context of the EU and its gender equality policies. Thus, I conduct an in-depth textual analysis of EU policies on gender-based violence while including at the same time detailed considerations of the political and discursive contextualization of the policy issues. Agency is covered through the specific view on EU and civil society actors' strategic framing of policy issues.

Whereas the potential of this methodological approach has been highlighted above, its limitations clearly consist in the reduced scope of policies that can be analyzed in-depth since the method is highly qualitative and can only be comprehensively carried out on a relatively small number of policy processes and documents. Consequently, this leads to a lack of potential for comparative analyses as no large data sets are included that could sufficiently form the basis of such analyses. Furthermore by focusing on frames, and emphasizing in particular their strategic components, there is a risk of reading too much into the intentionality of policy makers and civil society actors as well as overemphasizing the conscious shaping of all policies and policy-making efforts. Whereas frames more immediately lend towards pinpointing specific contents and agencies, a combination with proper discourse analysis would create a better balance between strategic efforts and broader structural developments.

Structure of the Book

The book is structured around eight chapters, including this introduction and the conclusions. The present introduction on challenges to EU gender equality policies has presented the aim of the book (i.e., exploring the interrelations between gender equality, diversity, and intersectionality at the European level as these are expressed through institutionalization and EU policy-making processes as well as women's transnational mobilization) and the methodological framework for analyzing policy problems underpinning the remaining chapters.

Chapter 1 embarks fully on developing a theoretical model for policy analysis at the transnational, European level, focusing on the dimensions of context, agency, and ideas. It goes on to present a dynamic, contextualized approach to intersectionality for the analysis of gender and diversity dimensions at the transnational level. It combines a dual focus on institutionalization and mobilization by focusing on institutional setup, policy making, collective action, and institutional/civil society interaction and the way in which these processes address and affect the interrelations between gender and diversity. The diversity challenge identified is related to intersectionality both in terms of processes of degendering in policy making (when other inequalities enter the stage) and in terms of increasing mobilization of minority intersectional constituencies in the transnational space, which is conceptualized as substantially different from the sum of European national spheres.

Chapter 2 focuses on the way in which intersectionality has been institutionalized in the EU. This refers, on the one hand, to article 13 of the Amsterdam Treaty as well as other key documents, which establish the multiple discrimination policy framework of the EU. On the other hand, the institutionalization of intersectionality refers to the influence on and interaction with civil society actors mobilizing at the transnational level around different and/or intersectional forms of inequality and their in/exclusion in the policy-making processes of the EU. Among other things the so-called hierarchy of inequalities is discussed, as is the competition/cooperation between civil society organizations.

In chapter 3 attention is directed toward minority intersectional constituencies within the panorama of women's collective mobilization at the European level. Political intersectionality is conceptualized as a complex and dynamic web of interrelations where institutionalized and noninstitutionalized actors mutually influence each other in discourses, policies, and practices of intersectionality. In the empirical analysis of transnational collective mobilization this refers not least to minority intersectional constituencies in European civil society and their interaction with other intersectional organizations, European umbrella organizations focusing on a single inequality ground and EU institutional structures. The chapter includes an empirical analysis of the ways in which both minority and majority organizations deal with diversity and the strategies employed to address ethnic minority women's concern, in particular. Furthermore EU/civil society interface is discussed in relation to the potential for inclusive policy-making structures, reflecting the empirical reality of differentiated demands and interests of diverse groups of women mobilizing at the European level.

Turning the attention toward policy-making processes chapter 4 traces the framings of EU policies on gender-based violence from the 1980s until 2010 by means of CFA. The policy area is characterized as a soft policy area, at the European level, in which the EU has no legal competences. Despite these legal constraints the EU has been able to act within this policy area and, as such, it is an example of the importance of political will as well as the role of ideational elements in policy-making processes at the transnational level. The chapter discusses differences in framings across the three main EU institutions (i.e., the Parliament, the Commission, and the Council) and highlights the development from framings of structural gender inequality to framings of human rights and public health within the policy area. Significantly, from the 1980s until now EU policies on gender-based violence have undergone a process of increased degendering at the level of official policies.

In chapter 5 different forms of degendering in policy-making processes are discussed both theoretically and empirically through the analysis of the implications of the framings articulated in EU policies on gender-based violence (as identified in chapter 4) as well as processes of frame contestation and policy negotiation in the development of policies. Despite the increased degendering of formal EU policies on gender-based violence, a strong gender equality understanding prevails in some of the EU institutions. Focusing on the institutionalization of frames, it is argued that the framing of gender equality policies can be divided in "background" and "foreground" framings as degendering occurs for strategic reasons in official policies whereas institutional discursive practices remain gendered, not least through the intervening capacity of the Commission.

Chapter 6 explores the theoretical notions of in/exclusionary intersectionality by analyzing the discursive articulation of European identity and the problematization of the "gendered other." The notion of in/exclusionary intersectionality highlights the relation between inequality categories, processes of in/exclusion, and power asymmetries between majority and minority groups. Immigration and integration policies typically represent migrant women as the potential "bearers of integration" whereas migrant men are conceived as the "violent other." Similarly a tendency toward the culturalization of the problem of violence is detected in EU policies whereby culture is increasingly articulated as the only explanation to violence in immigrant couples, leading to the risk of stigmatization of particular minority groups.

The concluding chapter sums up the main findings of the book in terms of the interrelation between gender equality, intersectionality, and diversity at the transnational level. Furthermore, the chapter discusses the EU variant of transnational intersectionality and, in particular, the saliency of certain interrelated categories and their intersections (like gender-and-ethnicity or gender-and-age), depending on the policy area. The conclusion addresses the dilemmas of degendering and diversity encountered and adds to these a new challenge, namely the one stemming from ideologically different organizations than the ones typically represented in EU policy-making processes so far. Thus the conclusion highlights the role and demands of conservative women's organizations in relation to mobilization as well as institutionalization of hitherto nondominant understandings of gender equality and women's interests.

1

Policy Making, Institutionalization, and Collective Mobilization: A Model for Transnational Intersectional Analysis

This chapter combines a discursive approach to policy analysis with the dimension of contextualization in relation to the particular setting of the empirical study of EU policy making. According to Kantola,[1] the agents articulating discourses "act not only within a discursive context but also within an institutional context, which constitute them as both subjects and actors" (2006, 45). There is an interrelation between the discursive and the institutional context in which policies are formulated and adopted at the EU level. This combination of discursive, institutional, and contextual dimensions of EU policy making is necessary in order to investigate the role of ideas within transnational policy processes and the importance of agency in the development of policies. Furthermore, in order to develop a contextualized approach to analyzing intersectionality at the transnational level, I argue that the particularities of the transnational space, the mobilization of civil society actors, as well as the institutionalization of diversity through policy-making processes and practices must be taken into account and integrated into a coherent model of analysis.

Context, Agency, Ideas: Analyzing Transnational Policies

The following sections direct the attention to discursive institutionalism, opportunity structures, and the particularities of the transnational space. The aim is to develop a model for analyzing policy making in a transnational perspective. The transnational space is substantially different from the national one and, thus, the theoretical take on dynamics of in/exclusion of ideas must be developed accordingly. On the one hand, I wish to pay closer attention to the transnational setting and the multilevel context of EU policy making, particularly within the field of gender equality. This calls, specifically, for an assessment of what opportunity structures mean, theoretically and empirically, in relation to multilevel settings. On the other hand, the discursive approach must also be theorized in relation to this multilevel setting. Different discourses are at work in relation to different actors or institutions, and they are articulated in policy making in interplay between various levels. Furthermore, organizational and suborganizational discourses are articulated, and the specific frames speak to these discourses and draw on them.

The key dimensions of context, agency, and ideas are discussed within the broader theoretical framework of new institutionalism, which seeks to shed light upon processes of continuity and change in the development of political institutions. I particularly discuss a new and still emerging dimension of this approach, namely, gendered discursive institutionalism and its potential in terms of undertaking analyses within the transnational space. Ideational processes are significant dimensions in dynamics of institutional and policy change: The institutional context as well as the transnational opportunity structures constrains and enables actors' possibilities of articulating certain frames within the space of political discursive struggles (see also Hobson 2003; Ruzza 2004; Tarrow 1998; 2005).

New Institutionalism: The Discursive Dimension

New institutionalism was developed as a paradigm in social and political theory in the 1980s with the aim of bringing institutions back in the theoretical spotlight of political science. Institutions should be understood broadly as stable, recurring patterns of behavior: whether material or ideational, they are dynamic social practices. As discourses, institutions are constructed (continuously) through human agency. At the same time, they impose limits on this agency. In other words, institutions shape political processes and outcome, delimiting the possibilities of action. Furthermore, institutions should not be regarded as unified entities, but rather as disaggregated yet related dimensions and practices. This means that (discursive) conflicts and tensions can arise both within and between institutions or institutionalized actors (Kantola 2006; see also Ruzza 2004).

Institutions can be seen as "embodied" (Dryzek 2005) or "sedimented" discourses, which are constituted through discursive struggles and work simultaneously as "fixed functional units" (Kulawik 2009). Institutions are, furthermore, considered to be "carriers of ideas and collective memories" and, as such, they are changeable and dynamic (Schmidt 2008; 2011). Institutional change and continuity are influenced by the (re)articulation of discourses and frames. Formal rules and informal norms interact in the institutional development; embedded norms are an important part of the institutions as they are the basis of inclusion and exclusion of actors (Kenny 2007; Mackay and Meier 2003; Orloff and Palier 2009). In sum, institutions are dynamic; they are constituted by ideas that have become institutionalized as discourses. They set the limits of in/exclusion, thereby both enabling and constraining action. Thus, ideas are institutionalized to comprise institutions, which in turn may perform agency.

Importantly, differences exist within institutions, such as the EU, as they are comprised of a conglomerate of different ideational or discursive institutionalizations. Dryzek (2005) considers institutions to be made up of discourses, which provide the context for social action, on the one hand, and formal institutional rules, on the other. In other words, structures (such as power, materiality, political realities) are as important as discourses. To Laclau and Mouffe (1985), though, there is nothing beyond discourses, and all structures are, consequently, discursive. The social constructivist approach can, however, be combined with an emphasis on the importance of strategic framing, attaining in this way a dual approach in which ideational change in institutions is seen as the result of an interaction between deliberative argumentation and political negotiation based on particular power interests (Elgström 2000). The theoretical position adopted here is inspired by this combination of ideational and material dimensions: Institutions are constituted by ideas and discourses while acknowledging at the same time the role of agency and intentionality—for example in the strategic framing of ideas. This is, furthermore, congruent with the CFA approach outlined above as opposed to the WPR approach, which does not conceive subjects outside discourse (see Introduction).

Within the new institutionalism paradigm (March and Olsen 1989), three different kinds of institutionalisms have been developed: The rational, the historical, and the sociological (see Hall and Taylor 1996; Nullmeier 2006). Schmidt (2008; 2011) adds a fourth version, namely discursive institutionalism. The basic proposition of discursive institutionalism is to explain institutional change and continuity through the analysis of ideas. It is, in other words, the "explanatory power of ideas and discourses" in a dynamic perspective (i.e., ideas explain change), which is under scrutiny here. Tracing changes in policy ideas over time will direct our attention toward shifts within particular institutions. Ideas and discourses can transform institutions, but the questions raised in discursive institutionalism are how, when, where, and why they matter (Schmidt 2008).

To these, we must add "whose" ideas and discourses matter in terms of fostering institutional change, in order to highlight the notion of agency. Ideas may enable actors to overcome the constraints of the institutional and political context. Schmidt argues that we must look at discourse as interaction and not only as content: "Discourse as an interactive process is what enables agents to change institutions, because the deliberative nature of discourse allows them to conceive of and talk about institutions as objects at a distance" (2008, 316). In this account, discourse is what you say to whom, how, why, and where in the process of policy construction.

The discursive process helps explain why some ideas fail and others succeed because of the way they are "projected to whom and where" (Schmidt 2008). There are, however, certain prerequisites for discursive dominance such as resources and "favorable conditions of access to discursive arenas" (i.e., the material or structural dimensions). The actors themselves may enhance their possibilities by using their diverse capacities to create discursive space and maintain or reproduce it (Nullmeier 2006). This idea resonates with Tarrow's theorizing on mobilizing actors' capacity for creating opportunity structures for themselves (1998; 2005).

Discourses become dominant within institutions based on criteria such as strength (frequency and repetition), resonance, adequacy, relevance, and coherence (Nullmeier 2006; Schmidt 2011). The idea of resonance in discursive institutionalism is parallel to that of frame theories: "The ideas in the discourse must "make sense" within a particular ideational setting [and] the discourse itself will be patterned in certain ways, following rules and expressing ideas that are socially constructed and historically transmitted" (Schmidt 2008, 313). Dostal (2004) argues that new policy ideas that relate to or resonate with the organizational discourse are more likely to be successful as it is the organizational discourse that supplies the policy frames upon which the policy change is based (see also Ruzza 2004).

The idea of organizational discourse is a way to bridge the gap between institutionalism and agenda-setting mechanisms, in a theoretical perspective. The organizational discourses are based on "discursive closure" (Dostal 2004) and they "inform the ideational grid through which the organisation...interprets the world" (Mahon 2009, 186). However, the organizational discourse should not be understood as a common whole: Different discourses are articulated within the organization and in its different directorates or sections. Again, internal institutional differences are highlighted. The concept is particularly useful for conducting analyses based on policy tracing with the objective of identifying the origin and development of policies that are currently dominant. It can help to determine in which institutional setting new policy ideas are developed, how they gain dominance, or how they foster policy change. In the empirical analyses presented in the remaining chapters of the book, I will explore the relationship between dominant discourses within the institutional realm and new frames, and the intrainstitutional differences in order to assess the internal dynamics of frame articulation within the EU.

However, the role of the institutional context needs to be further highlighted. Whereas the institutional context is not forgotten in discursive institutionalism, it does seem adequate to turn to one of its predecessors, namely historical institutionalism, for a strengthened emphasis on the role of institutions. Schmidt herself (2008) states that discursive and historical institutionalisms together explain change by directing attention to the critical junctures or windows of opportunity, which may shed light on the success, or failure, of certain policy ideas.[2] In other words, the institutional context contributes to explaining why certain policy ideas are adopted while others are not. This approach underlines the role of "macro structures and regularized practices" in the processes of shaping ideas whereas discursive institutionalism focuses on the micro level and the institutional development and the way in which discourses and ideas can reshape macro structures (Schmidt 2008; 2011).

Gendered (Discursive) Institutionalism

Feminist scholars have pointed to the fact that new institutionalist approaches, in general, lack a gender perspective. Theoretical debates have been initiated concerning the interplay between feminist political analyses and new institutionalism, with the aim of developing theoretical dimensions of the gendering of political institutions.[3] These attempts are, to a large extent, informed by the institutionalist turn taking place both in feminist political analysis and in mainstream political theory with the recent focus on processes of continuity and change in political institutions, as discussed above.

In the debates regarding the potential contributions that feminist political analysis and new institutionalism may lend to each other (Kenny 2007; Kenny and Mackay 2009; Kulawik 2009; Mackay and Meier 2003), it is emphasized that the two approaches share a basic interest in institutions and processes of change. Feminist political analysis highlights the concepts of gender, power, and change in their approach to the process of gendering political institutions (Kenny 2007). Power asymmetries are played out in institutional processes, for instance, through privileging certain agents and courses of action (Kantola 2006). When new institutionalism emphasizes how "seemingly neutral institutional processes and practices are in fact embedded in hidden norms and values, privileging certain groups over others" (Kenny and Mackay 2009, 274), a gender approach adds that these hidden norms and values are indeed gendered (Mackay and Meier 2003).[4]

Drawing on the theoretical developments of Nancy Fraser, Kulawik (2009) argues that politics is about struggles of interpretation over whom, what, and how to politicize as well as the representation of needs, problems, and identities. This emphasizes the importance of contestations and in/exclusions in the policy discourse development. In other words, the approach proposed by Kulawik focuses on institutional arrangements, actor constellations, and political discourse as well as the relations between them (ibid.).

In my account, I identify similar dimensions, namely, context, agency, and ideas. My concerns are how the EU interacts with civil society actors and whether or not the transnational space and the EU institutional context privilege certain civil society actors over others, for example. Power relations, which are more highlighted in feminist political analysis than in new institutionalist approaches, are asymmetrical and build on processes of inclusion and exclusion. These relations are reinforced through institutions. Kantola seeks to "gender" the theory of new institutionalism by posing the following research question: "What kind of resistance and possibilities do institutions provide for feminist struggles in particular contexts at particular times?" (2006, 34).[5] Institutions are gendered and they "reflect, reinforce, and structure unequal gendered power relations" (Mackay and Meier 2003, 2). Gender, thus, becomes a key analytical category as it is considered a central dimension of institutions and the institutionalization of (gender) power relations. I am particularly interested in two aspects in this regard: (1) the (de)gendering of policies (see chapters 4 and 5, in particular); and (2) the in/exclusion of civil society actors working to achieve gender equality (see chapters 2 and 3).

In relation to the latter, new institutionalism and feminist political analysis share a historical view on power relations and the idea that these are open to resistance and transformation through agency (Kenny 2007). In this way, the gendered version of new institutionalism places a particular focus on (collective) agency. Framing of feminist demands within dominant institutional discourses and the (collective) agency of women are common concerns in the synthesis between feminist political analysis and new institutionalism (Mackay and Meier 2003). Agency and the potential of (gendered) transformation of institutions become central dimensions of analyses and theorizing. The new institutionalist perspective is useful in terms of analyzing resistance as well as the interplay between actors and the institutional context as regards dominant discourses, constraints, and (re)framing of central concepts in order to convey new meanings within the institutional processes (ibid.).

Concepts of gender equality, for instance, change their meaning over time, and this contributes to institutional change. This is related to the inclusion and exclusion of political actors: The terrain on which actors struggle over representation is the universe of political discourse, a space in which identities are socially constructed. The universe of political discourse encodes an accepted set of meanings about who the legitimate actors are, the place they hold in politics, the appropriate sites of political struggle, and the form social relations ought to take (Jenson and Mahon 1993, 79).

The outcome of the struggles within the space of discursive political struggles over meanings and actor legitimacy depends on the institutional context—the asymmetrical power relations, the discursive and material resources of the actors, as well as their competences (Kulawik 2009). In addition, this highlights the interaction between the ideational processes and the institutional context in that "institutional arrangements interact with ideational influences as well, for example by affording actors with only certain worldviews a formal seat at the decision-making table, thereby selectively empowering some schemas and discourses over others" (Padamsee 2009, 423).

By focusing on change rather than continuity, feminist political analysis furthermore adds a more dynamic perspective on power to the theories of new institutionalism. Institutional change occurs in a context of political conflict, discursive contestations, and shifting alliances. Some meanings can be challenged and renegotiated, and herein lies the potential for resistance (Kenny 2007; Kenny and Mackay 2009). Gendered (discursive) institutionalism highlights, in particular, the hegemonic discursive constructions of gender. Kenny and Mackay argue that: "The 'discursive turn' in feminist analysis (e.g., Bacchi 1999) moves beyond power distributional perspectives, highlighting the complex interplay of discursive struggles over the interpretation and representation of needs, problems, and identities" (2009, 276). Gendered (discursive) institutionalism thus emphasizes the interaction between power, gendered discourses, and policy problem representations.

Gendered (discursive) institutionalism links up with the frame analysis approach outlined in the previous chapter as strategic framing is an important dimension of processes of institutional change: "Both NI [New Institutionalism] and FPS [Feminist Political Science] emphasize the importance of strategic agency in processes of institutional change, highlighting the ways in which strategic actors initiate change within a context of opportunities and constraints" (Kenny and Mackay 2009, 277). According to the new institutionalist paradigm, in processes of change, old ideas are deinstitutionalized and new ones institutionalized. This opens up the possibility for political actors to intervene in the space of discursive struggles over the definition of key dimensions like women's interests or the meaning of gender equality. This space is characterized by being "structured by power differentials" (Béland 2009; Kulawik 2009; Mackay and Meier 2003; Orloff and Palier 2009).

Power asymmetries must be taken into account in the institutionalization of new frames and policy ideas: Actors can formulate frames, but they cannot control them once articulated. In this sense, feminist gender equality contributions from collective actors in civil society may be turned into economic rationales when institutionalized within the context of the EU, for example (Orloff and Palier 2009). Specific actors use framing strategies in order to bring about institutional change through discursive struggles over meanings and definitions in politics. Collective actors of the civil society may formulate alternatives to existing policies, and institutionalized actors may use framing strategies in the intrainstitutional definitional struggles between different entities.

Kulawik (2009) warns us that discourses must be treated systematically, and that arguments related to "institutional fits" do not go deep enough in terms of identifying the underlying discourses and their reasons for being and gaining in dominance. While an in-depth analysis of the policy frames articulated in the policy-making processes of the EU, as the one conducted here, does not pinpoint dominant discourses (which depend on larger developments), it does identify dominant framings within the selected policy issue in detail. The analysis particularly focuses on how ideas become institutionalized, and what happens in the process in terms of inclusion and exclusion. The institutional context and the political and discursive opportunity structures constrain or enable these processes, privileging certain ideas and actors over others, particularly those that resonate with existing EU policies like the dominant gender equality discourse related to women's labor-market participation.

A key concern in the debate on feminist contributions to new institutionalist approaches and ideational dimensions of policy analysis is also the focus on social divisions or inequalities and their intersections (Béland 2009, Kenny and Mackay 2009). Thus, intersectionality aspects are another key point in the development of a gendered (discursive) institutionalism; here it is addressed as a transversal issue in terms of the intersections between gender and ethnicity as they are addressed in policy making and through civil society organizations.

Central to the arguments presented in this book is that discursive contestations and actor alliances/competitions may lead to institutional and policy change. Nevertheless, the importance that new institutionalist accounts attribute to causality in relation to the role of ideas in policy developments is questioned. Ideas may explain change, but a broader point of view must be adopted, asking what role ideas play in policy developments. Rather than focusing exclusively on causal relations I suggest the use of an interpretative take on the role of ideas in policy making as this is in line with the social constructivist foundation of my notion of ideational processes and policy analysis. Contrary to Schmidt (2008), for instance, I follow a constructivist logic of interpretation rather than a causal logic of explanation. This, furthermore, opens up for a broader take on the empirical material when asking (through CFA) how key concepts and ideas are defined and given meaning by different actors instead of limiting the empirical analysis to predefined theoretical notions and their causal influence on policy processes.

Policy Making in the Multilevel, Transnational Space

The theoretical development of the new institutionalist approaches focuses, to a large extent, on the national level and its political frameworks. Hence, the particularities of the context of EU policy making must be underlined in order to adapt the theoretical framework of gendered discursive institutionalism to this particular transnational context. This concerns not least multilevel governance and, in particular, EU policy-making processes as well as transnational opportunity structures.

The European integration processes and decision-making structures are an example of multilevel governance. The multilevel governance structure implies the involvement of a large number of actors in the policy process and the dispersion of authority among actors and levels (Hooghe and Marks 2001). Several levels of policy making are linked: National level policies, institutions, and discourses affect and influence the political development and the decision-making processes at the transnational level, and vice versa. This structure works both horizontally, where different institutionalized actors (the Parliament, the Commission, and the Council) participate in the policy-making processes, and vertically, since local, regional, and national levels are linked to the supranational one, for example through national representation, that is, the elected Members of the European Parliament (MEP). Furthermore, the supranational institutions also interact horizontally with actors such as organizations, networks, and interest groups at the transnational level and vertically with national civil societies.

In other words, different layers of the EU multilevel structure come together in processes of interaction, deliberation, and policy making. This means that when we set out to analyze policy processes in the current European context, we cannot ignore the fact that the different levels of decision-making structures are interrelated. According to Kantola, it is "important for feminist activists targeting the state and feminist scholars studying the state to understand the dynamics stemming from multilevel governance" (2006, 144). In the same way, Liebert points to the European dimension as an "embedded feature framing politics in states" (2003, 16), just as the national dimension influences policy making at the EU level. However, I do not take into account the vertical dimension here but instead focus specifically on the transnational level and horizontal dimensions of policy making within this context because this is a generally underexplored field of research.

Schmidt argues that the institutional setting of the EU is characterized by a compound structure (with a complex organizational setup and decision-making structure) and, accordingly, a weak communicative sphere (due to the lack of an elected government, for example) and a similarly strong coordinative sphere. Schmidt differentiates idea diffusion to the public in the communicative sphere from idea generation among policy actors in the coordinative sphere.[6] The former refers to the communication of ideas and policies from the political (elite) level to the public. Here, I focus on the latter, that is, generation of frames at the policy level. This concerns the policy-making sphere where ideas are negotiated: In the policy sphere, the coordinative discourse consists of the individuals and groups at the center of policy construction who are involved in the creation, elaboration, and justification of policy and programmatic ideas. These are the policy actors—the civil servants, elected officials, experts, organized interests, and activists, among others—who seek to coordinate agreement among themselves on policy ideas (Schmidt 2008, 310), and they are precisely the actors who are included here in the empirical data set as interviewees.

Policy Making in the European Union

The policy-making and decision-making processes of the EU are rather complex, and any analysis of these must take into account a number of differentiated procedures and regulations, according to the specific policy area under which decisions are reached in this multilevel governance structure. The institutional policy structure of the EU is typically divided into three pillars where the first is governed by supranationality and the second and third by intergovernmentalism. The second and third pillars cover common foreign and security policy as well as justice and home affairs, respectively, whereas pillar one includes the remaining areas.

The most common decision-making procedure is "codecision," which was introduced with the Maastricht Treaty in 1993 (article 251) and extended in the Amsterdam Treaty. In this procedure, the EP and the Council act as colegislators. The EC sets forward a proposal, which is then followed by two successive readings in the Parliament and in the Council. During this process, the relevant parliament committee elaborates a parliamentary report. If no agreement is reached during these readings, a conciliation committee is set up with representatives from the three main institutions. The proposal of the conciliation committee is debated in a third reading. The codecision procedure has been used for a number of areas within the first pillar. "Consultation" used to be another common decision-making structure in the EU: The EP comments on the EC proposals before the Council makes a decision.

Regarding the voting procedures in the Council, this depends on the legal basis of the policy issue addressed: Issues within pillar one require qualified majority voting whereas pillar two and three in general need unanimity for a decision to be adopted.[7] The legal basis is, in principle, decided by the EC, but this can be a highly debated dimension, and the EC must ensure that the legal basis proposed would be able to "resist court challenge" (Cini 2007). As of 2007, the qualified majority vote weighs the votes in the Council and requires 255 votes out of 345, the support of a majority of member states, and a minimum of 62 percent of the total population of the EU. Qualified majority voting has increasingly replaced the unanimity principle in Council voting (europa.eu).

The general framework for decision-making procedures has been modified with the Lisbon Treaty (2009), and codecision is now considered the "ordinary legislative procedure" as it applies to most policy areas (article 294) (europa.eu). The supranational competences and decision-making procedures have thus been extended over the years through the increased application of codecision and qualified majority voting (Balme and Chabanet 2008).

Transnational Political Opportunity Structures

The dynamic and complex policy processes of the EU, involving a large variety of actors, institutional levels and decision-making procedures, should be analyzed with a view to the institutional and discursive contexts. The presence of transnational civil society organizations and social movements addressing the European level directly has increased in recent years (Ruzza 2004). This can be interpreted as a potentially new expression of collective mobilization and political participation at the transnational level. Thus, activism and mobilization at the transnational level have a dual focus: On the one hand, they are directed at the state level, exerting pressure on national governments, and, on the other, they interact with international institutional structures, targeting these with specific demands.

In Tarrow's conceptualization of social movements (1998), these produce change and are, at the same time, influenced by change in the immediate context. In this way, the actions of the social movements depend on the specific, contextual political opportunity structure at a certain time and space in history. According to this reasoning, social movements act within a specific social and political context that may enhance or constrain their possibilities for action. The political opportunities are understood as dimensions of the political context that incite collective action in as much as they affect the expectations regarding success or failure. They are "a set of clues for when contentious politics will emerge" (Tarrow 1998, 20) and, thus, constitute the possibilities for emergence, interaction, and change that a social movement holds in relation to a specific social system.

The possibilities of influence in the political system depend on the interrelations between institutions and movements. Tarrow defines the political opportunities as "consistent—but not necessarily formal, permanent, or national—dimensions of the political struggle that encourage people to engage in contentious politics" (1998, 19–20) and political constraints as "factors—like repression, but also like authorities' capacities to present a solid front to insurgents—that discourage contention" (ibid., 20). These circumstances are dynamic and change over time and across different contexts, creating openings or closures in interaction with more stable social structures (ibid.). According to the dynamics of change, the social movements can also influence the environment themselves, increasing or decreasing their possibilities for favorable opportunity structures through the creation of social networks and coalitions of social actors.

In his first accounts of the concept of political opportunity structures, Tarrow theorized these as domestic. However, he has since elaborated further on his theory in order to include the transnational dimension as well (2005). Transnational activism is constrained by domestic relations and networks and might, at the same time, influence these. The transnational political opportunity structures can be defined as "the consistent dimensions of the international or transnational political environment that provide incentives or constraints for collective action" (Khagram et al. 2002, 18). This expansion of the theoretical approach to opportunity structures implies that the social movements for instance cannot operate in the domestic sphere independently of the events taking place in the transnational field and vice versa.

According to Tarrow (2005), it is internationalization in itself, defined as increased density of horizontal links between state and nonstate actors as well as increased vertical links at both the subnational, national, and international levels that creates these structures: "Internationalism provides an opportunity structure within which transnational activism can emerge. As internationalization increases, it can be expected to produce both new threats and new opportunities for activism" (ibid., 8).[8] Whereas the cited authors first and foremost focus on the interrelation between the domestic and the international, the purpose of my analysis is to investigate the transnational level in-depth. It is dependent on the domestic structures and processes, but transnational activism also takes on a "life of its own." Precisely, the interrelation between the two levels informs new paths of political change also on the transnational level where a new stratum of activists is developing, according to Tarrow (ibid.).

Here, political opportunity structures are perceived in a broader sense: They are conceptualized not only in terms of their institutional dimensions but also in terms of discourses. Frame analysis emphasizes the role of discursive opportunity structures that serve as the context in which framing processes and policy change take place: The frames articulated by specific actors must resonate with the "dominant cultural repertoire" of the society in question in order to be politically effective (Ferree 2009). Discursive opportunity structures are defined as "institutionally anchored ways of thinking that provide a gradient of relative political acceptability to specific packages of ideas" (Ferree 2003, 309). This ideational institutional framework is constituted by a series of legislative or authoritative texts (Ferree 2003; 2009). The discursive opportunity structures make certain framings more acceptable, depending on their relations with the dominant discourse. Thus, the concept links discourse and power (Ferree 2003; Ferree et al. 2002).

The discursive opportunity structures are also described as a "complex playing field [that] provides advantages and disadvantages in an uneven way to the various contestants in framing contests" (Ferree et al. 2002, 62). Thus, the "playing field" is dynamic and can change due to decisions made consciously by actors or because of the impact of events beyond their control (ibid.). Here, I conceive the dimension of agency broadly: Discursive opportunity structures not only relate to EU/civil society interaction but also to the general framing efforts of all involved actors, including the individual EU institutions.

Kulawik argues that looking at political opportunity structures from a discursive perspective underlines the importance of agency: "The 'objective' existence of opportunity structures is not decisive for the actual strategies pursued by actors, but how these opportunities are perceived" (2009, 268). In the context of this book, this means that frame articulation does not only stem from civil society: EU institutions may also use framing strategies and favorable opportunity structures to advance certain frames. In other words, the focus on political and discursive opportunity structures in the analysis of EU gender-based violence policies, for example (see chapter 4) relates both to EU/civil society interaction and to frame contestations between the key institutionalized actors.

A Theoretical Model for Analyzing European Union Policy making

The theoretical landscape outlined and discussed above is translated into a model to guide the analysis of EU policy-making processes (see figure 1.1). The model identifies the key dimensions to pay attention to in the empirical analysis of the role of ideas in transnational, European

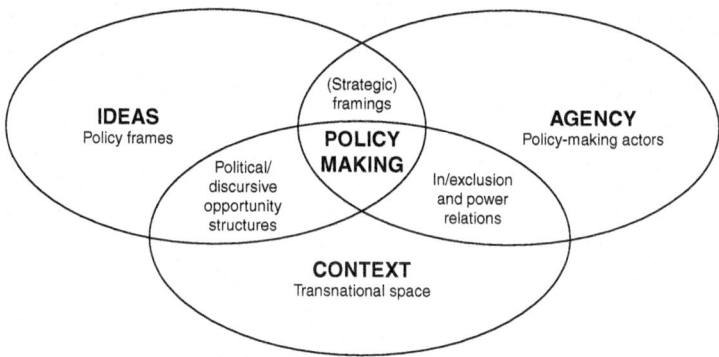

Figure 1.1 Theoretical Model for Analyzing European Union Policy making.

policymaking. It distinguishes between the three analytical dimensions mentioned above: ideas, agency, and context. Furthermore, it addresses the relations between the three dimensions; these interrelational fields, or the "space in-between" the three main dimensions, are to be considered the operationalization of the theoretical ideas for empirical analysis.

The dynamic aspects of the model—the interactions between the key dimensions as they are conceptualized in these interrelational fields—are the key dimensions of the analysis: strategic framing and the political and discursive opportunity structures of the institutional context. For example, in chapters 4 and 5, I focus on the policy development of the issue of gender-based violence, the institutionalization of frames within this area (emphasizing particularly shifts and contestations in these processes), and their implications, not least in relation to processes of degendering, as well as the opportunities and constraints of the institutional context within which frames are articulated by EU and civil society actors. The policy-making actors referred to are both transnational women's organizations, working on the European level to influence the EU institutions, and different institutional actors within the EU. A third interrelational field is included, namely, that of in/exclusions together with legitimacy issues in relation to civil society actors—these are exemplified in the empirical analysis of minority and majority organizations in chapter 3.

"Institutions" are not mentioned explicitly, but they are implicitly present in every part of the model, as a contextual dimension, an actor, and as the institutionalization of ideas through policy making. As mentioned above, I interpret institutions as being ideational; they are "sedimentations" of discourses. This sedimentation or institutionalization of ideas happens, among other things, through policy-making processes (i.e., the central field of the model where the three circles converge). Furthermore, as institutionalized ideas, institutions perform agency and are therefore also located among the policy-making actors. Finally, institutions are contextual in the sense that their political, legal, organizational, and discursive frameworks work as opportunity structures of the transnational space. In other words, the institutionalized framework of the EU serves as the main context of claims making, mobilization, discursive contestations, and framing strategies at the transnational level.

Similarly, gendered dimensions are also transversal and relevant in any of the fields or circles of the model (as gendered policy frames, gender actors, and as gendered power relations). The idea of gendering is a key dimension of the analysis of policy frames here. Policies are considered to be gendered when they include gender categories or take into account structural gender (in)equality as part of the diagnosis and/or the prognosis. However, in the theories, the gendering of institutions often refers to the institutionalization of unequal gender relations and power asymmetries (see above). Nevertheless, as institutionalized ideas, institutions can also be considered gendered if they include gendered policies as a part of the institutional framework. Thus, processes of gendering should be taken into account in relations to gendered policy frames, gender actors, and gendered power relations.

A Dynamic Approach to Intersectionality in the Transnational Context

The EU is, in many ways, marked by a diversity agenda. As Squires (2006) points out the diversity agenda refers both to social justice goals and to the business case of diversity management. To this, we might add the security agenda, which relates the management of diversity to social cohesion in multicultural societies. When linked to social justice, diversity concerns equity in society, when linked to management the goal is to enlarge the recruitment pool of companies or enhance the branding of a company or a product. In this sense, diversity is often associated with positive attributes whereas the notion of difference is more related to (a critical stance on) inequality. The specific idea of thinking different inequality grounds together is conceptualized in the EU as "multiple discrimination" (see for instance the 2007 EC report "Tackling Multiple Discrimination. Practices, Policies and Laws") whereas most academic debates are concerned with the idea of "intersectionality."[9]

The Concept of Intersectionality

I address the political dimensions of intersectionality (see also Borchorst and Teigen 2010; Crenshaw 1991; Kantola and Nousiainen 2009; Lombardo and Verloo 2009) by analyzing intersecting categories in policies, on the one hand, and minority intersectional constituencies in civil society, on the other. By "intersectionality," I understand the way in which the interaction between different inequality creating categories constitutes specific forms of oppression or empowerment. In other words, a woman is not just a woman; she is a woman of a certain age, ethnicity, social class, sexual orientation, and so forth and these aspects of her identity are inseparable. The specific positioning of each person is comprised of different intersecting, inequality creating categories, and the impact of these categories combined is different than the impact of their sum, that is, if we simply add them all together (as in the multiple discrimination approach). What follows from the intersectional approach is that identity categories (woman, man, etc.) are not homogeneous; rather, they are made up of a multiplicity of different positionings depending on each individual's intersectional belongings (Crenshaw 1991; Christensen and Siim 2006; Hancock 2007).

Intersectionality can be addressed at different levels: It addresses discrimination at the individual as well as the group level and the institutional level. Antidiscrimination rights are often individual as is the judicial perspective on the issue with a focus on litigation and court cases. There is a collective dimension to intersectionality for whole groups can be discriminated against in intersectional terms through structural discrimination. There is individual discrimination, as addressed in policies, for example, and systemic discrimination suffered by entire groups, as reflected in the demands of minority intersectional organizations. To some extent, this reflects the difference between individual cases and patterns of discriminatory practices toward intersectional groups, based on social structures and discourses.

Here, I focus particularly on intersectionality in policy making and the way in which intersectionality is institutionalized in the EU. This occurs on three different levels: (1) the policies and their intersectional categories, (2) the institutional setup, where gender, disability, and antidiscrimination are placed in separate units and there are no elaborate interinstitutional measures to combine the perspectives, and (3) civil society interaction where the EC favors an integrated approach and encourages cooperation between NGOs representing different inequalities, but directs no special attention to intersectional minority constituencies (see Introduction). In practice, this situation creates some degree of competition. In this regard, intersectionality addresses conflicts between and within inequality groups and contestations over gender equality, for example, but it also leads to new alliances.

Institutional intersectionality acknowledges the contextualization of how inequalities have been institutionalized (Ferree 2009). This refers, for instance, to the privileged position of gender and the way in which the institutional history of the EU affects the contestations playing out between civil society actors. It also relates to the EC preference for an integrated approach and a singular voice representing women. These dimensions are transferred to the interaction between the EU institutions and civil society organizations. And, finally, it reflects the way in which the privileged position of the European Women's Lobby (EWL) is contested as other women's groups who have not been recognized in the institutional context question the homogeneity of the women's interest represented in the EU. The way in which intersectionality has been institutionalized in the EU as well as the identification of particular grounds of discrimination shapes how it is understood in civil society, the claims set forward, and the struggles it entails. These dimensions of the institutionalization of intersectionality in the EU will be analyzed throughout the book.

Diversity and Inclusion: Mobilization and Institutionalization

The development of gender equality policies and the institutionalization of intersectionality in the EU have influenced the way in which intersectionality is perceived and practiced transnationally (Rolandsen Agustín and Siim forthcoming b): This includes the potential for mobilizing around gender-and-diversity claims at the transnational level. Integrating the concepts of difference, diversity, and gender equality into a coherent model for analyzing intersectionality at the European, transnational level is the main objective of this book. How can we analyze intersectionality transnationally? Which processes of intersectionality do we find at the transnational level? And what are the implications of these processes in terms of the gendering of policies and organizations? Focusing on these key questions, the book is based on an integration of different dimensions of analyzing intersectionality transnationally that focuses on mobilizing, on the one hand, and institutionalizing, on the other, including in this way both a top-down and a bottom-up perspective.

Through the lenses of intersectionality, mobilization concerns mostly the expression of a diversity of (intersecting) voices in civil society whereas institutionalization refers to attention to different inequalities in policy making as well as inclusion of a variety of civil society organizations and movements and the diversification of their channels of access to the political system. Thus, at a theoretical level I relate the intersections of gender and diversity to the mobilization and empowerment of women's organizations, for example, through the self representation of minority women in independent organizations, as well as to policy making, such as the recognition of minority women as policy interlocutors and the integration of their interests and concerns in policies. As regards institutionalization, I advocate for an enhancement of inclusive policy-making processes in order to reflect the empirical reality of diversity (of claims, demands, and interests among collective actors). I argue that diversity must be attended to at the transnational level in terms of collective mobilization (i.e., women's organizations) and contestation over policy meanings (i.e., women's interests) (see chapter 3).

The interrelation between collective mobilization and institutional structures may facilitate the expression of a diversity of voices (Rolandsen Agustín and Siim forthcoming b). This means that the model for analyzing intersectionality in a transnational context includes the consideration and integration of (1) the transnational space of mobilization and policy making; (2) civil society participation; and (3) institutionalization of diversity. Throughout the individual chapters, the book seeks answers to the ways in which intersectionality is institutionalized at the European, transnational level through EU policy making, civil society mobilization, and EU/civil society interaction. Thus, the book focuses on the interaction between policies, institutions, and civil society actors in relation to gender equality, diversity, and intersectionality.

The challenge is how to make room for diversity in policies (i.e., the content) as well as in policy making (i.e., the institutional processes). Using an intersectional model of analysis, which takes into account the particular context of the polity, two important dimensions of plurality can be adequately underlined: differences between women (as a heterogeneous group) as well as between women and other social groups (Rolandsen Agustín and Siim 2013; forthcoming b). Squires (2007) addresses the "turn to diversity" in political theory and argues that a model of inclusive democracy must acknowledge difference. This implies both power inequalities, and conflicts and tensions between different understandings of gender and other inequality categories. In other words, rethinking democratic inclusion from the perspective of intersectionality makes room for addressing contestation based on differences within the heterogeneous group of women (i.e., the actors) as well as "conflicting interpretations of gender equality and women's interests" (i.e., the discourses) (Rolandsen Agustín and Siim 2013; forthcoming b).

At the institutional level, one way of "making room for diversity" is to develop mechanisms of inclusive policy making in the EU/civil society interface. This would precisely take into account differences among social groups and address contestation over diverse interests. The current institutional setup at the EU level does not acknowledge the empirical reality of a diversity of demands from transnational civil society since it focuses on separate, rather than intersecting, inequalities (see chapters 2 and 3). Based on my empirical analysis of European women's organizations, I argue that the institutional structures of the EU do not match the practices and discourses of transnational women's movements. Since institutions play a crucial role in facilitating and encouraging expressions of diversity and their translation into the institutional realm, empowerment through articulation of diversified voices should be combined with the restructuring of current institutions with the view to address more adequately needs and demands emerging from multiple inequalities. Inclusive democracy implies precisely this recognition and incorporation of diversity and contestations as expressed through (intersectional) organizations. In practice, this would enhance the representation of diverse interests; however, the EU institutions have yet to come up with a solution for the complex inclusion of the diversity of interests and claims articulated in the transnational civil society.

According to Squires (2007), the political representation of women's movements always implies the exclusion of particular interests; the organizations that are included into institutional policy-making processes usually express a gender equality understanding, which resonates with the dominant policy of the institutions. In this way, "legitimate claims makers" are defined through processes of in/exclusion: The EU institutions decide who has a voice in policy processes and, thus, create their own interlocutors, that is, those who they represent (see Rolandsen Agustín 2008). Similarly, Young (2000) argued that diversity in perspectives, concerns, and belongings is a resource for democratic debate, rather than a division to overcome. Marginalized groups and voices from below should be included and given voice through mobilization. In this way, the diversity agenda can be perceived as a strategy to empower women who have been excluded from dominant gender equality discourses. A democratic model should focus on empowerment of women as social and political actors (Liebert 2007), on the one hand, and the restructuring of public institutions and policies (Squires 2007), on the other (see also Rolandsen Agustín and Siim 2013; forthcoming b).

What characterizes the transnational space is that it opens new possibilities for women's collective mobilization but it also tends toward exclusion of minority voices mainly due the difficulty of mobilizing at the transnational level, for instance, in terms of resources and the policy-making structures that favor elite groups and institutional advocacy or lobbying. Diverse women's groups' mobilization is a form of resistance against this tendency: Contestation and deliberation (from civil society) counteract the tendency toward exclusive interest representation and efficiency in civil society interaction (as practiced by the EC, for instance, through the preference for one unified organizational voice per inequality) (see chapters 2 and 3). There is a need to attend to diversity in a transnational model of intersectionality and inclusive democracy both in terms of contestations over policy meanings (i.e., diversity of women's interests) and collective mobilization (i.e., diversity of women's organizations). In this regard, I relate diversity to mobilization and empowerment of minority groups, in terms of the representation of intersectional constituencies, as well as to institutionalization and policy agendas, as regard the recognition of for instance minority women as interlocutors in policy making and as target groups of policies.

Contextualizing Intersectionality at the Transnational Level

With reference to Ferree (2009), I argue for the need to contextualize intersectionality in terms of how it has been institutionalized at the European level. The inequality categories upon which the idea of intersectionality builds take on different meanings depending on the contexts in which they are engrained, be they national, political, or institutional. Ferree argues that "national political histories of interpreting and institutionalizing class, race, and gender are dimensions of inequality, which are open opportunity structures that influence discourses in interactively intersectional ways" (Ferree 2009, 87–88). In relation to the EU this means taking into account its particular multilevel structure and its history of social and economic policies as a part of the context within which intersectionality is practiced and institutionalized (Rolandsen Agustín and Siim 2013; forthcoming b). The discursive opportunity structure of the EU has shaped the intersections between inequality categories, affecting the possibilities for political participation among civil society actors (Rolandsen Agustín and Siim 2013).

What characterizes the EU context of intersectionality is its status as "a complex hybrid," which has been shaped by the history of the EU and its internal struggles (Ferree 2008). The EU hybrid consists of a particular ideological combination: "An orientation to neo-liberalism and economic competitiveness on the global level, and a specific regional claim to the distinctive success of "Europe" as a model of modernity and social progress" (Ferree 2008, 237). Within this context of ideological hybridity, conflicts are carried out around the dichotomy of "citizen/noncitizen" in terms of framing equality policies and claims, rather than race like in the United States. (Ferree 2008; 2009). This means that gendered problems are primarily framed in relation to this dichotomy, thus excluding the "other," that is, the less gender equal noncitizens and non-Europeans (Rolandsen Agustín and Siim 2013; Rolandsen Agustín 2009; see also chapter 6).

Furthermore, Ferree (2009) emphasizes the potential, which lies in the EU context for feminist advocates to frame gender equality policies actively and strategically. The particular EU history of struggles and contestations over different interpretations and understandings of gender equality and women's interests as well as the turn from gender as the privileged inequality category—when it comes to policy attention (especially in terms of labor-market policies)—to a strengthened focus on diversity and multiple inequalities should be added to this contextualized perspective on intersectionality and the institutionalization of gender and diversity in the EU (Rolandsen Agustín and Siim 2013; see also chapters 2 and 3).

Underlining this contextualization is the recognition of the transnational space and the multilevel structure of the EU as key dimensions of the contextualized way in which intersectionality has been institutionalized at the European level. The transnational space is the space beyond the limits of the nation states—where actors, actions, and institutions cross nation-state borders. Transnational mobilization is different from national mobilization, for example, due to the territorial reference (where transnational activists usually mobilize collectively without living close to each other, for instance) and because the political system of the EU and its channels of access are different from those of the nation-state. However, transnational activists gain new possibilities of directing their demands toward multiple levels, or channels of claims making, (i.e., the local, the regional, the national, and the transnational) precisely because of the development of the EU as a multilevel polity. At the same time, the transnational space of mobilization, in itself, is strengthened in a process parallel to the institutional development of the EU: Civil society actors interacting directly with the EU institutions and seeking to influence these through lobbying efforts (such as the EWL) as well as organizations more distanced from or directly opposed to the EU as an institutional structure (like the European Social Forum) are influenced by policies and practices of these very institutions.

This, in turn, influences the way in which intersectionality is institutionalized and practiced. Yuval-Davis (2006; 2007) has been a pioneer in combining the intersectional and transnational perspective on multiple inequalities, focusing on people's multiple belongings and the different power structures, which underlie inequalities. This implies that an intersectional analysis is also a multilevel analysis, which takes into account different institutional, structural and individual perspectives (Christensen and Siim 2010). In a European perspective, we must pay attention to different institutional levels of policy making, inherent in the multilevel structure of the EU polity as well as different forms of collective claims making stemming from transnational civil society (i.e., the institutionalization and mobilization dimensions combined in the dynamic and contextualized approach to the analysis of transnational intersectionality applied here), which takes into account conflicts and contestations between different actors and frames.

On a methodological level the transnational perspective on contextualized intersectionality that is pursued in this book relates to a more general development in the social sciences moving beyond what Beck (2002) has entitled "methodological nationalism." The latter takes the nation-state as the exclusive starting point of (typically comparative) analyses and builds on "the explicit or implicit assumptions about the nation-state being the power container of social processes and the national being the key-order for studying major social, economic and political processes" (Beck 2002, 21). However, current local/global dynamics as well as processes of Europeanization, for instance, makes this approach obsolete to a certain extent, at least in what pertains to the exclusiveness of the focus on the nation-state. Transnational relations and multilevel politics need to be taken into account and incorporated in methodological approaches to analyze social and political processes in the world today whether they are empirically expressed at national or international level. Inherent in this approach is the acknowledgment of the ever important role of the nation-state combined with the recognition of the transnational space and transnational dynamics as something more than the sum of nation-states.

In the empirical analysis of the EU as focus point and catalyst of a significant part of the European debate on equality and diversity, the transnational perspective underlines the ways in which discourses, practices, and policy development at different levels are intimately related and mutually influenced by each other. This enhances the theoretical and methodological perspective by moving beyond nationalism and focusing on the interaction between local, national, and international contexts. Both methodologically and theoretically, the study of gender and intersectionality must be developed accordingly; as argued above, the transnational perspective calls for a rethinking of intersectionality at the European level (Rolandsen Agustín and Siim forthcoming b) and, at the same time, we must look empirically at intersectionality in its transnational context. Mostly our basic understanding and comprehension of the world and of its social and political processes and institutions are colored by the national framework; however, when looking to empirical evidence, such as for instance collective mobilization and civil society action at the European level, I find that practices are very much influenced by transnational dynamics (see chapter 3). Thus, the analysis of intersectionality through the dimensions of institutionalization and mobilization at the European level underlines the importance of transnational practices, which challenge engrained mental and institutional frameworks, rooted in (methodological) nationalism. This is precisely the endeavor of the remaining chapters of this book, that is, empirical analyses of the ways in which intersectionality has developed transnationally through processes of institutionalization and mobilization. These analyses take into account the dimensions introduced in the theoretical model for analyzing EU policy making presented above, namely those of context, ideas, and agency. In other words, they attend to the interrelational fields of strategic framings, opportunity structures, and processes of in/exclusion.

2

Gender and Other Inequalities in the Institutionalization of Multiple Discrimination Policies

With the introduction of article 13 of the Amsterdam Treaty (1997) on combating the six grounds of discrimination (sex, racial or ethnic origin, religion or belief, disability, age, and sexual orientation), antidiscrimination and multiple discrimination were cemented on the political agenda and policy-making processes of the EU. New legislation was introduced with the aim of putting the different grounds of discrimination on an equal footing in terms of protection. This has been perceived as a challenge for gender equality claims and policies as their development, to some extent, stagnated, while the focus was placed on strengthening the protection against other grounds of discrimination, such as race and ethnicity, which had previously been more neglected. However, these developments may also present an opportunity for institutions and organizations to establish new structures and alliances that are better equipped to address the multiple and intersectional perspective on inequality and discrimination.

The institutionalization of the idea of multiple discrimination in EU policies is characterized by a focus on the legal framework in terms of protection; on balancing out the levels of protection; on promoting the positive effects of diversity and rights through nonbinding policies and campaigns; and the favoring of an integrated approach to multiple discrimination in the institutional framework. I argue that the institutional take on multidiscrimination policies and the preferences laid out by EU institutions have influenced civil society organizations, initially creating competition between inequality grounds. This has slowly turned into more proactive stances and tendencies toward cooperation among organizations. However, the interface between EU institutions and civil society organizations in the transnational sphere shows inconsistencies: Whereas the EC, for instance, prefers interaction with one (umbrella) organization per inequality ground, the empirical reality of European civil society is characterized by plurality of organizations and diversity of demands. Thus, I argue that some organizations are privileged and others marginalized in the interaction between the EU institutions and transnational civil society, resulting in significant processes of inclusion and exclusion.

The scholarly literature on European women's organizations in recent years has focused on the implications of EU multiple discrimination policies, on the one hand, and on dilemmas related to the diversity of women's interests, on the other. I explore these issues at the transnational level and analyze the ways in which European women's organizations, operating in the transnational space of activism and mobilization, respond to the diversity challenge. The present chapter as well as the following concerns diversity as a challenge related to the development and institutionalization of intersectionality at the transnational level. This chapter, on gender and other inequalities in the institutionalization of multiple discrimination policies, focuses primarily on policies and institutional setup, thus adopting a top-down perspective on the development as well as on the EU/civil society interface; chapter 3 focuses on minority intersectional constituencies and women's collective mobilization at the European level and directs the attention more explicitly toward civil society strategies and the potential of inclusive policy-making structures, that is, the bottom-up perspective.

The Multiple Discrimination Policy Framework of the European Union

Gender discrimination has been on the EU agenda from the very beginning of the European integration process, whereas the fight against racism was introduced in the 1980s (Borchorst and Mokre 2013). It was not until the mid-1990s, EU institutions (pressured by the EP and by civil society organizations) started considering combating several and multiple grounds of discrimination (see EC Green Paper "Equality and Non-Discrimination in an Enlarged European Union," COM(2004)379). This led to the introduction of article 13 of the Amsterdam Treaty. Reflecting political and academic debates concerning discrimination and the attention paid to particularly vulnerable groups in policy making, the antidiscrimination article of the Amsterdam Treaty became a turning point in the legal development of

EU policies as well as in the institutional setup for handling different kinds of discrimination. Two directives were passed after the adoption of the article: The Racial Equality Directive (2000/43/EC), dealing with discrimination on the grounds of race and ethnicity outside the labor market, and the Employment Framework Directive (2000/78/EC), focusing on discrimination within the field of employment and occupation for the grounds not covered by previous directives, that is, belief, disability, age, and sexual orientation. Furthermore, the Goods and Services Directive (2004/113/EC), which was the first directive to address gender equality beyond the labor market, was also adopted based on the new antidiscrimination measures.

These developments reflect an effort to balance out the level of protection between the different grounds of discrimination while enhancing the multiple discrimination concerns in policy making. So far the results have not been convincing: Little thinking is carried out in terms of how the different inequality dimensions interact and how an accentuated competition between the different discrimination grounds in terms of the level of protection is playing out. Uneven levels of protection were already a reality before the signing of the Amsterdam Treaty with gender being the most developed ground. This hierarchy has changed with the new antidiscrimination measures and directives and race/ethnicity has taken over the "lead" (Bell 2002; Cunningham 1992; Fernández de Vega et al. 2008b; Kantola and Nousiainen 2009; Kantola 2010). The history and legislation for each ground of discrimination thus differ.

Especially in the 2000s, diversity and multiple discrimination have been on the agenda of the EU, both in terms of the legal follow-up on the Amsterdam Treaty aiming to balance protection levels and in nonbinding policies and initiatives. The framework of the latter was introduced with the 2001 Community Action Programme to Combat Discrimination (2000/750/EC). It addresses multiple discrimination even though no definition is given. The document deals with different discrimination grounds in parallel rather than their intersections. It also highlights the similarities and differences between different grounds of discriminations:

> Discrimination on different grounds can have similar features and can be combated in similar ways. Experience built up over many years in combating discrimination on some grounds, including sex, can be used to the benefit of other grounds. However, the specific features of the diverse forms of discrimination should be accommodated. (2000/750/EC: 1)

Thus, the efforts build on previous experiences with combating gender discrimination and, even though it is explicitly stated that there is no hierarchy of ranking between the different grounds, the document emphasizes that "women are often the victims of multiple discrimination."

In terms of activities, the Action Programme includes a funding program to increase awareness, support organizations and carry out research, and an information campaign aiming to "inform people about their rights and obligations and to promote the positive benefits of diversity" (see the 2008 EC report on the "For Diversity. Against Discrimination" information campaign. Five years of raising awareness in the European Union, 7). The information campaign "For Diversity. Against Discrimination," which has run since 2003, covers a number of activities promoting respect for diversity and raising awareness of rights, including a European Truck Tour through which the EC initiative collaborated with local partners to promote equality and diversity in national contexts of the member states (see also Borchorst and Mokre 2013). The EC activities combating discrimination were continued and strengthened with the 2007 European Year of Equal Opportunities for All—Towards a Just Society, which focused on raising awareness of rights, strengthen participation, celebrate diversity, and work toward solidarity. The decision to establish the year (771/2006/EC) emphasizes the concepts of "equal treatment" and "nondiscrimination," making few references to the idea of multiple discrimination. The different grounds of discrimination of article 13 of the Amsterdam Treaty are mentioned repeatedly, but only once is multiple discrimination addressed as "discrimination on two or more of the grounds listed in article 13," with the aim of promoting "a balanced treatment of all the grounds."

In terms of the institutional setup, the EC opts for a multiple perspective on discrimination: EC equality policies focus on addressing several grounds of discrimination together, adding them rather than looking at their intersections or the way in which they interact with each other. The 2004 EC Green Paper "Equality and Non-Discrimination in an Enlarged European Union" (COM[2004]379) highlights in particular the need for "a coherent and integrated approach" in order to effectively address multiple discrimination. Again the similarities of the different grounds of discrimination as well as the possibility of learning from previous experiences combating one ground are mentioned as significant elements of the multiple approach.[1] The 2007 EC report "Tackling Multiple Discrimination. Practices, Policies and Laws" addresses the idea of multiple inequalities more directly by differentiating between multiple discrimination (discrimination on more than one ground) and intersectional discrimination (several inseparable grounds interacting with each other). The EC focuses on addressing several grounds together and they opt for the multiple discrimination approach.[2]

Some traits of intersectionality can, however, be found in EU equality policies even though these articulations are still "embryonic" in the EU context: Intersectional dimensions of discrimination and different forms of inequality "are increasingly present but they are treated implicitly and from a separate perspective" (Lombardo and Rolandsen Agustín 2012). This means that there is no in-depth articulation of intersectional relations, such as for instance the way in which inequalities can be perceived as inseparable from each other; in general, more articulated understandings of intersectional dimensions, such as structural or transformative perspectives, which could challenge status quo, and existing privileges, are lacking from EU policy texts. Furthermore the increased attention to a wider range of inequalities often leads to the degendering of policies. In other words, when multiple inequalities enter the policy stage, gender tends to move to the background or entirely disappear from the texts rather than being incorporated into a multiple or intersectional perspective on the interaction between gender and other inequalities (ibid.).

Singular or integrated equality bodies, addressing all grounds of discrimination (as opposed to bodies dealing with each ground separately), have been set up in most member states, as recommended by the EC (2004), whereas others have chosen separate bodies. Advantages of the integrated equality bodies include emphasis on complex interrelations between inequality grounds; disadvantages concern the potential rationalization in terms of funding as well as overlooking distinctive traits of the singular grounds. Within its own institutions, the EU has maintained a separate framework regarding gender discrimination (the European Institute for Gender Equality (EIGE) and, in the DG Justice, Unit D1, Gender Equality, previously DG Employment, Unit G1 Equality between Men and Women and Unit G2 Equality, Action against Discrimination: Legal Questions) and integrated bodies for most of the remaining discrimination grounds (the Agency for Fundamental Rights (FRA) and DG Justice, Directorate D, Equality, previously DG Employment, Unit G4 Action against Discrimination). Concerning the EC, the Equality Directorate of DG Justice treats gender and disabilities separately in its institutional structure whereas nondiscrimination and combating discrimination against Roma are placed in another unit. Vulnerable groups and ageing are reflected in the institutional setup of DG Employment but there is no directorate explicitly targeting gender and the labor market. In the EP, the FEMM Committee is in charge of gender related issues (Ahrens 2008; Fernández de Vega and Lombardo 2008; Kantola 2010; Kantola and Nousiainen 2012; Squires 2010).

Having analyzed the policy framework on multiple discrimination, and with this its institutionalization in terms of directives, policies, and institutional setup, I will now direct the attention toward mobilization. This concerns in particular civil society organizations' reactions to the policy framework, the influence exercised by the EU institutions on organizations, as well as the EU/civil society interface in terms of gender and intersectionality. In practice multiple discrimination policies promoted by the EU have affected civil society relations in the sense that an accentuated competition between organizations combating different grounds of discrimination can be detected. Here, women's organizations seem to have been to some extent paralyzed by the critical stance that, in a first instance at least, impeded more progressive action and new alliances to develop between organizations. I will focus precisely on these reactions and courses of action taken within transnational civil society as a response to EU policies and preferences on multiple discrimination.

Transnational Civil Society and European Women's Organizations

The transnational space opens up new possibilities of claims making as another layer of political decision making and opportunity structures is incorporated and organizations are able to direct their demands to this European, transnational level. In other words, the EU has provided new opportunities for civil society mobilization as well as for new alliances to be forged (Helfferich and Kolb 2001; Lang 2009; Williams 2003; Woodward 2006). The transnational space of activism is constructed vis-à-vis the development of the EU as a political institution. Simply by multiplying the levels of interaction, the transnational space is, in itself, characterized by complexity, a complexity of participation, and policy making within which civil society actors manage to navigate.

Social policy provisions in the EU are, in general, limited as this is mainly an area of member-state competence. Nevertheless, a propitious environment for gender equality and social policy issues characterized the beginning and middle of the 1990s though the latter mainly translated into a focus on antidiscrimination policies (Kantola and

Nousiainen 2009). The antidiscrimination provisions of the Amsterdam Treaty have provided civil society actors with a new arena for setting forward demands vis-à-vis the EU institutions beyond the employment/economy framework (i.e., relating gender equality to women's participation in the labor market) as EU competences are enhanced in equality and nondiscrimination areas. In this vein, Woodward and Wiercx (2003) argue that article 13 has enhanced the political opportunities for European social movements and increased the "basis for social action" as more attention was directed toward social policy in the EU in general in the 1990s. According to the authors, this was mainly due to the strength of left wing governments in the 1990s, the Nordic enlargement, and the increasing sense of a democratic deficit in the EU institutions (ibid.). However, a strong emphasis on economic growth and competitiveness increasingly began to develop toward the end of the 1990s (Van der Vleuten 2007).

Authors agree that new transnational opportunity structures have emerged in the last two decades. Woodward and Wiercx (2003) talk about "exponential growth" in the mid-1990s of European organizations trying to influence and become "sparring partners" of the EU. In particular, the 1990s witnessed the establishment of a number of umbrella organizations promoted by the EC.[3] Thus, from the mid-1990s onwards more and more civil society organizations have engaged with the EU system and gained presence in the transnational space (Woodward 2007).

The European women's organizations are a particularly relevant empirical case in terms of transnational activism because the "European women's movement was one of the first to see the EU as an arena for political claims making in the 1970s" (Thiel and Prügl 2009, 10). It is often highlighted as an example of a high degree of transnational activism and one of the fastest expanding areas (Keck and Sikkink 1998; Woodward 2006). It is considered one of the most active and successful movements, providing new innovative ideas to EU policy making and legitimacy to its institutions (Lang 2009; Ruzza 2004; Woodward 2007). The favorable environment of the 1990s also affected the women's movements at the EU level: In the EU, transnational women's networks are part of a surge in advocacy fuelled by the "rights based" takeoff phase of European integration in the early 1990s and the shift from the "community method" to more open multilevel governance processes. The new focus on rights gave women's groups more political leverage and mobilization tools while multilevel governance extended the institutional spaces and settings for advocacy (Lang 2009, 328).

Cichowski (2002) argues that the EU framework has enabled women's activists on the national level to participate in transnational debates.[4] Thus, the EU has become a key gender equality actor both at the national and at the transnational levels, for instance in its role as agenda setter and impulsator in relation to equal pay provisions. The prominent role of the EU within the field of gender equality policies is one of the reasons why it is imperative for women's organizations to address the European level directly or through umbrella structures. Though the women's organizations have not always been successful in their attempts to influence EU policy making, pressure has, at times, led to change and progress, and a mutual strengthening between the EU institutions (gaining legitimacy) and the civil society organizations (furthering access to policy making) has taken place (Van der Vleuten 2007).

Competition and Equality Hierarchies

However, increased mobilization at the transnational level has resulted in processes of both cooperation and competition between civil society organizations due to the multiple discrimination framework set and defined by the EU as well as the organizations' reactions to this. So far, few studies have been conducted within the field of multiple discrimination and European mobilization. They concern mainly the relations between umbrella organizations, covering different, single discrimination grounds, and their internal competition and/or cooperation (Pristed Nielsen 2010; Woodward 2006; 2007; Woodward and Wiercx 2003). The transnational civil society "landscape" has changed, and a "new arena for contention and cooperation to move the equality agenda forward" (Woodward 2006, 5) has emerged. Legal and organizational structures favoring multiple discrimination policies and organizations each representing one ground of discrimination[5] as well as the EU enlargement have led to changes in organizations, resources and discourses. There is an increasing pressure at the European level for organizations to work across issues and discrimination grounds and to recognize diversity. Thus, cross-issue alliances are increasingly emphasized. However, Woodward (2006) argues that organizations know little about each other, they are not aware of each others' contributions, and umbrella organizations overshadow all other civil society actors in the field.

As mentioned above, race and ethnicity have, to some extent, taken over the policy spotlight from gender issues within the EU (Woodward 2007). Gender equality policies and mainstream women's organizations are challenged (or consider themselves to be challenged) by the diversity and multiple discrimination approach. The issue of equality hierarchies is contentious, and the women's movement makes a "territorial defense" of its policy gains: "This is the most thorny and controversial issue for the women's movement, how to retain a gender focus and continue work progress, while also agreeing that other sorts of discrimination need to be tackled" (Woodward 2006, 16). While acknowledging the need to address crosscutting issues, some women's organizations, like the EWL, at least initially feared that other discrimination grounds would gain priority over gender (Woodward 2006; 2007; Woodward and Wiercx 2003). In particular, the EWL was concerned that the greater emphasis on other inequalities and discrimination grounds than gender would develop at the expense of the goal of gender equality (Cullen 2005).

The recent developments can also be perceived more positively as an opportunity for gender equality policies (Squires 2007) to address intersectionality concerns and differences between women more adequately. Furthermore, "the new configurations of the European Union offer unknown possibilities for policy inventiveness" (Woodward 2007, 169). Whereas intersectional thinking and the introduction of multiple discrimination policies in the EU are generally assessed in positive terms by feminist scholars, certain concerns have also been voiced: "The emergence of multiple inequalities agendas...has raised anxieties that gender equality considerations will be marginalized, and even undermined, by the pursuit of other equality claims" (Squires 2007, 19). Thus, multiple discrimination policies may present a threat to gender equality goals, by marginalizing them, or an opportunity to develop greater sensitivity toward intersectional dimensions (ibid.). Kantola (2010) mentions two positive aspects of the development: EU legislation on other inequality grounds may be brought up to the same level of protection as gender ("upward harmonization"), and the institutions gain increased competences in handling cases of multiple discrimination when all discrimination grounds are considered together.

Skeptical accounts focus on the marginalization of gender, the competition between grounds, and the inadequacy of using the same tools for discrimination grounds, which are different in nature (ibid.). In general, the academic debates in political science on EU, multiple discrimination, and intersectionality have focused on aspects such as the potential degendering of policies and the disappearance or dilution of gender when other inequality grounds enter the political stage (Dombos et al. 2007; Lombardo and Meier 2009;

Lombardo et al. 2009c; Mazey 2002; Schwenken 2009; Verloo et al. 2007; Woodward 2006; 2007), the lack of adequate attention to the substantial and conceptual differences between the inequality grounds (Kantola and Nousiainen 2009; Verloo 2006; Walby 2005), as well as the potential of diversity mainstreaming (Kantola 2010; Schwenken 2009; Squires 2007; 2010; Woodward 2008), that is, combining gender mainstreaming with multiple discrimination or, in other words, taking all inequality grounds into consideration when elaborating policies.

Potential for Cooperation

Since the introduction of multiple discrimination policies in the EU civil society actors working at the transnational level have undergone changes in their focus as a result of their attempts to make use of and/or adapt to this new policy framework. As explained above, feminist activists and European women's movements have both applauded and criticized the multiple discrimination approach. Initial skepticism and resistance toward the diversity approach has over time translated into a need to adapt and, most recently, more willingness for cooperation and proactive attitudes vis-à-vis the policy developments and the potentials and opportunities they represent. Initially women's organizations were particularly concerned with the status of gender within the policies and their potential degendering (Bygnes 2013; Kantola 2010; Woodward 2006). They were caught in a dilemma between addressing women's diverse interests by focusing on crosscutting issues, for instance, and preventing gender being overshadowed by other inequalities, thus wanting to maintain a separate focus on each discrimination ground.

In the mid-2000s, the EC started to push the European level umbrella organizations to work together across inequality grounds. This was a strategy to foment the perspectives of multiple discrimination. Thus, the umbrella organizations were asked to "take into account multiple discrimination in designing the [annual] work programmes" that form part of the requirements of their funding schemes (EC official, DG Employment, interview January 2008). At the same time, the DG Employment antidiscrimination unit G4 came to constitute a channel of institutional access for minority intersectional organizations (EC official, DG Employment, interview December 2007). EU institutions clearly favored cross-issue alliances (between discrimination grounds) and encouraged umbrella organizations to adopt this approach to their relations. The 2004 EC Green Paper on Equality and nondiscrimination in an enlarged EU explicitly states that: "Funding made available to NGOs under the Community action programme to combat discrimination has also helped to focus attention on the new EU anti-discrimination policy framework and the need to deliver results in accordance with this framework." The EC Green Paper also comments on skeptical reactions from certain sectors of civil society, implicitly referring to women's organizations: "It is clear that some organisations that have a tradition of working with particular target groups have found the transition to [the integrated] approach challenging." Several of my EC interviewees underline the fact that umbrella organizations need to think more of "how to work on transversal issues or crosscutting issues" (EC official, DG Employment, interview December 2007); in particular the EWL was highlighted as an organization in need of restructuring in terms of inclusion of minority women. The EC G4 interviewee emphasized that umbrella organizations needed to start thinking "globally" and looking at individuals as whole persons with multiple identities in order to include diversity and avoid competition between discrimination grounds (EC official, DG Employment, interview December 2007).

In the EC report on multiple discrimination, recommendations were made for "the European Commission [to] develop funding sources for multiple-ground NGOs" in order to "address the needs and represent the interests of intersectional groups," and "build their voice" (2007, 7).[6] However, the recommendation was rejected in a consultation of NGOs as these preferred the inclusion of all groups in umbrella organizations as well as cooperation between the umbrellas instead of broadening the scope of financing and participation to include more and smaller groups (EC official, DG Employment, interview January 2008). Thus, the EC opts for cooperation between umbrella groups in order to address multiple discrimination instead of financing minority intersectional groups, for example. In this regard, Woodward and Wiercx argue that diversity issues risk getting lost through the EU's turn to umbrella organizations and the homogenization of demands:

> [W]hile trans-national and trans-issue groups may move the social agenda of Europe forward, it will come at a loss of the very diversity it strives to encourage. Simplification and homogenization of both issue accents and national accents is a necessity in such trans-issue and transnational alliances. (2003, 30)

The implementation of an integrated approach to a range of discrimination grounds strengthened the need to incorporate different inequality dimensions in organizations and policies. In the beginning, this led to the EWL feeling threatened by other inequality umbrella organizations whose interests and discrimination grounds might have overshadowed that of gender and the privileged position held by gender advocates so far. Tensions did indeed arise between the EWL and organizations within other fields of discrimination, precisely because of the development of EU equality legislation (Mazey 2002). Whereas the EWL preferred to maintain a separate focus on each inequality ground, other umbrella organizations were swift to take on board the multiple discrimination approach, which was seen to further their cause and eliminate the "equality hierarchy":

> I think that LGBT people have been very creative and very progressive and very dynamic...I think that if women, women's associations, are not taking into account these multiple identities, they are losing some of their forces and their strengths because today I think that the discussion is far more advanced than always taking to the gender issues...I think that if the women's associations are not taking this on board they will be left on the side of the road. Okay, gender pay gap is an issue but...but there are so many different issues that women, young women, older women, are living and going through. So, it's a question of strategy and it's a question of...of momentum. (EC official, DG Employment, interview December 2007)

Another EC interviewee also perceived the EWL to be more focused on its own battle (i.e., gender equality and women's rights) and not "feeding into" other forms of discrimination (EC official, DG Employment, interview January 2008). Other studies show that the organizations focusing on race and ethnicity were more prone to cooperation across discrimination grounds (Pristed Nielsen 2013b), having more to gain from the change in policy focus than the gender organizations. However, the EWL for instance has definitely caught up, making changes in priorities and policies concerning diversity and multiple discrimination, which has resulted in a "sharpened focus" on these issues (Pristed Nielsen 2013a) and the need to enter strategic alliances across discrimination grounds. I will return to this point in chapter 3.

Interaction between Civil Society and European Union Actors

Civil society actors are, to some extent, included in EU policy-making processes. This is largely due to the fact that the EU needs legitimacy to counteract the perceived democratic deficit from which it suffers as well as the need for information transfer into EU institutions that do not always have the resources to gather enough information themselves (Ruzza 2004; Schmitter 2000). Furthermore, the civil society actors provide new and, at times, innovative policy frames, and they connect the multiple levels of governance of the EU structure (Ruzza 2004).

The emphasis placed on civil society inclusion in EU policy making and citizen participation in recent years by the EC[7] should be seen in this light. It underlines the need to combat the image of a distant bureaucracy, far away from the daily life of European citizens. Formal consultation processes are typically applied whereby civil society organizations can submit online comments on EC policy proposals.[8] The EP involves civil society organizations in the policy-making process through hearings, organized by the parliamentary committees. Due to its nature as a parliamentary site of political debates and ideological struggles, the EP is, to a certain extent, the most prone to deliberation and contestations over diverse understandings of gender equality and women's interests of the three main EU institutions. It has also been characterized as the most open of the institutions where civil society actors have the easiest access to transnational policy-making processes (see for instance Richardson 2006).

Civil society organizations are also represented in advisory committees and expert groups within individual policy areas. Furthermore, ad hoc consultations and informal lobbying activities by organizations and interest groups are major fields of civil society (attempts at) input into the EU policy-making processes as well. However, none of these measures are legally binding, and they impose no formal commitment on the EU institutions. The European Economic and Social Committee works as the official body of the EU, bridging institutions and civil society organizations, even though the European Economic and Social Committee has a limited role in decision-making processes.

I will argue that the particular structure of EU/civil society interface and, importantly, the preferences of the individual EU institutions in terms of their dialogue with organizations have created and continue to reproduce significant processes of in/exclusion whereby some women's organizations, for instance, are privileged over others. This, in turn, leads to the exclusion of certain demands and a reduction of the potential plurality of women's interests represented in EU policy-making processes.

Privileged and Marginalized Civil Society Actors: Processes of Inclusion and Exclusion

Within the limited research on European women's organizations, the EWL has been a particular subject of analysis (see for instance Helfferich and Kolb 2001; Hoskyns 1991; Pudrovska and Ferree 2004; Strid 2009).[9] On the basis of these and other analyses covering several European women's organizations (see for instance Lang 2009; Pudrovska and Ferree 2004; Roth 2007)[10] or women's European, transnational activism in general (see for instance Hoskyns 1996; Kantola 2010), the main characteristics of the panorama of women's collective activism at the European level can be identified.

The 1980s was characterized by the diverse interests and fragmented groups of the European women's movement. When the EWL, encouraged and facilitated by the EC, was founded in the early 1990s, an actual transnational focus was, for the first time, developed by women activists, trying to influence and interact with EU policy structures directly (Bretherton and Sperling 1996; Hoskyns 1991; 1996; Woodward 2006). Since then the EWL has been privileged in its interaction with the EU, being the main interlocutor within themes of gender equality and women's rights of the EC and Unit G1 Equality between Men and Women of DG Employment in particular (before the institutional restructuring of the EC in 2011). Thus, the EWL has a very strong position within the panorama of European women's organizations, being the largest umbrella body with direct relations to the EC: "[T]he EWL has come to be accepted as representing the political and social interests of European women. When women's interests are debated in the institutions of the EU, those interests appear to have become the same as the interests and policy areas of the EWL" (Strid 2009, 253).

Strid argues that this role provides the EWL with unique opportunities to formulate women's interests though the lobby is also constrained both in terms of having to adapt these interests to those of the EU and regarding the remaining European women's organizations that are restrained in their possibilities of gaining voice and access. Pudrovska and Ferree (2004) define the feminism of the EWL as "less radical" and "more liberal" and therefore better fitted to the framework of the EU than other organizations. Empirically, however, Strid (2009) finds that the EWL does push the gender equality agenda forward, also beyond the immediate interests and agenda of the EC.

Symptomatically, the women's advocacy networks at the European level tend to be oriented toward "institutional advocacy" such as lobbying rather than public debate, for instance (Lang 2009). Thus, the representational weakness of the umbrella organizations is constantly discussed, and their ability to reach the national grassroots levels is questioned. Woodward suggests that "[t]here is some justice in a critique that while the European women's organizations became more consolidated and more interlocked with policy makers, they also lost touch with issues of difference between women" (2007, 181).

Processes of exclusion play out in policy making and in the interaction between EU institutions and civil society organizations. This concerns the ways in which certain frames are in/excluded in the process of institutionalization of policy ideas as well as the constitution of legitimate interlocutors in civil society, resulting in both discursive and institutional dimensions of in/exclusion of civil society actors. In general, processes of exclusion occur both due to institutional structures (*who* is in/excluded?) and to discursive limitations (*which claims* are in/excluded?). The institutional and discursive frameworks both enable and constrain the ways in which civil society organizations act and set forward claims. They must adapt to dominant discourses in order to gain resonance for their claims; resonance in practice depends on similarity to EU institutions' interests, priorities, and policies. EU institutions recognize certain actors as more valid interlocutors than others. Similarly some claims are recognized as more legitimate than others because they resonate with dominant policies and institutional discourses. This means that the EU institutions limit claims making through the channels of participation and funding as well as the conditions, which apply to these, and through discursive means of resonance. Through these processes of in/exclusion the EU institutions constitute legitimate claims makers among the organizations mobilizing in civil society. Jenson and Mahon (1993) and Ruzza (2004) both employ the term "legitimate actors": The former from a political-discursive perspective (defining an "accepted set of meanings" about these actors), the latter in relation to the aims of movement coalitions (i.e., recognition and inclusion into policy-making processes). EU institutions implicitly define "legitimate claims makers" through processes of in/exclusion, whereby some actors and ideas are prioritized over others in the EU interaction with civil society actors. The legitimate claims makers are those included in consultation processes; their claims are transferred into policy processes depending on their ability to frame them according to institutional discourses.

To exemplify this we can see how women's interests are defined in resonance with already established EU policies; one of the most visible and significant examples of this is the way in which civil society organizations in the field of gender equality use framing strategies to make their claims fit the overarching economic growth discourse of the EU institutions. This does not mean that the equality objectives of the organizations disappear. Rather they are adapted to convince policy makers who first and foremost look for economic arguments in order to set forward potentially new policies, for instance in the way in which women's participation in the labor market and strengthened care policies are seen as a way to gain economic growth while, at the same time, advance gender equality goals. This occurred in the civil society consultation carried out in relation to the EC Green Paper on Equality and nondiscrimination in an enlarged EU, published in 2004. The EC Green Paper focuses on reducing discrimination in order to enhance labor market access and participation aimed to create economic growth. Relating to this dominant discourse, European Women Lawyers' Association (EWLA), in their response to the EC Green Paper, frames their gender equality claims as good economic policy: "The progress towards effective gender equality is still slow. This, inter alia, endangers the achievement of the Lisbon economic and social goals." Gender equality is the aim but it is converted into a means of job growth in order to make claims resonate with EU institutional policies and preferences.

Similarly, the preference of the EC for an integrated approach to multiple discrimination, as described above, contributed to the constitution of legitimate claims makers. Some organizations, such as the Social Platform, criticized the economic consequences of this approach: "Instead of a more coordinated approach this has simply led to cuts in the overall budget allocated to the fight against discrimination and less resources to deal with complex issues." ILGA and ENAR, on the other hand, showed support for the integrated approach by criticizing the "unacceptable hierarchy of protection" between different grounds of discrimination. ENAR furthermore used strategic framing to reframe the understanding of the concept of diversity, combining equality and difference in a dual approach that would pay particular attention to several grounds of discrimination simultaneously: While accepting the framework of the integrated approach, ENAR argues that there is a need for "safeguards against excessive 'merging' of the complex problems caused by different forms of discrimination." The women's organizations, on the other hand, were more skeptical toward the integrated approach, among other things because of the risk of downplaying gender dimensions: The EWL in particular argued that "different equality agendas have their specific dynamics of inclusion, exclusion, and marginalization—and consequently need specific analysis and actions" (see also Rolandsen Agustín 2008).

The functioning of the interaction between the EC, especially, and civil society organizations leads to a certain homogenization of claims and of the definition of women's interests since the EC prioritizes efficiency (i.e., one voice per ground of discrimination) over pluralization of claims or processes of deliberation and contestation within civil society. Subscribing to the normative assumption that it is an objective of civil society to allow for an expression of a plurality of ideas, empirical evidence for this plurality among women's organizations can be found at the transnational level. Activism in the European, transnational space is indeed characterized by a pluralism of demands, claims-making activities on multiple levels, and through multiple institutional channels as well as the postnational nature of some of the policy demands.

Summing up, civil society actors use framing strategies to fit their claims to the institutional context, thereby aspiring to gain recognition as "legitimate claims makers." The EU institutions hold the power to attribute voice to the different civil society organizations, and they set the discursive limits for the content of their claims if these are to be taken into consideration in policy making. Consequently, there is a permanent risk of including only the privileged groups whereby minorities are marginalized and the capacity of disadvantageous groups to include inequality concerns on the agenda is limited. Empirically speaking, this happens to a certain extent at the European level, and progress toward more inclusive policy making is slow. Furthermore, the processes of in/exclusion have an effect on civil society participation as a means to enhance the substantive representation of women's interests at the institutional level. An explicit assumption of the theoretical perspective adopted here is that civil society participation generates greater potential for the substantive representation of women's interests. Political scientists within the field of gender studies pose the question of how women's interests are represented in policy making and how the diversity of women's interests can be ensured in these processes. Squires (2007) argues that the political representation of women's movements always implies the exclusion of particular interests; the ones included are usually the ones with a gender equality understanding that resonates with dominant policy frames. There is a need to emphasize the significance of informal exclusion processes; formal access alone does not result in a translation of the plurality of civil society claims into policy making. Instead Phillips' (1999) notion of an "empowerment of the already powerful" can be found also at the transnational level.

The conditions of access to participatory processes, mobility policies affecting transnational activism, funding requirements, and resource shortage as well as discursive limitations all constrain transnational collective mobilization and result in a lack of inclusion of the diversity of claims emanating from the transnational civil society. Furthermore, my interviews confirm that gaining and maintaining legitimacy and voice is a continuous effort for civil society organizations, and it requires continued presence in Brussels, constant maintenance of networks, and contacts within the EU institutions as well as financial security (EWLA representative, interview May 2010).

Regarding the discursive dimension, the criteria for legitimacy in claims making seem to be predominantly about resonance and not deliberation, for example. Thus, "women's interests" are first and foremost defined in a way, which resonates with the dominant institutionalized policies and discourses of the EU and its individual institutions. The scope of contestation of the dominant discourses nevertheless varies among the different EU institutions. There are important differences both between and within the individual EU institutions. They differ in the processes of in/exclusion of (legitimate) interlocutors as well as in the level of access; the EP is the most open, the EC more formalized and granting access to a limited number of organizations, whereas the Council is a very closed institution where lobbying activities can backfire if embarked upon. Thus, the EU cannot be perceived as one unified entity with a single voice in matters of gender equality. Important contestations are encountered, and the EU institutions play different roles in this regard.

As mentioned above, chapters 2 and 3 are interrelated in the sense that they both address what I have labeled as the diversity challenge. Here I have discussed the policy framework constructed around multiple discrimination at the European level as well as the ways in which this framework has influenced civil society actions and ways of organizing. I will now focus more exclusively on the civil society perspective by analyzing the ways in which majority and minority women's organizations, respectively, deal with diversity, the demands they set forward as well as the potential for inclusive policy-making structures at the European, transnational level that would enable reflecting the diversity found in civil society in the institutional structures and processes.

3

MINORITY INTERSECTIONAL CONSTITUENCIES AND WOMEN'S COLLECTIVE MOBILIZATION AT THE EUROPEAN LEVEL

Transnational civil society at the European level is characterized by a plurality of organizations and diversity of their interests and demands when it comes to gender equality and the definition of "women's interests." I argue that transnational mobilization holds constraints in itself—of economic and political nature—though the possibility of organizing at this level is both enabled and hindered by the EU and its institutional and financial framework. The empirical reality shows that majority and minority women's organizations mobilizing transnationally in Europe differ not just in terms of their constituencies but also in relation to their demands, claims-making efforts, and, not least, their ways of dealing with diversity internally and externally. In particular, I focus on majority organizations' strategies for addressing minority issues, and minority intersectional organizations combining ethnicity and gender identities and claims as well as their interrelations with majority organizations. Thus, the chapter assesses the potential of the transnational, European civil society panorama in terms of defining and representing the diversity of women's collective interest vis-à-vis the EU.

In the literature, the field of women's transnational activism typically refers to global transnational feminism with a focus on broad debates surrounding the notion of global sisterhood, global inequalities, postcolonialism, and/or the UN framework (see Grewal and Kaplan 1994; 2000; Keck and Sikkink 1998; Mendoza 2002; Mohanty 2002; Naples 2002). My approach differs as I direct my attention toward a specific kind of transnational activism among women, which is delimited regionally by the political and public space surrounding the EU.[1] The EU is considered to be a transnational construction in relation to which a transnational civil society sphere has emerged and still continues to develop. There is, however, a gap in the research on the variety of civil society organizations on the transnational, European level.[2] The relations between civil society actors and state structures at the national level have been studied and theorized intensively (see for instance Outshoorn and Kantola 2007).[3] Considerably less research has been undertaken into these aspects at the European, transnational level (see however Ruzza 2004), not least in relation to EU gender equality policy making as a specific field. Whereas it is common to refer to the general significance of women's activism at the European and international levels, few studies focus on the actual dynamics of the EU/civil society interface (see however Strid 2009; Zippel 2006) or the specific transnational panorama of women's organizations in Europe.

Organizing Majority and Minority Intersectional Constituencies in Europe

The following empirical analysis centers on two of the main organizations within the area of women's rights and gender equality at the European, transnational level. One, the European Women's Lobby (EWL), is categorized as a majority organization, that is, representing women's issues broadly, and the other, the Black European Women's Council (BEWC), is characterized as a minority organization because it focuses specifically on a particular group of women. Whereas the EWL is the main majority organization in the field, BEWC is one of the most important "newcomers" with a clear minority intersectional constituency, in this case representing a gender-and-ethnicity intersection.

According to their website (womenlobby.org), the mission of the EWL is "to promote real and effective equality between women and men, in all spheres of public and private life, across the EU." Equality is related to rights, personal integrity and choice, resources, caring responsibilities, and representation. The EWL furthermore specifies its values as equality, solidarity, respect for difference and diversity, parity, freedom, peace, justice, empowerment, cooperation, accountability, transparency, and independence. The organization was established in 1990. It differentiates between full members—with voting rights and organized into national coordinations—and associate members—with access to EWL activities and observer status in the general assembly. The full members comprise a count of 30 national coordinations (the

27 EU member states and 3 candidate countries) and 21 European-wide organizations. Associate membership is currently granted to 34 organizations from across the world. The membership structure thus combines "a geographical framework," which has expanded in parallel with the EU, and representation of "specific groups" through associate membership. The EWL receives 83 percent of its budget from the EC Progress program and relies also on membership fees and contributions from independent sources. The organizations mainly engage in lobbying activities, advocacy work, projects and raising awareness on women's rights, and gender equality broadly.

The BEWC, on the other hand, was founded in 2007 in relation to the European Year on Equal Opportunities for All and the organization was officially launched the following year, within the framework of the European Year of Intercultural Dialogue. The organization explains its purpose and objective in the following manner:

> Our main challenge is to identify and address critical needs of Black European Women and children, by raising public awareness both at the national and international level underlining the challenges faced by Black Communities across Europe ensuring that we are recognized on the agenda of the European Union... Together, we will have a stronger voice and a stronger impact and only together, can we bring about change. We can empower one another by working closely to achieve our goal of full inclusion and respect. (bewnet.eu)

The BEWC board currently consists of nine members from eight different EU member-states,[4] whereas members from sixteen member-states participated in the founding congress in 2007. Members come from a number of different organizations, ranging from social, cultural, and political organizations to health organizations. The BEWC has received funding from Filia, The Global Funds for Women, and the EC program Europe for Citizens. Key activities include lobbying, networking in relation to EU institutions, workshops, as well as empowerment and capacity-building activities concerning the needs and interests of black European women and children. General assemblies as well as strategic meetings are held biannually. Whereas the BEWC was off to a strong start with strategic networking activities within the EU institutions, this was followed by a period of less activity, where the organization struggled to gain visibility and maintain participation. At the 2010 strategic meeting the need to "reactivate the BEWC again and to define common goals, an organisational structure, duties and a strategic plan" was highlighted (bewnet.eu).

In terms of diversity, the EWL, when first established in the early 1990s, represented mainly the majority of white, middle-class working women: Ethnic minority and migrant women were not included, and their concerns were not high on the EU agenda. As the focus on multiple discrimination policies and cooperation between umbrella organizations was emphasized, migrant women's issues gained a significant space on the EU policy agenda. The EWL responded by incorporating migrant issues into their policies and encouraging migrant women's selforganizing (Kantola 2010; Schwenken 2009; Woodward 2006; 2007).[5] Williams (2003) analyses how the EWL has dealt with the issue of ethnic minorities. She argues that the black, ethnic minority and migrant women's struggling to gain recognition, voice, and visibility vis-à-vis the EWL "contributed to the reformulating of feminist politics in ways that can account and organise for difference and diversity between women" (2003, 142). The minority women are marginalized, but they also challenge the dominant meanings of citizenship through their attempts at combining a "multipositioned constituency within a multilevel polity" (ibid.).

Furthermore, the EU antidiscrimination policies, and especially the article 13 of the Amsterdam Treaty concerning the six grounds of discrimination (sex, racial or ethnic origin, religion or belief, disability, age, and sexual orientation) and the subsequent directives on equal treatment, have impacted the organizational landscape of European civil society. Large umbrella networks already existed or were set up at the European level in the years following the signing of the Amsterdam Treaty in 1997. They cover different, separate grounds of discrimination and are partly funded by the EC. However, as the EC preferences toward a multiple discrimination approach that perceives the six grounds of discrimination as integrated rather than separate develops (see EC Green Paper "Equality and Non-Discrimination in an enlarged European Union," COM[2004]379), it should be expected that the civil society landscape would modify itself accordingly. This is indeed happening and in two different ways: The big umbrella organizations, which continue to be organized around one of the discrimination grounds, cooperate among themselves or with other smaller organizations to deal with intersecting inequalities (for instance the cooperation between EWL and several migrant women's organizations)[6] or new organizations emerge (such as the BEWC) that, in their self definition and objectives, already cover and deal with several discrimination grounds and as such are intersectional in their approach.

Thus, the decade of the 2000s was characterized by the emergence of organizations with intersectional constituencies, though some ethnic minority and migrant women's organizations began to emerge already in the 1990s (Hoskyns 1996). They were established in a vacuum of unattended difference and diversity concerns. These organizations are understudied in the literature in general. Schwenken (2009), however, refers briefly to intersectional organizations with a focus on migrant women. She argues that the Amsterdam Treaty "improved the institutional setting for migrant women, as the separation of racial discrimination from gender discrimination was partly challenged. Hence, migrant women's demands gained increased legitimacy" (2009, 81). Thiel and Prügl suggest that "[i]ntersectionality may open up diverse venues for making claims toward the EU, but it also often leads to exclusions" (2009, 13), for instance, of migrant women who are not properly represented by any of the single discrimination ground organizations.

As mentioned, the EWL has worked to combat racism and gender inequality since the late 1990s, even though this focus has strengthened in recent years. This is an effect of the EU multiple discrimination agenda more than an internal policy development: "We have to do multiple discrimination, and we're doing multiple discrimination...It's a challenge for any organization" (EWL representative, interview December 2007). Thus, a main challenge for the EWL as a mainstream organization is to avoid homogenizing the category "women" and attend to differences. This occurs both in terms of addressing intersectionality as a pertinent theoretical perspective on difference and diversity and by implementing it as an explicit policy strategy (see EWL Position paper on Strengthening women's rights in a multicultural Europe; and Vassiliadou 2008)[7]:

> Despite the fact that intersectional discrimination has been recognized, the concerned international bodies have not developed corresponding legal instruments. As a result, the intersectional experience of discrimination is not recognized and treated properly in legal and institutional frameworks built around single types of discrimination because discriminations are seen as one-dimensional and as affecting all people—men and women—in the same way. (Vassiliadou 2008)

Taking on this perspective, and reflecting the changes undergone within the EWL in recent years in relation to the issue of diversity, the website of the organization states as an aim to "take into account the needs, specific inequalities, and perspectives of different groups of women, and the diverse experiences of women at all stages of their life cycle" through the development of the EWL as an organization as well as in its relations with "organizations that represent the many women that face multiple discrimination in the European Union and globally."

Next I will turn the spotlight on political intersectionality and diverse constituencies in European women's organizations that combine gender and ethnicity in collective claims making. Key elements are constraints on transnational mobilization, on the one hand, and diversity demands set forward by transnational women's organizations in the European sphere and the collective representation of ethnic minority and migrant women, on the other. Thus, claims-making efforts of majority and minority women's organizations, operating in Europe, will be analyzed using documents, such as reports and position papers published by the organizations, and elite interviews with key representatives (see also Rolandsen Agustín 2012; Rolandsen Agustín and Roth 2011).[8]

Constraints on Civil Society Mobilization in the Transnational Sphere

Lack of resources and the difficulties of connecting the national and transnational levels are some of the problems encountered by European women's organizations in general. Transnational organizing is, to a large extent, an elitist endeavor for resourceful, privileged groups (Bretherton and Sperling 1996; Hoskyns 1996). This is promoted, directly or indirectly, by the EC through its construction and institutionalization of certain civil society actors. The EC insists on maintaining informal contacts with civil society organizations, instead of formal contacts and a strong civil dialogue comparable to the social dialogue applied to European trade unions and employer organizations. The EC prefers resourceful, transnational civil society organizations, and it prioritizes one unified voice per discrimination ground (Kantola 2010).

An additional two problems seem to be salient regarding the constraints placed on transnational mobilization in the European context: funding and access. These problems reflect two different bases of the risk of exclusion, namely economic and political grounds. The EU serves as a framework for civil society organizations both in discursive terms, when they formulate demands and policy proposals, and in a more structural sense, with respect to organization and funding. At a general level, the EU institutions seem more receptive to a particular kind of organizing, closely related to interest group representation. According to Marks and McAdam (1999), lobbying is a more efficient form of pressure than activism partly due to the limited institutional access, the absence of media at the EU level, the emotional detachment with which many citizens perceive the EU, and the interest of the very institutions in receiving information from the lobbyists that may enhance their receptiveness toward this kind of interaction. This affects the particular opportunity structures that the organizations and networks may make use of at the transnational level. The EU institutional context, thus, calls for a particular kind of mobilization, organization, and claims-making activity due to its delimitation of the arenas and access points made available.

The political and institutional framework of the EU can work both as a facilitator and as a constraint on the organizations' demands and activities. First, the EU is often articulated as the main space for gaining visibility and recognition at the transnational level. This is reflected in the BEWC's selfdefinition as an organization of Black European Women (i.e., Black Women living in Europe):

> This definition is part of the political strategy of Black European Women to position themselves in the political landmark of Europe, and claim and reinforce their rights to have access to goods and services, and to take part in all sectors of European society. (www.bewnet.eu)

The EU institutional structure for civil society participation influences the emergence of actors at the European level and it also influences the funding of the networks and organizations. The BEWC initiated its activities in the realm of the European Year for Equal Opportunities for All and made its official launch during the European Year For Intercultural Dialogue, which, according to the organization itself, presented an opportunity to create alliances with institutional and organizational actors. A BEWC representative reflects upon the importance of the EU framework and the use the organizations can make of it in the following way:

> We have to go out to tell the EU "we are here" and not waiting until the EU recognizes our presence...The good opportunity to do this at the European level was last year [2007]. Last year was the European Year of Equal Opportunities for All so I saw it as a good opportunity to invite black women so that we can together look at the European concept of equal opportunities for all from our own perspectives. (BEWC representative, interview November 2008)

The BEWC used EU institutional contacts extensively during its launch and the first year of its existence and it focused heavily on strategic lobbying vis-à-vis the EU institutions.

The EWL has, for a number of years, enjoyed financing from the EC on one of the continuing grants, an operating budget from the Community Action Programme. Several of the other transnational organizations articulate their concerns and problems related to the financing of activities across borders. Here the projects emanating from the European institutions, such as the EC, are thought to facilitate the transnational mobilization largely as project funding makes travelling and reimbursements for activity participation easier. However, some tensions also arise around the EU membership regarding the relations between the national and transnational dimensions. First, there is a problem of down-prioritizing the national level due to the added value attributed to the "international": "In some countries they would never fund a women's shelter but if they fund like travelling to a conference, an international conference, they have the ability to say 'okay, we funded this for an international conference, then people get money'" (WAVE representative, interview November 2008).[9] Second, there is a problem with the allocation of responsibilities. This particularly relates to EU candidacy and accession processes when the EU passes the responsibility of funding onto the state level, once countries become members. The states nevertheless do not feel obliged to take over funding responsibilities that previously were assumed by EU external or candidacy programs. For member-states, the EU only takes on the obligation to fund transnational projects (WAVE representative, interview November 2008). This has negative consequences for the activity at the local and national levels, which cannot, be upheld in some cases.

Regarding the second element, namely that of access, constraints concern EU policies on mobility and, more concretely, visa policies. One of the problems that are mentioned most frequently by the civil society organizations in relation to transnational activism relates to the issue of visa requirements:

> One thing that we have been facing, one problem, is the visa issue. Visa issue for Eastern European participants travelling to the member states of the European Union and for migrants, now with the Schengen area, a migrant residing in Italy can travel easily to France or to the Schengen countries but a migrant person living in the UK will be needing a visa to enter Italy, for example. So, visa was a big issue.

> Visa and visa obstacles were there all the time...And having especially like a migrant person, a refugee from Rwanda, living in St. Petersburg, travelling to here, was really difficult...So the visa, it's a tricky thing. (WFM representative, interview December 2008)[10]

Even when there is funding available, the visa policies restrain the possibilities of mobility and, thus, of transnational political participation, beyond the economic constraints. The organizations may try to direct particular attention to participants from countries with less funding possibilities but, nevertheless, the lack of access and mobility rights is often an obstacle:

> Visa procedures are really restrictive...The goal would be that from every country one representative could participate at the WAVE conference but we couldn't fulfill it...Visa is also a big exclusion criterion. Often, I mean we have to sign guarantees for visas for people. We are covering everything till if they stay in a hospital, I mean it is also a big risk...It was always a problem, visa. But this is about the same exclusionary issue as money because often even if we have money, people cannot access the European Union, to learn from good practice examples from the European Union countries, because they just don't get visas even if we sign all guarantees because people like to play the power and whatever...We still strive to include everyone and to get funding for everyone but this is always also a big challenge." (WAVE representative, interview November 2008)[11]

The limitations in the access to participation in transnational activities in the European sphere seriously restrain the access to the EU territories for non-EU citizens who are nevertheless considered to be covered by the activities taking place in the civil society. The EU has the institutional power to define who is included and who is excluded, and restrictive immigration policies have repercussions in relation to this distinction (García Agustín 2008). The organizations may have broader definitions as regards to their constituencies but the access is constrained through the visa policies and the definitions set forward by the EU. The women activists, especially migrant women and non-EU citizens, are constrained in their capability of moving freely and this affects their possibilities for political participation.

In sum, the main obstacles identified in relation to civil society participation and empowerment at the European level are related to the institutional framework of the EU institutions. The shortcomings of this framework are both of political and economical nature. The economic dimension is related to the funding and resources available to the civil society organizations. In this sense, the EU both restrains the possibilities, by setting a particular agenda for the organizations to conform to, and enhances them, through particular programs and project funding opportunities. However, the funding processes also seem to have a negative spillover into the national arenas in some cases via a tendency for member-states not to prioritize the areas of participation and service provision offered by the organizations when the EU withdraws its contributions. This is an implication of the diffusion of responsibilities that is particularly prominent at the transnational level. Another kind of institutional constraints are the political ones, here best reflected in the visa regulations governing the access into EU territory. This is both a problem of lack of mobility, which results in a lack of participatory opportunities, and a problem of the right to define the European space. The latter is more restricted in the EU notion than in the organizations' selfperception of their constituencies, which are often times defined as going beyond EU memberstates. Both of these aspects restrain the possibilities of mobilization at the transnational, European level.

Majority and Minority Differences in Demands and Claims Making

Focusing on how organizations deal with diversity at the European level, I argue that there is a specific complexity to their claims-making efforts due to the dual dynamic of transnationalism, the multilevel structure of the EU and European civil society, and intersectionality. According to Soysal (2004), the sites for claims making have diversified within the context of multilevel structures, decoupling participation and citizenship practices from the national level. Similarly, Hobson et al. (2007) argue that

> as individuals and groups utilize trans-national legal frameworks, discourses and forums, we expect changes in the practice of citizenship, in terms of group identities, agency and power. Trans-national dialogues among mobilized groups often result in political learning. New strategies can emerge. Trans-national venues open up new political opportunities and new brokerage partners. Perhaps most importantly, trans-national institutions offer recognition movements new forms of leverage politics, as governments become more and more integrated in structures of multi-level governance. (ibid., 445)

The demands of some of the European women's organizations relate to diversity and are, as such, intersectional. In the empirical cases presented below, this concerns specifically the intersection between gender and ethnicity, which combines (particularistic) claims on identity and belonging with (universal) claims on human rights, citizenship status, and inclusion.

Contrary to Soysal's (2004) notion of universalized rights related to inclusionary forms of membership that are increasingly combined with particular identity claims, as exclusionary practices, in the national-transnational nexus, I argue for the complex transnationalization of both rights and identity. Universal dimensions of the gender-and-ethnicity intersection, that is, women's rights and citizenship rights, are combined with the particularistic dimensions engrained in the idea of this being a specific group of women that is at the center of demands, namely ethnic minority women and their particular needs (see also Rolandsen Agustín 2010). The intersectional nature of the transnational diversity demands calls for a complex dualism in claims making as particularism is necessary for recognizing women as a heterogeneous group whereas both "gender" and "ethnicity," as well as the demands to be included (as citizens) in the European society, highlight the universal dimension of claims and rights. I argue that the combination of transnational mobilization and diversity claims leads to complex claims-making processes due to the multilevel and intersectional nature of the demands. This includes recognition and voice of minority groups, on the one hand, and rights and inclusion into the European society, on the other.

Two types of demands can be discerned in the claims-making efforts of majority and minority women's organizations: One refers mostly to universal claims on human rights, and the other to issues of identity and belonging. The first type can be related to EWL practices of defending migrant women and their rights, mostly by promoting a gender sensitive approach to EU policies on migration and integration:

> *By maintaining a 'gender neutral' approach to immigration, women's human rights and the experiences and needs of women are being ignored in the current debates and policies around immigration...* A gender aware approach to immigration policy introduces a shift from the predominant view of female immigrants as simply the wives and children of male immigrants to incorporating an understanding of women's human rights and of the unique experiences of women immigrants themselves. (EWL Position paper on integrating a gender perspective into the EU immigration policy 2004, 3; original emphasis).

This type of demands focuses on the need to strengthen migrant women's labor-market participation and to gain full economic and legal independence for migrant women. Rights are individualized in the sense that the focus is placed on migrant women as individuals and their access to employment. These demands around the intersectional category of "ethnic minority and migrant women"[12] can be related to the way in which Ferree (2008; 2009) has depicted the EU intersectionality model as organized around the citizen/noncitizen dichotomy (see chapter 1): Citizenship status becomes the main marker of differentiation and conflict, and demands on behalf of migrant women are set forward by the EWL against this background, combining gender equality aims with the objective of equality through full citizenship status to marginalized women.

The second set of demands is articulated primarily by the BEWC. It relates to the recognition of rights and inclusion into a European society, which is characterized by plurality and multiculturalism. As the previous type of demands, the overall frame is that of citizenship and human rights but an increased focus is placed here on the notions of belonging and identity:

> These diversity identities which you can find in one person and to be able to say, okay, this person can say "I am a woman," "I am a lesbian," "I am handicapped," "I am old," you know, the six grounds of discrimination. We have to start looking at them from a different perspective and say these are six identities which may be the identity of one person. (BEWC representative, interview November 2008)

This clearly relates to the EU framework of combating multiple discrimination. It is an explicit aim of the BEWC as a minority women's organization to gain influence by placing this particular group of women on the policy agenda of the EU institutions. They seek an institutional recognition that has so far not been sufficiently acknowledged:

> This definition is part of the political strategy of Black European Women to position themselves in the political landmark of the EU, and claim and reinforce their rights to have access to goods and services, and to take part in all sectors of European society. (www.bewnet.eu)

The fight to gain visibility and recognition is both related to inclusion at the individual level, that is, the sense of belonging, and at the social level, vis-à-vis the plural European society:

> "European, when you use this phrase honestly what picture comes to mind? I would say that 99% of you with the exception of the members of the [BEWC] see a Caucasian person of different ethnic background

but with features familiar to yourselves in some way. We are hoping that in time we can be included in your description too. Our aim is for European society to begin to include in its definition of itself all of its members, to also include those that don't look like you. (Jarvis 2008)[13]

In this type of claims making, the distinction between minority women (as European citizens) and migrant women (as noncitizens) is important: The aim is to be recognized as citizens and to be included in society and this means taking distance to the exclusive definition as "migrants" that inevitably means being considered "the other," and not a part of "us," that is, European citizens.

> Many women who migrate to Europe they have been given lots of names, they have been defined in different ways, they are foreigners, they are strangers, they are "l'autoctone" in other countries, they are immigrants, they are all these names, they are Black women, they are African women, so there is this big confusion and now we come to say 'we are Black European women'... It is just a strategic working definition and it is a future definition for children who are being born here. (BEWC representative, interview November 2008)

All in all the type of demands set forward by the BEWC combines particularism and universalism by using identity as a strategic way to support universal claims to citizenship rights, and social and political inclusion into the European society in the name of a collective subject, namely minority women as a group rather than as (marginalized) individuals (see also Rolandsen Agustín 2010).

Dealing with Diversity among Women's Organizations in Europe

Having identified the constraints related to transnational mobilization as well as the demands set forward by and on behalf of ethnic minority and migrant women, I now turn toward the responses, that is, the ways in which diversity is dealt with at the European level. This concerns both the strategies used within majority and minority women's organizations, respectively, as well as the responses emanating from the institutional, political structures of the EU.

Practices and Strategies of Transnational Women's Organizations

Transnational women's organizations mobilizing at the European level make use of four different strategies in order to address diversity related to the intersection of gender and ethnicity: (1) minority inclusion into majority organizations; (2) intersectional agenda setting and self representation by minority groups; (3) coalition building among majority and minority organizations and between umbrella organizations covering different inequality grounds; and (4) dual strategy of inclusion and simultaneous self representation (see also Rolandsen Agustín and Roth 2011). The combination of strategies aims to achieve representation, recognition, and empowerment of ethnic minority women, for example.

Until recently, the strategies of the EWL were a typical example of *minority inclusion into majority organizations*. The organization explicitly states that one of its objectives is to "empower migrant women through mutual support and sharing of information" (EWL 2006). This means including minority issues on the agenda of the organization and cooperate with external partners, instead of inviting them into the institutional structures of the EWL itself. However, in terms of the representation of interests of the diversity of women, I find that certain groups of women, such as the black European women of BEWC, do not feel represented by the EWL.[14] While the EWL explicitly emphasizes the importance of not homogenizing the group of women, the organization has for years fallen short in terms of making minority intersectional groups of women feel represented and recognized. The EWL mainly incorporated minority concerns into policies and spoke on behalf of the minority women whereas the latter claim their right to an own voice. Organizations such as the BEWC argue that interests were not articulated *by* them but *for* them. Their critical stance on the practices of the EWL in the 2000s ultimately led them to set up their own independent organizations.

In the meantime, the EWL has changed their structures and practices: In the last few years the EWL has made significant efforts to include minority women, among other things, by allowing both individual supporting members as well as European women's NGOs and women's sections of European umbrella organizations into the lobby, thus addressing the structural, organizational issue (former EWL representative, interview October 2010).

> Yes, the critique [of the EWL for addressing mainly white, middle-class working women] is quite legitimate, but it is an internal issue for us as well, and I think there have been improvements and it is done through specific projects, specific funding and strategic reviews, etc., and it is not at all something that we are ignoring. (EWL representative, interview December 2007)

Furthermore, the European Network of Migrant Women (ENoMW) emerged out of the EWL project "Equal Rights. Equal Voices. Migrant Women in the European Union" (2006). Though it was initiated at an EWL seminar in 2007, the network has become independent with associate membership status of the EWL. It was officially launched as such in 2010. The network has member organizations in 16 European countries. Financially it does not count on an EU operating budget like the EWL but depends exclusively on funding from specific projects and programs. The purpose of the ENoMW is "to establish across Europe a democratic and effective network which represents the concerns, needs, and interests of migrant women in the European Union." This relates both to the promotion of immigrant women's rights and to attempts to influence EU policies on immigrant women's lives as well as strengthening their voice in the EU institutions and through migrant women's organizations. Thus, the network focuses on migration policies specifically (asylum, integration, undocumented immigrant women, etc.) as well as mainstream policies seen through an immigration lens (employment, education, health, etc.). Through joint activities and collaboration with the EWL, the ENoMW has quickly managed to gain a voice in relation to immigrant women's position and rights at the European level. The collaboration between the EWL and the ENoMW takes different forms: Recently, the EWL and the ENoMW coorganized a public hearing in the EP on "Family Reunification Legislation in Europe: Is it Discriminatory for Migrant Women?" (2011), and together they launched a joint lobbying campaign aiming to make EU policies on family reunification more gender sensitive by emphasizing the need for immigrant women's autonomy (2012). In this way the ENoMW draws on the extensive experience and knowhow of the EWL in terms of lobbying strategies, institutional insight in EU administration, networking relations, etc. (see also Rolandsen Agustín 2012).

The BEWC does not believe that the ENoMW suffices in terms of representing and recognizing minority women. An interviewee from the BEWC compares the network initiative to creating "a ghetto within the structures" instead of integrating migrant women fully into the EWL. Furthermore, she emphasizes that "some of us are not immigrants, we are European population" (BEWC representative, interview November 2008). This again underlines the need for recognition, participation, and inclusion into the European society.

All in all, the relationship between the organizations is characterized by "love and hate": Most women's organizations are or were keen to collaborate with the EWL, but at the same time the modes of operation and the allegedly deficient democratic procedures, as well as the impossibility of being involved in the policy work undertaken by the lobby on a more continuous or daily basis, receive strong critique. The membership criteria for transnational organizations wanting to be included in the EWL are also considered too demanding since these are required to have member organizations in all EU member states. Trends of cooperation and competition thus coexist though most civil society interviewees feel that the former needs improvement (BEWC representative, interview November 2008; EWLA representative, interview May 2010).

The response from some of the dissatisfied minority women was to set up the BEWC, thus pursuing the strategy of *intersectional agenda setting and selfrepresentation by minority groups* as a way to deal with diversity. This enabled them to speak on their own behalf, as a minority group seeking legitimacy and empowerment. The ultimate aim is to achieve equality through active participation, the use of citizenship rights and inclusion into European society (in line with the abovementioned identity related demands). The BEWC wants to cooperate with the EWL on an equal footing, as partners. The general assembly of the BEWC passed, for example, a resolution urging the EWL to take into account the "diversity of Europe, with particular reference on visible minorities" in relation to the EWL 50/50 Campaign for Democracy, aiming to ensure equal representation of women and men in the EP and the EC, prior to the EP elections in 2009. The BEWC also stresses the need for the EC to support minority groups, which are an empirical reality of the transnational civil society, in order to recognize their voices and enhance EU democracy.

The elements of identity and empowerment are crucial in the activities of the BEWC:

> I want a roundtable discussion where I have someone there talking about black women, a black woman, where I have someone talking about Muslim women, she's a Muslim woman, someone talking about the challenges of European women so that we can have this broad perspective. Only when we get there can we then talk about equal opportunities... So if we agree that we are so diversified and that one, two, three organizations are, honestly, not in a position to represent the needs of the diversity we have, then people will automatically see that the emergence of selforganized networks is absolutely necessary. It's actually a kind of richness in the society. This is participation. And the European policies are constantly talking about participation, they're talking about European citizenship, they are talking about spreading European values, the sense of belonging. When we start doing this it's

because we realize that we are Europeans, we're living in a European context, we identify with the structures. (BEWC representative, interview November 2008)

In this way, demands articulated around identity are related to inclusion into European society. Participation and empowerment, to become active citizens, are important aspect of the selfrepresentation. This is all about making one's own voice heard:

> We know best what our challenges are, and we have better solutions for them than anyone else. Let's make use of our know-how to fight for our place in Europe, "our home"...The key is that black women organise themselves, identify their needs and fight to make them visible, they must stop playing the role of victims, a role they are most often forced to play, and become active players. (Achaleke 2007, 24)[15]

The two strategies identified so far, that is, minority inclusion and selfrepresentation, are nevertheless combined with *coalition building among majority and minority organizations and between umbrella organizations covering different inequality grounds*. This means that diversity is also addressed through cooperation. This is practiced through practical cooperation, exchange of information, common statements, and activities, for example, often with the common goal of setting an intersectional policy agenda in the EU. Whereas the EWL seems to prefer broad coalitions, supporting minority issues by collaborating with single-issue umbrella organizations, the BEWC to a further extent opts for coalitions build around like-minded organizations with intersectional constituencies. According to Cullen (2005), the first type of coalitions is common to the European, transnational level, where NGOs manage differences (rather than transcending them) by the use of bridge leaders, articulation of transversal issues, and network participation.

Finally, a *dual strategy of inclusion and simultaneous selfrepresentation* is also found at the transnational level. The organization Young Women from Minorities uses a combined approach of representation and recognition that allows them to speak on their own behalf while, at the same time, working toward minority integration into majority organizations both in terms of policy issues and individual representation of minority women:

> Having a minority person in these mainstream organizations, you know, bringing forward the agenda for minority issues is very, very difficult because when you reach to that level, then you're asked still

to speak for everyone but then the minorities are asked to speak for everyone but then the majorities sometimes are not talking for the minorities. So, I think also for a political representation...there is a need to establish minority organizations or minority women's organizations or migrant minorities because I think people need to raise their voice, first of all, and fight for their active citizenship, for their political participation. Of course, minorities cannot do everything by themselves. I think the collaboration with other organizations is important, I mean, especially the mainstream organizations. And a role also of these organizations is actually to mainstream minority issues in the mainstream organizations because we are not here to create islands of separated organizations, we need also to have more minorities also in the other organizations, more representation of the minorities in the big organizations. (WFM representative, interview December 2008)

This perception reflects the need to create opportunities for participation along with empowerment through selfrepresentation.

In sum, dealing with diversity from within the organizations means addressing both representation and recognition. This is done most efficiently and satisfactorily by a combination of strategies, including coalition building, intersectional agenda setting, and selfmobilization (see Rolandsen Agustín and Roth 2011). To this we must add the institutional responses as the EU in itself is the other counterpart in the interface with a responsibility of recognizing majority and minority voices in civil society through institutional interaction.

Institutional Responses and the Potential of Inclusive Policy-making Structures

Initial skepticism among well-established, transnational women's organizations over the integrated approach to multiple discrimination policies and a focus on disadvantages are slowly turning into changes (such as plurality of voices and increased cooperation) in the civil society field. What remains unresolved, however, are the institutional responses in terms of achieving (complex) inclusion of the diversity of civil society interests.

The EWL is still privileged (at least informally) as an interlocutor of the EC, which has also managed to limit the voice of ideologically divergent groups outside the sphere of the EP. The minority organizations are struggling with organizational and financial challenges and seek, to a large extent, alternative channels into the transnational space of policy making such as the European Economic and Social

Committee (BEWC representative, interview November 2008) or the Council of Europe (WFM representative, interview December 2008). These are also important sites of struggle for less privileged majority organizations such as EWLA, in the case of the European Economic and Social Committee (EWLA representative, interview May 2010), and WAVE, in that of the Council of Europe (WAVE representative, interview November 2008).

In general, cooperation among the large umbrella organizations still remains the exception rather than the norm (Schwenken 2009). According to Hancock (2007), a multiple discrimination approach like the one adopted by the EU, is more likely to lead to competition than cooperation because the discrimination grounds are added and not seen as inseparable. The result is a competition over resources instead of a transformation of the "entire logic of distribution" (ibid.). Looking to the institutional setup and the EU/civil society interface, one of the main problems is, as mentioned earlier, that there is a mismatch between civil society demands and ways of organizing and the institutional channels established to direct their demands into policy-making processes. Kantola and Nousiainen (2012) mention in particular the fact that the change in policy focus has not lead to a parallel change in legal framework and institutional structures.

According to Lombardo and Verloo, policy makers need to be aware of "how institutions could promote intergroup co-operation to address the intersection of multiple inequalities" (2009, 81). The EU institutions, thus, have a role to play in promoting either competition or solidarity between the different civil society organizations (Verloo et al. 2007). The empirical diversity of women's interests in the civil society sphere, which I have encountered, does not match with the EC's preference for a single voice and representation of interests through one organization exclusively. The EU institutions overall do not reflect the pluralization of demands emerging from a more diversified civil society, partly because this is not prioritized, partly due to the lack of resources to attend to this higher level of complexity in civil society inclusion.

However, also here we find significant differences between the EU institutions and even between the individual units of the general directorates:

> We [unit G1 of the DG Employment] share the views of the gender equality organizations that gender should not be covered at the same... or it could be covered at the same time as antidiscrimination policies, but it should not be put into the diversity package and that

we share the views that it will be diluted if it's included in this diversity package and that, we're always recalling the typical argument that women are not a minority...We are a bit worried about what will be the place of gender equality in this more and more visible diversity thing...We would always ask to have a specific paragraph, a specific section with gender inequalities as such. That's clear. This we will do each time. Then afterwards, when it is the question of [gender] being there or not, being there a little bit or not being there at all, we prefer being there a little bit, that's the idea. (EC official, DG Employment, interview January 2008)

An interviewee from unit G4 of the DG Employment, however, argues that umbrella organizations have to think more on "how to work on transversal issues or crosscutting issues." As mentioned above, several interviewees find that the EWL, in particular, needs to be restructured to include also nonmajority women as there is a lack of diversity within the lobby. The EC G4 interviewee emphasizes that in order to avoid competition between the discrimination grounds, the umbrella organizations need to start thinking "globally" and looking at individuals as whole persons with multiple identities (EC official, DG Employment, interview December 2007).

Kantola (2010) states that ethnic minority women do not have a voice in EU institutions, which lack a mechanism to ensure their participation. As mentioned above, I find empirical evidence that shows that minority women themselves also perceive a lack of voice and representation at the transnational level. Intersectional references are increasingly present in EU policies though this does not automatically lead to the gender equality policies being more inclusive. Thus, introducing practices of "intersectionality impact assessment" as a measure to enhance the attention toward intersecting inequalities in policy making could be one way to make policy making more inclusive as civil society organizations with minority intersectional constituencies would be able to participate formally in EU policy processes. The aim would be to strengthen both the content of the policies and the feeling of being recognized and represented among minority women, emphasizing the need for EU institutions to better reflect the empirical reality of mobilization in the transnational sphere and the urgency in attending to the demands of civil society constituencies that do not fit into single inequality categories. Inclusive policy making at the EU/civil society interface would take into account the diversity of claims articulated in the transnational sphere as well as the need to avoid stigmatization in policy outputs (see Lombardo and Rolandsen Agustín 2012).

Having addressed one of the two challenges identified in the introduction, namely that of the diversity in women's interests, addressing both institutional aspects as well as the expression of civil society voices within this field, I now turn toward the analysis and discussion of the challenge of degendering in the following chapters. Both challenges are related to the developments, which have characterized processes of institutionalization and mobilization as dimensions of contextualized transnational intersectionality.

4

Gender-Based Violence and the Framing of Equality Policies

The challenge of degendering that followed from the introduction of the multiple discrimination approach in EU policies with article 13 of the Amsterdam Treaty was, in particular, expressed through civil society organizations' concern over the potential downplaying or disappearance of gender as a consequence of increased attention to diversity and multiple inequalities. The following three chapters will address the challenge of degendering in terms of policies and policy making. The present chapter analyzes the framings of policies on gender-based violence articulated in the Parliament, the Commission, and the Council from 1980 to 2010. Chapter 6 addresses the culturalization of these policies that is related to the theoretical dimensions of inclusionary and exclusionary forms of intersectionality. Chapter 5 analyzes and discusses the strategic use of (de)gendered frames as well as the implications of degendering within the particular institutional setup and institutional context of the EU. Civil society actions, reactions, and interaction with the EU institutions are addressed across the three chapters.

The ideational processes related to gendering of political institutions are a key concern in the constructivist analysis of EU gender equality policies and their development in terms of continuity and change. Focusing on the articulation of frames and discourses through discursive struggles and contestations over meaning, I analyze, in the present chapter, the ideational content of EU policies as well as EU institutions and civil society organizations as key actors and frame producers within the processes of policy making. In other words, I look at the detailed levels of differences and nuances in the ways that policies are formulated and framed.

The object of analysis of this chapter are policies on gender-based violence and, in particular, the DAPHNE program of the EC. The main framing of the policy issue over the years, from the 1980s until 2010, shows significant differences between the individual EU institutions and shifts over time, moving broadly from a structural gender inequality framing of violence, over a general human rights framing developed at the UN level, to a public health framing specifically related to the adoption of the DAPHNE program. There is a broad scope for articulation of ideas within this area since most policy documents are nonbinding, and even the binding ones, such as the DAPHNE program, do not entail legal changes at the national level. Furthermore, civil society is expected to have more possibilities of providing input in a soft policy area. The DAPHNE program is particular in the sense that it is, formally, a piece of binding legislation, launched as an initiative of the EC and negotiated in the EP and the Council as part of the legislative codecision process. It does not, however, have any direct effect on member-state legislation since it is a program adopted to fund transnational NGOs in a project-based manner.

The area of gender-based violence, or violence against women, at the EU level is, in general, characterized by a high degree of consensus.[1] There is a basic agreement on the issue of violence because it is a broad problem that is relevant to all member states and easy to gather around when it is phrased in terms of "human dignity," for example. This makes it an ideal case for looking into the specificities of policy framings because conflicts and contestations between actors and ideas are played out in the frame nuances that require a close textual analysis. Furthermore, the traditional imbalance between member states, dividing them into a gender equality progressive North and a backward and slowly developed South, does not apply in this case. Member-state legislations differ as do the problem perceptions (see for instance Krizsán et al. 2007), but there is a consensus on the aim of combating gender-based violence.

The analysis shows that ideas, agency, and context, in terms of political and discursive opportunity structures, interact in policy-making processes at the EU level, and specific frames are articulated strategically by EU and civil society actors. As mentioned above, several significant shifts in framings have characterized the field since the issue was first put on the EU agenda. However, the dominant frame of the DAPHNE program—public health—has maintained a broad scope whereby articulations of simultaneous framings, such as women's rights as human rights, have not been completely marginalized. Importantly, gender-related frames still prevail in the selection of projects to be funded under the DAPHNE program. These struggles over framings show how ideas (frame content), agency (EU and civil society actors articulating frames) and context (institutional, political, legal and discursive constraints, and opportunities) interact in the institutionalization of the policy issue of gender-based violence.

Approaching Policies on Gender-Based Violence

The ways in which the issue of policies on gender-based violence is approached theoretically differ. We can, however, identify a number of common frameworks that, in one way or another, relate to social movement theories. These are, for instance, frame analysis, agenda-setting mechanisms, political opportunity structures, and transnational norm diffusion.

Thus, concepts such as advocacy coalitions, transnational advocacy networks (Zippel 2004; 2006), and velvet triangles (Locher 2007) are recurring in the literature on EU policies on gender-based violence. The transnational advocacy networks are "those relevant actors working internationally on an issue, who are bound together by shared values, a common discourse, and dense exchanges of information and services" (Keck and Sikkink 1998, 2). These networks can be considered either structures, in that they constitute patterns of interaction, or actors, since they consist in a particular agency not equal to that of the components (ibid.). They use information and idea generation to influence the value context of politics. They seek new allies and access points into the political systems at the same time as they articulate new ideas and discourses, and negotiate the meaning of politics.

Domestic and international opportunity structures interact according to the idea of boomerang patterns: Social movements may find obstacles in their attempts to influence politics or articulate demands at the national level. The obstacles may consist of a repressive or authoritative regime or a lack of responsiveness that result in a lack of voice. They can, however, be remedied by turning to the international level for support, thus creating transnational advocacy networks to counteract the inaccessible national level. These networks might succeed in convincing the international institutions to put pressure on the domestic government or regime (ibid.).

Several empirical accounts of EU policies on gender-based violence build on Keck and Sikkink's theoretization of transnational advocacy networks and boomerang patterns, developing these theories further. Zippel (2004; 2006) argues that a ping-pong effect takes place whereby transnational advocacy networks use the opportunities of influence created at different levels when policy action "cycles" back and forth between the national and the supranational institutional realms in the development of policies and measures. Similarly, Montoya (2013) argues that internal domestic factors interact with external international ones. This creates two types of processes not envisaged by the original framework of Keck and Sikkink: One is the "umbrella pattern" that occurs when transnational advocacy leads international organizations to put pressure on several states and not just the one that "triggered" the advocacy processes. Reforms are thus initiated from above, at times without the necessary domestic structures (in civil society, for example) to respond to these. This may lead to the second process conceptualized by Montoya, namely the reverse boomerang: International organizations use capacity-building measures to strengthen domestic advocates, enabling them to play a role in the reform processes. This would potentially contribute to closing the gap between policy rhetoric and policy practice (ibid.).[2]

Velvet triangles, on the other hand, are defined as the informal relations between femocrats (feminist bureaucrats, and politicians), academics, and women's organizations (Woodward 2004). Locher (2007) uses the concept to identify the "winning coalition" of norm entrepreneurs who successfully implemented the antitrafficking norm. Using qualitative network analysis, Ahrens (2010) finds that both formal and informal gender equality policy networks exist at the European level, but the term "velvet triangle" might not apply any longer as academic experts are deemed less relevant at the supranational level. Instead, "multifaceted networks" with strong insider/outsider distinctions are identified, and within them only a few women's organizations are recognized (ibid.).

Two of the most comprehensive studies on EU policies on genderbased violence address each their subissue within the general field: sexual harassment (Zippel 2004; 2006) and trafficking (Locher 2007). In a comparative analysis of sexual harassment policies in Germany, the United States, and the EU, Zippel (2006) analyses transnational norm diffusion and the translation of ideas into policies. She particularly addresses the interaction between social movements and institutions in EU policy making. The objective is to do a "fine-grained, contextual analysis of the paths through which the politics emerged and of the opportunities for feminists to shape policy approaches" (2006, 30). Zippel concludes that, through their interaction, the women's movements were shaped by the political opportunity structures of the EU institutional realm. At the same time, they impacted the political opportunity structures by using transnational exchange and expertise, on the one hand, as a resource to construct new meanings and alternative discourses, and the institutional access granted, on the other hand, to contribute to the shaping of policies within the field (Zippel 2004; 2006).[3]

Similarly, in her analysis of EU policies on trafficking, Locher (2007) focuses on agenda setting and norm diffusion from the international level, where the norms were created, to the European level. She particularly studies the transition from norm adoption to norm implementation. Based on theories on social movements, discourse analysis, and feminist theory, she identifies actors (norm entrepreneurs and institutions), frames (norms and language), and political opportunity structures as intervening variables. Locher's main conclusion is that previously adopted but "dormant" antitrafficking norms were revitalized through the introduction of new norms in the 1990s that were easily adopted because they fit with the already existing, dormant norms. The interplay between the international and the European level was highly influential for the development of EU policies, and norm entrepreneurs were important for the mediation between the different levels. Political opportunity structures played a role in the norm development as well. However, the real decisive factor, according to Locher, was the power of norms (ibid.).

Analyzing other policy areas (antiracism, environmentalism, and regionalism), Ruzza (2004) sets out to assess the role and modes of operation of transnational movement advocacy coalitions that he considers to be networks of movement organizations and EU allies. The success of movement coalitions is assessed based on their "ability to achieve policy objectives and the ability to gain recognition as a legitimate policy actor, that is, as a source of valid policy ideas, and therefore be included in decision making" (ibid., 138). The movement coalitions are faced with institutional filters that constrain the influence on policy making; these filters are both structural (rules of in/exclusion) and discursive (frame bridging into dominant discourses). Regarding the latter, Ruzza argues that the multiplicity of institutional roles that actors play at the European, transnational level facilitates frame-bridging processes, due to the proximity of EU and civil society actors. He furthermore finds that there are significant differences between the policy areas as regard institutional openness, "previously institutionalized ideas," and incorporation of movement actors. Ruzza concludes that movement coalitions do not affect the EU policies in a strong manner, but they are able to introduce new frames and inspiration into the policy-making process as well as shape the preferences of EU institutions.

While inspired by these approaches and their focus, I have chosen a different theoretical path that, to a greater extent, emphasizes the constructivist dimension. I place the main focus on policy making and consider ideas, agency, and context to be important dimensions in the interpretation of policy development. Within this theoretical framework, I include political opportunity structures to be part of the discursive and institutional context. I place a strong focus on detailed textual analysis of the frames articulated in the policy processes; I find this approach necessary in order to avoid conflating or diffusing the concept and role of frames. Frame dynamics and frame relations are key dimensions of the approach, and therefore the main focus is placed on the level of policies.

I follow Locher (2007) in her attempt to "bring agency back in" by underlining the role of EU institutions and civil society actors that are in/excluded from policy-making processes. However, I subscribe to the assumption that discursive struggles are constant in policy making, and that discursive closure is never reached (Laclau and Mouffe 1985). Therefore, my approach differs from Locher's in that I am not looking to identify "winning coalitions" of actors. Similarly, instead of focusing on "norm success," I aim to interpret frame relations internal to policy making, that is, how simultaneous frames are articulated and compete with each other, as well as the establishment of dominant and nondominant frames and the implications of these relations for policy making and policy development. I consider policy making to be a part of the institutionalization of ideas (as legislation, policies, and frames); this is a continuous process, a constant negotiation between a variety of actors and an ongoing (re)interpretation of meaning. I will consider the ways in which civil society actors provide input into these processes, but I do not aim to assess their degree of actual influence or impact on the policies. The object of analysis here is the policy issue, and I seek to identify and interpret the framings that are found empirically in the policies; I do not establish significant norms or frames a priori in order to follow their development across levels, institutions, or policy areas.

The Framework of European Union Policies on Gender-Based Violence

The development of EU gender equality policies from exclusively employment related to addressing issues beyond the labor market led, among other things, to an increased focus on gender-based violence. The issue emerged on the agenda of the EU already in the 1980s, but the policy options were not really explored until the 1990s. Thus, it was a rather new field to be cultivated politically within the framework of the EU in the 1990s, and the political and legal ground has at times been "shaky" as definitions and competences were debated and negotiated. As Zippel (2006) argues, new policy fields are typically characterized by political struggle over the definition of concepts and the identification of laws to be applied as these both concern the question of which version of reality is going to be articulated in policies.

Gender equality is typically articulated as a means to the end of economic growth and, similarly, hard law within the field has been related to employment. However, soft law is identified by several authors as significant to the policy development of EU gender equality issues. Soft law has been used to explore and expand new areas of policy making beyond the direct competences of the EU and, subsequently, develop hard law measures within these areas (Kantola 2010). Walby concludes that even though the competence of the EU outside the realm of the economy is limited, the "noneconomic nature of [gender equality] issues has merely slowed (rather than prevented) EU engagement with these domains" (2004, 22) because of the interconnectedness of economic and noneconomic domains.

Particularly in relation to civil society and the role of its actors, Strid argues that these are instrumental to the EC efforts to move forward in areas where there is no EU competence:

> The lack of a legal remit can, somewhat paradoxically it may seem, be argued to have strengthened women's civil society organising through EU soft law measures, funding of civil society and for example violence against women programs carried out and implemented by women's civil society organisations in Europe. (2009, 256)

Gender-based violence has been a priority for women's movements at the European level since the 1970s and they have focused, in general, on feminist accounts, emphasizing power relations, structural causes, and female empowerment while denouncing and challenging gender-neutral approaches to the issue (Elman 2007; Hoskyns 1996; Kantola 2010; Van der Vleuten 2007). Civil society organizations are considered to have been particularly active and successful in terms of putting the issue of gender-based violence on the EU agenda (see for instance Hoskyns 1996; Kantola 2006). Furthermore, the area of gender-based violence sets itself apart by recognizing the importance of including and consulting women's organizations, an aspect that is not considered to the same extent in any other policy area (Fernández de Vega et al. 2008a). In the literature, feminist activism and international references are, thus, seen as determining factors for the agenda setting of the issue of gender-based violence in the EU, and the UN development is typically conceived as an opportunity structure for European women's organizations to raise attention around the issue (Hoskyns 1996; Kantola 2006; 2010; Krizsán et al. 2005; Locher 2007; Van der Vleuten 2007).

As a political and theoretical concept, gender-based violence covers a wide range of violence forms occurring in the private and/or public sphere, such as sexual abuse, battering, (marital) rape, sexual harassment, trafficking, and female genital mutilation.[4] In the scholarly literature on gender-based violence policies in the EU, studies are usually thematically related to one of these subfields, most prominently sexual harassment (Collins 1996; Gregory 2006; Zippel 2004; 2006), trafficking (Askola 2007; Elman 2007; Kantola 2010; Locher 2007; Wijers 2006), and domestic violence (Kantola 2010; Krizsán et al. 2005; Krizsán et al. 2007; Lombardo and Meier 2008; Paantjens 2007). While analyzing the policy area of gender-based violence broadly, I will, when relevant, address the subissue of domestic violence more in detail. The nature of the sexual harassment issue is different in the sense that it relates directly to the dominant employment and labor market focus of the EU, and binding, legislative documents have been adopted within this area at the EU level.[5] While the issue of trafficking is mentioned in very early texts of the EU as well, it is not fully articulated as a policy issue in the 1970s and 1980s (Hoskyns 1996; Van der Vleuten 2007).

Within the field of gender-based violence, most of the nonbinding legislation and policies concern domestic violence. Here I conceptualize gender-based violence as a social problem, expressed at the individual and at the systemic level. At the individual level, domestic violence can be defined as a pattern of coercive control, linked to an abusive household, rather than single incidents (Stark 2007). This underlines the power dimensions of the problem. On the systemic level, (Walby 2009) violence is a social system exercised by states, groups, and individuals. In this way violence permeates societies, something that is particularly visible in times of discourses on security and counterterrorist measures. Furthermore Walby directs the attention toward violence in relation to multiple inequalities and the way in which these forms of violence (marital rape, for instance) are not effectively criminalized and prosecuted.

Conducting Critical Frame Analysis on European Union Policies on Gender-Based Violence

In the subsequent analysis, I am particularly interested in the discursive framings of the policies: The policy area chosen is, by definition, gendered, but it may contain both gendered and degendered framings. I am not analyzing the potentially gendered impact of so-called gender-neutral policies, for example. Rather I wish to analyze and discuss how policies are created, formulated, and articulated in the policy-making process, focusing exclusively on input/output dimensions and not the outcome of the adopted measures.[6] Attention will, thus, be paid to the input into the policy-making process and the discursive negotiation taking place prior to and during the decision-making process that leads to a specific articulation of the policies. Here, I focus particularly on the interaction between agency and ideas in the strategic framings of policies articulated by different EU and civil society actors in the transnational context and the shifts in policy frames that occur over time.

In particular, I analyze the adoption of the DAPHNE program. The main aim of the program is to fund European projects within the field of violence against children, young people, and women.[7] The DAPHNE programs as well as their negotiation and adoption expand over a period of more than ten years, and thus it is possible to follow a rather detailed and long policy-making process. The development of the DAPHNE program has contributed to the continuity of gender equality policies in the EU and the policy development in itself shows significant shifts over the years. Furthermore, the adoption of the DAPHNE programs is the only legislative process within the field of domestic violence policies that has resulted in binding legislative texts though they have not resulted in legal transposition into the national frameworks due to the nature of the programs (i.e., the objective is to provide funding for organizations transnationally).

The methodological approach followed takes it point of departure in the QUING project and its CFA.[8] This is based on a close-to-the-text coding of key policy documents, asking sensitizing questions[9] that determine the aspects of the texts that are in focus in the analysis. The basic codes are gathered in story grammars that together make up supertexts. The latter reflect the logical and argumentative structure of the coded text. The frame is understood as a configuration of positions to be mapped: The main analytical categories in the supertexts are voice, diagnosis, prognosis, and main messages (normativity, balance between diagnosis and prognosis as well as overall interpretation). Each category has its own code set or story grammar, focusing on elements such as actors (responsible actors and target groups), problem representation, policy action, policy goals, underlying norms, and causalities. This has enabled bottom-up constructions of frames as frame elements were identified in the coding and combined into actual policy frames that could then be compared across countries and across policy fields (gender equality machinery, intimate citizenship, nonemployment, and gender-based violence) and types of policy texts (law, policy reports, parliamentary debates, and civil society texts). Each frame is identified by one or several primary markers (i.e., a specific code like for example the "active actor") along with a set of additional markers. The primary markers are the ones defining the frame. A structural gender inequality frame, for instance, was identified within the policy area of gender-based violence and its primary markers consisted of "men" as the active actor (the one causing the problem), "women" as the passive actor (the one affected by the problem), and gender equality as the main norm (Dombos et al. 2009; Krizsán and Popa 2008; Krizsán and Verloo 2006; 2007; Lombardo et al. 2009b; Verloo 2005b; 2007).

Here, I have chosen to reelaborate the QUING methodology since the aim of my analysis is quite different: I conduct an in-depth analysis of a limited number of EU related policy documents within a specific policy field, without the need to do comparisons across large multinational data sets. This made it feasible to do in-depth qualitative analysis without the need for standardizing the codes or quantifying certain elements for comparative purposes. Consequently I have coded the relevant policy documents according to the following dimensions: agency (voice and standing); diagnosis and prognosis (problem, active actors, passive actors, and solution, responsible actors, and target groups); context (references to documents and actors, political opportunity structures, and participatory processes); specific policy content (concept of gender equality, silences, and intersectionality); as well as interpretation (summary, internal coherence between diagnosis/prognosis, normative framework, (non)gendered political strategies, overall interpretation, and immediate frames).

A (critical) revision of CFA needs to ask how far this approach can take us if we wish to move beyond the analysis of the frames "at face value," that is, as they appear in the policy documents. CFA can uncover details of policy texts and problem perceptions as well as the voice given to different actors in the policy process. However, its main shortcoming is the lack of scope: It deals with text-based analysis exclusively, but it does not tell us much about what is going on outside the text, in the political and institutional context. This translates, among other things, into a lack of focus on power relations. I therefore suggest combining CFA, based on analysis of policy documents, with the analysis of interview data. As mentioned in the Introduction, I have chosen to conduct elite interviews with officials and politicians from the three main EU institutions (the Council, the Commission, and the Parliament) as well as with representatives from a number of transnational women's organizations. These interviews contribute to the contextualization of the analysis of the policy documents by shedding light on aspects such as the policy process, the institutional framework, the opportunity structures of the transnational space, agenda setting mechanisms, and the strategic reflections and framings made by key actors in the development of the policies under scrutiny. Furthermore, through the contextualization of the policy processes, the interviews are expected to reveal patterns of (potential) conflicts and silences (i.e., unarticulated policy issues or frames) in the textual material by articulating issues such as intentions and actor relations. In other words, the interviews give an insight into some of the aspects that the documents do not reflect.

Combining textual analysis of policy documents with the contextualization provided by expert interviews, elements such as agency, silences, political context, and actor interrelations are emphasized in my take on CFA as an approach to policy and policy-making process analysis. This makes for an analytical framework that takes into consideration tensions between frames and between actors, shifts over time, and discursive and political dimensions of the opportunity structures. Particularly relevant for the area of gender-based violence is the focus on actors in the diagnosis and the prognosis: The perception of victims and perpetrators (and their identification as gendered or not) is a key point in the policies within this area.

As regard the documents selected for analysis, they cover a period from the late 1970s, when the issue of gender-based violence first appeared on the EU agenda, up until 2007 when the decision on the third version of the DAPHNE program to combat violence against children, young people, and women was adopted. Overall, the analysis covers 137 policy documents from the main EU institutions and a number of European women's organizations.[10] This includes both documents related to gender-based violence and key EU documents on gender equality policies in general. The latter were mainly used to provide contextual information. A detailed CFA was conducted on 23 EU and civil society texts within the area of gender-based violence policies (using the coding schema outlined above). The 23 documents were selected because they are key documents within the policy area and they reflect the general development of gender-based violence policies in the EU. Furthermore, a particular analysis was made of the policy-making process in relation to the first DAPHNE program (adopted in 2000) as the most important shift in framings took place in relation to the adoption of this program. In this case, I applied a complementary method of in-depth policy tracing, following a specific policy issue (i.e., gender-based violence and, particularly, the DAPHNE program) over time and tracing the debates and negotiations from agenda setting to decision making. Thus, draft versions of the policy documents were analyzed with specific attention toward textual modifications as the documents passed through the hands of the various relevant institutional actors.[11]

Soft Law, Lack of Competences, and Ideational Changes in the Policy Area of Gender-Based Violence

Gender-based violence was never directly related to the main areas of interest of the EU, namely economy and employment. As such it remains a soft policy area where programs and best practices have been developed but no binding legislation envisaged. The lack of legislation has been criticized by NGO actors, for instance, whereas other institutional actors take a more optimistic view, arguing that the fact that European policies exist within the area is a huge achievement in itself. The purpose of this analysis is not to evaluate whether the glass is half full or half empty; my interest lies in the way in which the issue has developed and been strategically framed within this particular context, being able to be included within the realm of EU policies without surpassing the division of competences between the EU institutions and the member states.

In principle, the EU has no competences within the field of gender-based violence, and there is no explicit legal basis to cover actions regarding gender-based violence at the EU level. There is no common legislation on the issue and no common frame to refer to. Member-state competences thus prevail, and their reticence to make changes in the direction of harmonization and EU legal action is clear. The question remains, however, how and why the broadening of the policy area of gender-based violence beyond the direct competence of the EU came about. There is a common agreement in the literature that a shift in framing within the area of gender-based violence at the EU level occurred, moving from human rights to public health, as the issue was articulated in binding policy documents in the late 1990s. This was mainly because the EU holds no legal competences as such in gender equality policies outside the labor market (Krizsán et al. 2005; Krizsán et al. 2007; Lombardo and Meier 2007; 2008; Paantjens 2007). Kantola (2010) argues that the gender-neutral public health framing has "narrowed down" the definition of the policy areas and the measures proposed for its solution. In an earlier study of EU, British, and Finnish national discourses on gender-based violence, Kantola (2006) found that feminist definitions were "losing ground" and the issue was increasingly depoliticized. This may be an effect of the focus on multiple discrimination, as described above, or it can be interpreted within the general policy development in the EU in the 2000s that is characterized by the enlargement processes, the saliency of economic imperatives, a lack of prioritization of social policy issues, as well as a right-wing turn both in the Council and in the Parliament.[12]

The lack of a clear legal basis for EU gender equality policies outside employment seems to have led to processes of degendering (Lombardo and Meier 2007; 2008) whereby gender is ignored, silenced, or excluded from policies that would be relevant to gender equality concerns: The area of gender-based violence reflects "a lack of competence and the subsequent need to adopt measures...that are linked to policy matters for which the EU has legislating power, which facilitates the co-optation of gender equality concepts and principles by other concerns" (Lombardo and Meier 2007, 72). Lombardo and Meier (2008), furthermore, argue that the broadening of the EU agenda on gender equality that happened with the introduction of the principle of gender mainstreaming in the Amsterdam Treaty has not led to a deepening of the gender equality frames articulated at the EU level. Krizsán et al. (2007) find policies on gender-based violence to be particularly prone to degendering as compared to other policy issues: It is a general trend that when gender-based violence enters the policy agenda, it is defined in gender-blind terms (for example "domestic violence") (Krizsán et al. 2005).

Whereas the literature accounts for interesting policy developments within the field of gender-based violence, additional questions arise and certain gaps can be detected. These include the way in which the main policies were negotiated as well as the reasons behind the shifts, such as the one from human rights to public health. Whereas others have identified the main frames and, to some extent, the shifts taking place during the policy development, there is a lack of focus on the detailed level of negotiation that goes beyond the textual level and takes into account the institutional context, the interplay between the main actors, the role of civil society actors, as well as the reasoning behind the frame articulation.

Consensus or Contestation in a Discursive Battlefield of Policy

A salient feature of the policy issue of gender-based violence in the context of the EU is the apparently low level of disagreement. Even though there are significant variations across the EU member states in terms of how they deal with the issue of domestic violence as gendered or nongendered (Krizsán et al. 2007; Verloo et al. 2007), several of my interviewees from the EU institutions emphasize an existing consensus on the main objectives within the area. Thus, one of the MEPs from the FEMM Committee argues that there are no significant political struggles over the content of the issue of gender-based violence within the EP:

> There is a very strong consensus on what kind of issues should be addressed and we also learned from the best practices of some countries, we are all trying to go for a European Year against violence against women and we all want that the European Union comes forward with legislation on violence. (MEP, Socialist Group, interview December 2007)

Another interviewee from the Council says that nobody disagrees that something has to be done; it is a matter of which measures to use to combat the problem (Council official, permanent representation, interview May 2010). To phrase it in frame analysis terms, the key actors may disagree on the policy actions but not on the objective.

However, beneath any kind of discursive consensus, we can expect to encounter exclusions or silences (Laclau and Mouffe 1985). Even though there may not be significant contestations regarding the objective within this policy field, the potential disagreements on a more detailed level of policy making invite us to look deeper into the ways in which the problem of gender-based violence is represented. Thus, my aim here is to uncover the underlying content of the frames articulated. Even though an idea or a frame has become institutionalized, it does not follow that its significance is the same to all actors. In this sense, institutionalization is ongoing since the content and the meaning of the frames are always contested. This theoretical presumption is confirmed by the following quote from another MEP: "There isn't any agreement in the [FEMM] Committee. We disagree on many things. Right down to how we should define it, whether as gender-based violence or as domestic violence... [The definitions] tell a lot about the perceptions of gender" (MEP, Socialist Group, interview January 2008).

One of the disagreements thus concerns the way in which the problem is defined. At times, it is phrased as "domestic violence" other times as "violence against women" or "gender-based violence." This is a central question as the denomination or definition entails a particular perception of the problem (Bacchi 1999) as well as a specific view on its gendered or nongendered nature. "Gender-based violence" highlights the gender equality content but it also leads to discussions over the idea of gender and what it covers; "violence against women" makes the category "women" explicit and underlines the direction of the violence, while covering both the public and the private sphere; and "family violence" deliberately excludes the gendered dimensions of violence, as anyone could be a victim in this problem representation, and delimits it to the private sphere. Notions where "women" or "gender" are mentioned point more explicitly to the problem as one of gender inequalities, male dominance, and human rights. In theory, the term "violence against women" denotes a structural problem, suffered by female victims because of their gender, and supported by specific (patriarchal) social structures. The term "domestic violence" in itself does not address these structural issues and is considered by some of my interviewees to lack a critical content toward gender-based asymmetries in the society. Furthermore, as Bacchi (1999) points out, the term implies a differentiation between public and private spheres and their respective forms of violence.

If we turn toward the empirical evidences of the different uses of the terms within the context of the EU, it is clear that the use of "violence against women" is far more widespread than "domestic violence," whether the policy documents address structural gender inequalities or not. Both the Zero Tolerance campaign of the EP and the DAPHNE programs, managed by the EC, which are the two most significant policies within the field, use the term "violence against women" in their document titles. "Gender-based violence" and "violence against women" can also be considered as the broad definitional framework of the policy field, and "domestic violence" as a subarea or subissue. This is the categorization that is used here and I consider "gender-based violence" and "violence against women" to be synonymous in this regard.

The question of victims/perpetrators and, particularly, the role attributed to men are also contested. The problem of gender-based violence can be perceived as a matter of dominance; in this case the prognosis is often related to helping women, for instance through empowerment measures. However, the problem can also be perceived as pathological, relating it to psychological problems of the perpetrator. Here the prognosis relates to the treatment of men. Some actors, like the Nordic member states in the Council of the EU, combine a structural problem perception with a dual perspective on both victims and perpetrators: "Because they very much felt that, yes, we need everything for the victims, but unless you deal with the perpetrators, you're not... we're not ridding ourselves with the problem" (Council official, General Secretariat, interview May 2010). Thus, including the perpetrators in the prognosis can be a way of addressing the structural root causes of the problem.

As mentioned above, another disagreement within the field of gender-based violence concerns the distribution of competences between the member states and the EU and the question of whether or not legislation should be envisaged at the supranational level. Some member states think that the EU should coordinate in the field of social policy and put gender equality issues on the agenda, but they consider legislation a matter for the national level. Other member states favor a more active role for the EU as the one leading the struggle against gender-based violence and, as such, the legislative role of the EU should be stronger. This is reflected in the following interview quotes:

> [Violence against women] is something that touches us all... All member states welcome the talk on the topic. It is just how you talk about it is different and unfortunately sometimes, when you go for too much, you get less. Sometimes, I mean, it is unfortunate but sometimes when you push one agenda which would be for example a legislative one of a certain kind, then you get just reactions which are, which might be like saying 'legislation is not the way ahead for us'... Sometimes instead of advancing all together slowly toward the target, you end up stalling in terms of the discussions on whether legislation is the way out... In the social area in general sometimes the EU is not moving forward very much because of the debates on legislation that divide member states when the actual aim, we all share... sometimes we might be moving further away from the aim by debating at length on having or not having legislation whereas if you talk about much softer measures, you have member states engaged. (Council official, permanent representation, interview December 2010)

I don't think there is an EU member...I mean everyone is against gender violence and nobody of course, nobody is going to say "no, I don't want to deal with this," even in the EU level. The question is the way you want to deal with it...If you want to produce just another paper that states "fight against gender violence is important," "EU should do something as well as member states," well, nothing is going to happen. (Council official, permanent representation, interview May 2010)

To a certain extent, the disagreements in terms, competences, and legislation are linked to the member states' approach to the EU in general and to the area of social policy in particular. In other words, the degree of skepticism vis-à-vis the EU is reflected in the member states' position on adopting legislative measures or not within the field of gender-based violence.

In sum, the disagreements within the field, and the discursive contestation, are located within the policy process more than the policy content. The dispute refers to the distribution of power and competences within the EU institutions. The framings of the issue are intertwined with these institutional interests. Furthermore, the prevalence of member-state competences within the area fits the overall tendency within the Commission and the Council to treat the issue as a private and individual matter. This means that the framing does not legitimize excessive state intervention. Overall, there is a consensus on the EU level regarding the relevance of the topic and the ultimate goals of the policy actions but not on the key definitions, the policy measures, and the division of competences. Therefore, it is relevant to look into the framing processes that play out in the field of gender-based violence and conduct a more detailed textual analysis of the most important policy documents and the actors behind them.

Framing the Policy Problem of Gender-Based Violence within European Union Institutions (1980–2010)

The EU policies on gender-based violence can be divided roughly into three phases: The early documents of the EP (1980s), the documents related to the Zero Tolerance of Violence against Women campaign (1990s), and the documents relating to the adoption of three successive DAPHNE programs on violence against children, young people, and women (2000s). The most recent phase has, to a certain extent, been dominated by the actions taken under the Spanish presidency of the

Council in Spring 2010. Using a similar classification, Montoya (2013) adds a useful perspective on the institutional context of the different stages:[13] In the 1980s, there were no EU competences in the field of gender-based violence, the EP was weak, and no international documents were yet addressing the issue. In the 1990s, the EP had gained strength, and in general the EU was more active within the field of gender-based violence. The 2000s, in turn, were characterized by a general security discourse and cultural framings of the issue. Montoya argues that a stronger role of the EU is developed over time (ibid.).

The European Parliament and the Structural Gender Inequality Frame: The Early Years and First Campaign (1980s and 1990s)

The main frames found in the three phases are structural gender inequality, women's rights as human rights, and public health. The early documents of the EP in the 1980s, which refer to violence against women, are elaborated by the FEMM Committee and its antecedents. They emerged in a context of economic crisis and increasing unemployment, a fact to which almost all of them refer. These circumstances are considered to affect women particularly hard, to threaten the progress achieved in terms of gender equality measures, and as a pretext for the lack of implementation of already adopted legislation.

In general, the EP documents in the early years perceive women's dependence as one of the fundamental problems of gender inequality: Women are economically dependent and oftentimes socially isolated when they dedicate themselves to housework exclusively. The problem is considered to be structural, and unequal distribution of work at home and in the labor market is seen both as an individual and as a collective problem. Particular historical, cultural, political, economic, and social developments have created gender inequalities, and the modern industrial societies and industrialization have "given rise to new forms of alienation and imbalances" (EP Resolution on the position of women in the European Community, OJ C 50, 09.03.81). The 1986 own initiative report and resolution of the FEMM Committee on violence against women (A2–44/86; A2–0044–86)[14] focus on structural rather than individual explanations of the problem. The weak economic position of women as well as their dependence is what causes unequal power distribution and, through this, violence.

These kinds of causal relations (and, correspondingly, a very developed diagnostic dimension) are much more frequent in the early, more developed and comprehensive documents than in subsequent ones. The prognostic elements are, correspondingly, the improvement of women's economic position and the abolishment of unequal power relations. More concretely, the measures mentioned are information and awareness raising, in order to increase the number of actual reports of violence, and the training of professionals, to improve the way in which the reports are received. In order to get at the deeper causes of the problem, in terms of gender inequality, the sharing of professional and parental responsibilities, educational measures to ensure respect, mutual responsibility and the elimination of gender stereotypes, as well as the harmonization of laws are mentioned. The problem is seen from a multidimensional, integral perspective in the sense that social, cultural, and economic gender roles are considered to be related to gender-based violence.

Thus, the problem of gender-based violence is mainly framed as a structural problem of gender inequality and economic dependence in the early documents of the EP. This is a very different kind of economic framing than the one that would become prevalent in the 1990s and 2000s (focusing on economic cost and decreasing productivity):

> Violence against women is expressed in a variety of ways and in a variety of situations... However, what all these forms of violence have in common is that they are bound up with the position of women in our society. Violence against women is the sexualized expression of the oppression of women, the dependence of women, the difference in power between men and women. In other words, the sexual and economic dependence of women are related. (A2–44/86; A2–0044–86)

A diagnostic relation is articulated between the sexual and the economic systems whereby the weak economic position of women makes them more prone to stay in a violent relationship in order to maintain their jobs, family, and home.

When the issue of gender-based violence was first introduced on the EP agenda, the predominant framing was clearly in tune with the civil society demands of relating gender-based violence to structural gender inequalities. In the first years of the institutional history of the policy issue, it is fair to say that the dominant framing was developed by civil society actors and articulated institutionally by the EP and especially the FEMM Committee who was the driving force behind getting the issue on the official EU agenda. Civil society actors had been at the forefront and active in developing and formulating demands, also before the issue reached the EU agenda. This happened not least through the shelter movement in the 1970s and its increasing pressure for states to take action. Simultaneous mobilization at the national and the global levels in the 1980s and 1990s put pressure on the EU to develop policies within the area (Elman 2007; Hanmer 1996; Locher 2007). The EU developments of the 1980s were particularly inspired by the Dutch case where femocrats had placed the issue on the political agenda, emphasizing state responsibility in attending to the problem (Elman 2007). Thus, the civil society actors contributed to voicing the issue, and in the 1986 EP report (A2–44/86) it is underlined that the issue is no longer a taboo.

It is important to bear in mind that the EP was still a young institutional body at the time when gender-based violence was first introduced in its policies.[15] The field of women's rights and gender equality policies were being explored for the first time within the framework of the EP, and the scope of the policies was still to be defined. During this period, the FEMM Committee (and its antecedents) thus looked quite actively to civil society organizations for input, and the first reports are actual research exercises into problems, dynamics, and opinions within the field. Several of my interviewees talk, in different ways, about the EP/civil society-tandem when it comes to putting issues such as gender-based violence on the EU agenda:

> The issue of violence, which was not... in the Commission's competences at all, at the beginning was brought in by, I remember, Hedy d'Ancona who used to be an MEP in the 1980s, produced, I think it was in [1986], she produced the first report on violence and it was really thanks to the push of people, I mean, the MEPs, the Women's Committee has had a tremendous sort of impact in pushing new issues and relaying a lot of things that were coming from civil society. (EC official, BEPA, interview January 2008)[16]

In general, my interviewees oftentimes consider civil society actors to be the "original" producers of novel ideas. These ideas, emerging from civil society, are transferred through the FEMM Committee, which is attributed a central role as agenda setter. In other words, the push forward in terms of gender equality and gender-based violence policies is perceived as emanating from parliamentary and activist sources:

> [The civil society] organizations are very dedicated and very determined, they have an agenda and they are pushing their agenda to EU

policy makers. I think that over the years definitely they have been a driving force in the field of violence against women. Yeah, I would say so...if nothing else, they have really drawn the attention of policy makers to this problem and made it clear, loud and clear, that this is a European problem and it needs to be addressed at an EU level. (EC official, DG Justice, interview May 2010)

Returning to the development of gender-based violence policies in the EP, the first documents on violence against women and their strong framing of the issue as structural gender inequality and women's rights as human rights were followed by years of silence. However, the same frames reappeared when the issue was brought up again at the EU level in the mid-1990s through the Zero Tolerance of Violence against Women Campaign of the EP (1997). The campaign framed the policy issue as one of gender equality, democracy, and human rights:

> Gender-based violence not only reflects unequal gender power relations in our society, but also forms a formidable barrier to efforts to overcome inequality between women and men...A society that claims to champion human rights and work for equality must seriously tackle the widespread violence which directly and indirectly affects a majority of the population—women and children. (A4–0250/97, 16.07.97; A4–0250/1997, 06.10.97)

There is a focus on the structural dimension of gender inequality through the articulation of patriarchy and gendered power imbalances. The problem is represented as universal since the male perpetrators come from all backgrounds, cultures, and social classes, and the problem affects all citizens. Women should be treated as survivors of violence, not as victims. Together with the focus on women's empowerment, this makes for a rather feminist framing of the issue. According to Locher (2007), the campaign in general reflected a new strategy of the femocrats to include men in the articulation of the problem of violence, thus converting it into a problem for the entire society, not just for women.[17] A public health frame and a related frame on economic costs are also present, to a minor degree. The combination of legislation and campaigns (awareness raising and funding) is the main prognostic dimension as the objective is to remedy the insufficient national level instruments, on the one hand, and change individual, collective, and institutional attitudes, on the other.

The European Commission and the Public Health Frame: Introducing and Consolidating the DAPHNE Program (1990s and 2000s)

Whereas the EP had been the main protagonist in the development of policies on gender-based violence in the 1980s and 1990s, the EC, too, started to launch initiatives in the 1990s[18] and 2000s. The EC DAPHNE initiative on violence against children, young people, and women was launched in 1997 as a result of increased attention to the issues of domestic violence and trafficking on the EC agenda in the late 1990s. Sweden and Finland were included as new EU member states in 1995, just prior to the revitalization of gender-based violence policies. These two member states are often mentioned in EU policy documents as examples of good practice at the national level (see Fernández de Vega et al. 2008a). Furthermore, the presence of so-called "good women" (EWL representative, interview December 2007), or norm entrepreneurs, such as Anita Gradin (Commissioner 1995–1999), Anna Diamantopoulou (Commissioner 1999–2004), and Maj Britt Theorin (Chairwoman of the FEMM Committee 1999–2002), strengthened the opportunity to advance EU policies on gender-based violence in the late 1990s (Kantola 2006; Krizsán et al. 2005; Locher 2007). Furthermore, in 1996, the Dutroux affair, that uncovered a number of sexual abuse crimes against young girls in Belgium, caused public and political commotion, also at the EU level. The same year the first World Congress against Commercial Sexual Exploitation of Children was held in Stockholm, and in 1997 a hearing on trafficking and sexual exploitation of children with key European level actors led to a call for EU action and NGO funding within this area.

Immediately afterwards, the EC launched the DAPHNE initiative that was to fund NGO transnational cooperation to prevent violence, commercial sexual exploitation and trafficking, and protect the victims. The focus was on children, but due to the parallel development of EP initiatives in the area of gender-based violence (as described above) the agendas were merged and actions aimed at children, young people, and women:

> It was a Parliament/Commission initiative and it was the result of a public outcry following the Dutroux affair...There was a public reaction in the sense that the EU needs to do something about it, so this initiative started, it proved to be very successful. (EC official, DG Justice, interview May 2010)

The narrative of the origin of the DAPHNE program is diverse, however; some interviewees talk about the need to address the issue of sexual exploitation of children at the European level, whereas others highlight the "feminist agenda" and the civil society fingerprints on the development of the policy issue and program (EWL representative, interview December 2007; EC official, BEPA, interview January 2008).

The DAPHNE initiative ran for three consecutive years, and in 1998 negotiations to adopt a multiannual program within a clearly defined legal base were initiated. Thus, the first DAPHNE program was adopted in 2000 (293/2000/EC). This document clearly frames the problem of gender-based violence as a public health issue with social and economic costs:

> Physical, sexual and psychological violence against children, young persons and women constitutes...a serious threat to the physical and mental health of the victims of such violence; the effects of such violence are so widespread throughout the Community as to constitute a major health scourge...It is important to recognise the serious immediate and long-term implications for health, psychological and social development...and the high social and economic costs to society as a whole. (293/2000/EC)

In the document, there is a dual focus on individual well-being, and social and economic development. The gendered framing is almost gone, except for a reference to women and girls among the prime victims. Responsibilities are not discussed as the main focus is on the victim. The solution to the problem lies mainly in information: Providing the victims with information and the police and health care professionals, among others, with better training will enhance the possibilities of prevention, protection, and adequate support.[19]

The second DAPHNE program (803/2004/EC, 21.04.04) reproduces to a large extent the same frame content, but the women's rights as human rights frame gains relative importance in this document compared to the first DAPHNE program. Furthermore, EU level action within the field is promoted. The third DAPHNE program (779/2007/EC, 20.06.07) ensures the continuity of the policy. Similarly to the first two programs, it is marked by the public health frame, with rights and economic costs as secondary frames. Insufficient national action within the area of public health is mentioned as member states are articulated as responsible actors in the prognosis. Synergies are sought with other community instruments such as immigration and health protection policies. All in all, the document is fairly degendered: References are made to equal opportunities and equal treatment, but they have no impact on the policy proposals. Similarly, human rights and (gender) equality are mentioned as objectives, but this is not elaborated upon.

The Council and Recent Developments: Presidencies and Agenda Setting (2000s and 2010s)

The Council of the EU has been involved in the negotiation of the DAPHNE program as the key documents of the program are legally binding. All other EU documents within the subarea of domestic violence are nonbinding, soft policy texts, and therefore the Council has had no role in their elaboration. The Council does influence EU policies on gender-based violence in general. Kantola (2010) points to a dual tendency whereby the Council, on the one hand, often blocks gender equality initiatives and, on the other, keeps domestic violence, for example, high on the agenda.

One of the ways in which the individual member states may seek to set the policy agenda in this area is through the Council presidencies—each member state holds the presidency of the Council for a period of six months on a rotation basis. Through work programs, priorities, and Council conclusions, the individual member state has a possibility of influencing the Brussels debates. The role and importance of the presidencies are underlined by the interviewees from the Council:

> [In the Council] it's the presidency that leads for six months, so the presidency might table initiatives in its priority areas like we have these Council conclusions on violence recently under the Spanish presidency, very much a presidency led priority that they pushed through... but it was prepared for a little bit by... under the Swedish presidency, because they had... a conference on violence—but it was, you know, a Spanish initiative to have conclusions on this topic and, you know, that is a very good and typical example of how the Council works—it's the presidency that can, you know, give a sort of political push to an individual sector. (Council official, General Secretariat, interview May 2010)

The agenda-setting powers of the individual presidency as well as the significance of creating continuity between subsequent presidencies within thematic policy areas are underlined. The political will and commitment of the individual government holding the presidency are also considered to be decisive.

Gender equality has always been a part of the presidency programs, but gender-based violence as a specific policy area has also been prioritized or emphasized by successive presidencies over time. Austria, Finland, Germany, Greece, Portugal, and Spain are mentioned in the literature as particularly active presidencies in terms of advancing the gender-based violence agenda (Kantola 2006; 2010; Lombardo and Meier 2007). My interviewees point to Spain, Portugal, Italy, the Netherlands, and the Nordic countries as the ones pushing the agenda within this area (Council official, General Secretariat, interview May 2010; EC official, DG Justice, interview May 2010). Typically, the policy issue has been framed as a human rights issue, and the need to study the deeper root causes of the problem is also highlighted by several presidencies as gender-based violence is considered to be an obstacle to gender equality in the EU.[20]

As mentioned above, the culmination of the gender-based violence focus of several Council presidencies came in 2010 with the spring presidency led by the Spanish socialist government. The "Council conclusions on improving prevention to tackle violence against women and care to its victims within the scope of law enforcement," adopted in April 2010 (8310/10), frame the problem of gender-based violence in terms of gender equality and human/fundamental rights. Gender-based violence is seen as an obstacle to equality and progress, and legal references are made to article 2 of the Treaty of the EU (the fundamental rights upon which the EU builds)[21] and to the Charter of Fundamental Rights. The presidency conclusions contemplate the possibility of creating a common European hotline for victims of gender-based violence and the establishment of an observatory within the same field. Even though no binding agreement was made within the Council regarding these proposals, the Spanish presidency did contribute to putting the possibility of EU legislation on gender-based violence on the table. Thus, plans are in the making for a specific strategy to combat gender-based violence that could lead to actual European legislation within the field. In sum, the framings found in the Council presidency documents suggest that the three main EU institutions use gendered framings of the issue of violence against women. The public health frame is indeed absent and was only articulated by the Council in a significant way in relation to the legislative adoption of the DAPHNE programs when the division of competences between the EU and the member states was at stake.

Other recent initiatives within the area include an EP declaration from September 2010 proposing the establishment of a European

Year of Combating Violence against Women (0020/2010) as well as a resolution pushing for a directive against gender-based violence (2010/2209[INI]).[22] These are ways for the EP to maintain pressure on the Council and the Commission to keep the issue on the political agenda. In the EC Communication "Delivering an area of freedom, security and justice for Europe's citizens. Action Plan Implementing the Stockholm Programme" (COM[2010]171), a strategy to combat violence against women, domestic violence, and female genital mutilation is envisaged and scheduled for 2011–2012. The Strategy for Equality between Women and Men (2010–2015) (COM[2010]491) specifically includes, among its key actions, the aim to: "Adopt an EU-wide strategy on combating violence against women...supported by a Europe-wide awareness-raising campaign on violence against women." However, this kind of strategy is still to be developed by the EC. On the positive side, the directive on the European protection order was adopted in December 2011 (2011/99/EU); it was promoted by the Spanish presidency of the Council in Spring 2010 with the aim of protecting victims of gender-based violence, among others, from perpetrators, across EU member-state borders. Thus, the directive ensures that protection orders issued in one member state apply in the entire EU territory.

In general, the scope of the gender-based violence frame is widened with the adoption of the Lisbon Treaty. The declaration on article 8 of the Treaty on the functioning of the EU, which is annexed to the Lisbon Treaty, states that in the "general efforts to eliminate inequalities between women and men, the Union will aim in its different policies to combat all kinds of domestic violence." Domestic violence is, thus, particularly highlighted as a problem of gender inequality:

> The Lisbon Treaty seems to give more emphasis in this area and we are working toward expanding actions in the field of violence against women on an EU level...Over the years, [there] has developed a discussion on what could be a strong legal basis for action at the EU level on combating violence against women and that is still under discussion...and we feel the Lisbon Treaty gives more room for action...The right kind of momentum has been building up for the last few years and given the political support we have right now I would say that this is a natural timing for action. (EC official, DG Justice, interview May 2010)

The idea of the EC is to develop a more comprehensive policy framework for the issue of violence against women, and in this development the results of the DAPHNE program, that is, the knowledge that has accumulated over the years from the different projects funded under the program, will have "a critical role to play" (EC official, DG Justice, interview May 2010).

In the process of adopting the DAPHNE program, the framing of the policy and the overall development from structural gender inequality, of the early EP documents, to the dominant public health framing of the DAPHNE texts have been decisive. The next chapter analyses precisely how this came about by tracing the policy issue through institutional negotiations and policy-making processes.

5

TRANSNATIONAL POLICY FRAMINGS: (DE)GENDERING IN THE CONTEXT OF INSTITUTIONALIZATION

As the frame analysis in chapter 4 shows, the main EU policies on gender-based violence differ in terms of the dominant frame articulated, that is, that of structural gender inequality, women's rights as human rights, or public health. On the one hand, these differences can be attributed to the institutional authorship of the texts, as the EP documents articulate frames related to gender equality and human rights whereas the EC focuses on public health. However, a shift occurred, also in the Commission perspective, from gender equality and human rights frames to public health. This shift was first and foremost related to the question of which would be the most adequate legal basis for EU policies within the area of gender-based violence and the division of competences between the EU institutions and the member states. In particular, during the process of negotiation of the DAPHNE program, the EC tried to persuade the Council to use a general legal base that would legitimize EU level action. The Council did not accept this and recurred to the legal base of public health protection instead. Given the impossibility of advancing in a different direction, the EP used the framework of public health to a maximum by broadening its scope and articulating human rights concerns.

In order to assess whether the shift in policy frames within the area of gender-based violence had any impact beyond the purely discursive level, we must look at the implications of the framings and, in particular, the institutional context in which they are inserted. In other words, this calls for a detailed look at frame nuances, differential institutionalizations of frames, contextual dimensions, and the immediate implications of the framings at the policy level. I argue here that no clear processes of degendering transcend; rather, I find that gendered understandings of the policy issue of gender-based violence are still significant within the EU, even though they are articulated in a moderate fashion, not including feminist perspectives on structural inequalities, for example. The key binding documents within the area subscribe to a public health related framing, but violence against women is still predominantly articulated as a gender related problem. I argue that this is due to the instrumental use and weak institutionalization of the public health frame, which was first and foremost articulated with the aim of passing legislation, and the simultaneously prevalent gendered understanding of the problem within the EU institutions. This results in the public health frame not spilling over into one of the outputs of the policy-making process, namely the selection of projects for funding under the DAPHNE program. The EC, with pressure from the EP and implicit support from several Council presidencies, maintains a gendered understanding of the issue. These findings, in turn, feed back into the methodology of CFA.

Frame Contestation within the Context of Multilevel Division of Competences

Given the basic consensus among member states within the area, the case of gender-based violence, and particularly that of domestic violence, is an example of how far the EU institutions are able to take the policies in an area of limited competences. Progress is possible within this policy area although it is based on a complex combination of frames in a field of legal and institutional constraints but with some degree of political consensus and will to build policies, most recently demonstrated by the Spanish presidency (see chapter 4). The case is interesting because of the tension between the apparent impossibility of advancing policies within the area, due to legal constraints and member-state reluctance to develop EU competences in relation to the policy issue, and the simultaneously strong political will, emanating from specific actors within all three major EU institutions.

The tension is not least reflected in interviews with Council officials who, at the end of the day, are the ones who deal with the detailed policy negotiations of the binding texts, finding a way to make all member-state interests converge:

> Competence at EU level on violence doesn't really exist. So, in some ways it couldn't really be taken. Although if you look at what the

Spanish presidency is doing now, you see? They can set up a European Observatory, they can do this, they can do that. So even with some of these sort of institutional constraints if there is really a political will then sometimes they find their ways around it. So, I mean, I think it does depend on the seriousness of the issue, the political will, particularly of the presidency... But it means that then they have to be able to persuade all the others that this is acceptable, this is what they wanted. And... some people have been a little bit, you know, surprised: "Gosh, this is really going quite far!" (Council official, General Secretariat, interview May 2010)

When we first saw this topic coming, you know, I personally thought this would be really difficult because it is a crosscutting issue–it is both a social questions issue,... but it has also got a justice and home affairs dimension, where the member-states are very, very careful to retain and to protect their competences, because it is, you know, a question of the national courts and national legislation and it is much, much harder to get agreements in areas where there is very, very limited European Union competence, but we got these conclusions [of the Spanish presidency] unanimously agreed and as you know the conclusions call for a strategy to combat violence including this idea of an observatory and the Commission is invited to consider the possibility of proposing legislation on it too. (Council official, General Secretariat, interview May 2010)

The struggle over competences is crucial but even when the competence is lacking, it is still possible to broaden the scope of institutionalized framings and "sneak in" policy measures, given that there is a strong political will across the EU institutions to do so. In other and more theoretical words, policy development is possible, even in contexts, which are institutionally and discursively constrained, through the way in which key actors articulate ideas as strategic framings. The negotiation of the DAPHNE program is an example of this.

When the first DAPHNE program was being set up in the late 1990s, the legal framework of the program was initially thought to be consistent with the human rights framing promoted by the Parliament. Both the 1997 EP Zero Tolerance Campaign and the 2005 EP report on violence against women argue that, for this policy issue, human rights is an adequate competence ground that legitimizes EU level action.[1] In the process of negotiation and institutionalization, however, violence against women was reframed from a human rights issue to a public health issue due to competence considerations:

> The matter of competences is crucial in the EU, and the limits of the legal basis need to be respected: The first thing member states ask

themselves when they receive a new proposal for directive is...whether there is actually any competence. We just have to look into that, we just have to look into whether the EU can actually do anything here, from the point of view that they shouldn't if they cannot do so and therefore the Commission will always articulate the problems in such a manner that there is a competence there. (Council official, permanent representation, interview June 2010).

Each time something is negotiated...it is done within the context of the competences and that's...that's always a major part of the discussion. The Council will be...you know, the member states challenging the Commission on the competence issue—the member states take it really seriously—you know, they won't accept legislation or decisions that disregard the division of competences. This is sacred to the member states, so, you know, what policies there are have been structured in such a way that they respect the competences—it's just the way it is. (Council official, General Secretariat, interview May 2010)

The public health frame resonates institutionally with already existing policies and respects the division of competences whereas women's rights as human rights would create a new field of competence at the supranational level. Furthermore, the public health frame draws on the dominant economic discourse of the EU by highlighting the economic costs of ill-health. The Commission is constrained by the framework and need to be strategic when articulating and framing the problems in order to gain acceptance from the Council. In the case of the first DAPHNE program, this meant that the EC had to come up with a suitable policy frame under which the program could be adopted (due to pressure from the Parliament and civil society, see below) without interfering in member-state affairs and altering the established balance of competences.

Policy Negotiation Process

The timing of the negotiation process between the Commission, the Parliament and the Council (from 1998 to 2000) coincided with that of the adoption and entering into force of the Amsterdam Treaty. The Commission had originally proposed to launch the DAPHNE program under the new article 308 (ex article 235) that allows the Council to "take the appropriate measures" if needed in order for a community objective to be addressed, in case the treaty did not provide "the necessary powers." The human rights frame would comply with this and give the EU the necessary competences to implement the program.

Whereas most member states were positive toward the proposal for a program combating violence, some found the use of the legal base of article 235 too far-reaching and were reluctant to pass a program within a policy area where the EU had no explicit legal basis or competences to refer to. Thus, the Council Legal Service suggested using article 152 (of the Amsterdam Treaty) instead: This article allowed the EU to take initiatives to improve public health without harmonizing national legislation or changing member-state competences with regard to health services. Most member states (such as Finland, Greece, the Netherlands, and Sweden) did not find any of the two legal bases suitable. The French delegation argued "the use of Article 235, by artificially expanding the Community's power of action, would constitute a dangerous precedent." Other member states did not find article 129 on public health suitable as it did not resemble the actual content of the policy proposal. Only Spain fully accepted the suggestion to use article 235 as the legal base of the DAPHNE program (5610/99).

The Council Legal Service argued that the concept of public health could be interpreted broadly, and with the pertinent changes in the proposal for a decision on the DAPHNE program, article 129 would be a "justifiable legal basis": "Insofar as the DAPHNE programme did not cover measures aimed at combating violence as such, but preventive measures targeting victims and potential victims of violence...Article 129 might provide adequate legal cover" (5610/99). Belgium and Denmark supported the choice of article 129, whereas France and the Netherlands were still skeptical. The latter specifically questioned that violence would fit the wording of article 129, and it was emphasized that the public health programs of the Union had not covered violence, up until this point (5994/99). The EC preferred article 235, but it also perceived a risk of blockage in the Council and, in the end, the chosen frame turned out to be that of public health. The wording of the program was changed in order for it to show the aims and content more precisely and in this way adapt it to the use of article 129 as the legal base (7124/99). Thus, the DAPHNE program was, from the outset, restricted to a focus on victims and not structural gender equality perspectives as had previously been the case within the area of gender-based violence.

Institutional Embeddedness of Policies

The general shift in framing from human rights to public health had institutional implications in the sense that DG Justice[2] would take over the policy from DG Employment, where the gender equality unit was placed. The immediate institutional context of the DAPHNE program was, thus, the DG Justice, which did not have a specific unit dealing with gender equality policies like the DG Employment did. This institutional embeddedness of the policy issues within different DGs makes for a complex setup in terms of framing; given that the DG Justice had the competence on violence, the issue was often framed in relation to crime and justice, which is most visible in terms of policy actions, target groups, and responsible actors (i.e., the prognosis). This diminished the gender (in)equality perspective that DG Employment, and especially the Unit on Equality between Men and Women, would have contributed with. The institutional embeddedness of specific policy issues within the individual EU institutions is important: Decisions and framings are predominantly left to the EU institution where the issue is embedded. This imposes a constraint on the possibilities of contesting the chosen frame from within the EU institutions in the sense that the institutional embeddedness determines to a certain extent the content of future policies.

Discussions regarding the institutional embeddedness of the policy, similar to the ones of the EC, emerged in the Council in relation to the adoption of the third DAPHNE program in 2006:

> There were...questions about the way [the DAPHNE program] was being proposed because it was now going to be part of what they called the fundamental rights [program]. So that changed things quite dramatically. Because it was...before it was dealt with by the Social Affairs Working Group. And then when it went to be under the fundamental rights programme, there was a question whether...should it be Justice and Home Affairs Group that's dealing with it, because it was in the Commission...So there were some discussions about the legal base, some discussions about whether it should be the Social Questions Working Party or not and in the end it was decided that it was, but I...I remember them not being clear for some time about whether they could do it or not. And I think the gender people wanted to deal with it because they felt it to be a gender issue and to be sure that it would do the right things.[3] (Council official, General Secretariat, interview May 2010)

Some may have feared that the gender perspective would disappear as violence policies were moved into another institutional realm. However, Council officials point to the fact that all social issues are complex, and that policy makers can handle the multiple dimensions they entail (interviews May 2010).

However, recent institutional changes in the EC seem to push gender equality toward the fundamental rights and justice perspective. The Gender Equality Unit of the EC has been moved from DG Employment to DG Justice (along with the rest of the Directorate on Equality). This suggests a move toward a partial reframing of the gender equality perspective of the EU or at least a strengthened focus on rights and justice. The concern here would be whether this means returning to a formal equality perspective or if the substantive equality aspects can be sustained and developed. DG Justice focuses more on rights and securization whereas DG Employment relates gender equality to social policies and the labor market. Furthermore, DG Employment is considered to be more open in terms of civil society consultations (Ruzza 2011). In terms of gender-based violence this institutional restructuring may lead to a more unidimensional perspective on protection of rights and prosecution, and less on prevention and support. Policies to combat violence that would include a broad series of measures, if considered from a gender equality perspective, such as housing, labor market inclusion, etc. are less likely to be linked to this area. The same would be true for a number of other areas. However, increased attention to women's rights in relation to violence as well as effective criminalization for instance might be positive developments as well even though they cannot stand alone.

Nevertheless, the interinstitutional coordination has not been very developed in any case and the DAPHNE program was already situated within DG Justice so, on the other hand, the new institutional setup may create more coherence in the field and bring the multidimensional perspectives on violence closer together (even though Gender equality and DAPHNE are situated in two different directorates of DG Justice). Another parallel dimension to this is the fundamental rights and citizenship program, also within the same unit. The strong focus on this program draws the framings of the DAPHNE projects and the EC policies on gender-based violence in general toward a human-rights centered approach, which is often degendered. The institutional focus in general on fundamental rights may pull the gender-based violence framings toward implicit gender equality framings (instead of explicitly feminist or structural framings) though it also leaves room for gendered analysis to be used in implementation processes.

This interpretation is supported by some of the latest developments in the institutional setup of the EC. In the spring of 2010, with the increased focus of the Spanish presidency of the Council on policies on gender-based violence, the EC was invited to develop an actual policy strategy within the area. There was political support behind this, for instance from the Commissioner of Justice, Fundamental Rights and Citizenship, Viviane Reding, and plans were initiated. However, in the process the plans for a gendered strategy have been inscribed into the general program on fundamental rights. So the plans to develop an independent strategy on violence seem to have been haltered, at best (see also chapter 4).

Gendering the Degendered Frame of Public Health?

As mentioned above, women and health was always an issue in the early EP texts on women's rights, but usually it never concerned gender-based violence. In these documents, health was related to pregnancy, contraception, and specific risks for women, like breast cancer, as well as the need for a European policy on health care for women. However, in the very first report of the Ad Hoc Committee on Women's Rights, the increase in violence against women is mentioned in the health section. The problem is here perceived as dual in the sense that the causes are the unequal power relations and the consequence the ill-health of women (Doc. 1–829/80 part II, 29.01.81). So, even though health and gender-based violence are usually separated in policy documents, this reference suggests that public health was already a potential framing for the policy issue of gender-based violence and it could, thus, more easily be taken up by the EC later, in accordance with Locher's (2007) notion of dormant norms that are activated through the introduction of new norms.

However, framing the issue of gender-based violence as a public health matter has several implications. As the public health frame takes over from the human rights frame, a nongendering of the policies also takes place: Whereas the first EP documents were feminist in their expressions, the structural gender inequality dimensions are omitted in the later EC documents. The public health frame does not attend to gender inequalities as a cause of violence against women (Krizsán et al. 2007; Lombardo and Meier 2007). It often deals with the victims and the target groups in rather generic and nongendered terms (as "victims," "human beings," "individuals"). Thus, the DAPHNE program does not address the separate particularities of the three main target groups, that is, children, young people, and women (see also Krizsán et al. 2005).

In the process of frame negotiation, some of the EU institutions used their possibilities of strategic framing to broaden the scope of the (nongendered) legal basis chosen for the DAPHNE program and the dominant frame that followed from this (i.e., public health). The strategic uses of different frames highlights the significance of agency (in this case mainly parliamentarians and civil society organizations) within the development of policies and the way in which policies are attributed meaning. The FEMM Committee was not satisfied with the chosen legal base because it did not reflect the complexity of the issue of violence nor its structural gender inequality ground. Having accepted, however, that a change in the legal base would risk a blockage of the entire proposal in the Council, the 1999 EP report on the DAPHNE program (A4–0188/99), elaborated by the FEMM Committee, suggested a number of complementary amendments to the Commission's proposal in order to expand the scope of the public health framing. Initially the MEPs protested against the shift of legal framework because they felt that it was too limited:

> Our Committee is very worried that...the scope of the programme will not be adequate to the scale of the problem. We would like it to deal with all possible legal aspects...If the legal basis is the promotion of public health, we want guarantees that the Commission will actually be able to create a programme...in which violence against women is not merely reduced to a health problem. (Heidi Hautala, MEP, Group of the Greens/European Free Alliance, EP debate 08.03.1999)

Most importantly, the report suggested adding (human) rights to the public health problem definition of the program. Furthermore, references were made to the UN and the World Health Organization (WHO) with the clear aim of broadening the definition of violence. The WHO defines health as "the complete physical, mental and social well-being." The Council rejected this for some time but ended up accepting the inclusion of the broad definition, which, in principle, made the main public health frame and the secondary human rights frame compatible. In this way, all forms of violence could be covered under the public health frame, and the MEPs involved succeeded in their strategy to use the new frame and its legal framework to a maximum. According to Locher, this was not least due to the "determination of committed feminists in Parliament" (2007, 282).

The new legal framework would, potentially, allow the EP to influence the policies more: With the previous article the Parliament would only be consulted, whereas the new article 152 of the Amsterdam Treaty on public health is covered by the codecision procedure,[4] giving the Parliament more competences in the area. Strategically, the EP needed to make the text a reality in order for the institutionalization of the policy issue to take place. The EP aimed at preserving as much of the original, human rights content as possible, in order to maintain a multidimensional approach to the policy issue of gender-based violence, while accepting the legal framework that would give them a more prominent role within the area. This is an example of strategic bargaining with the acceptance of a less gendered framing of the problem based on a pragmatic reasoning as to what could be achieved politically. As one interviewee underlines, the degendered public health frame was "just a way to have the action taken" (EC official, DG Justice, interview May 2010). The EP gained more both in content and in influence than might have been the case by gendering the policies further and having to fight the resistance of the member states. The broadened scope of public health protection was used as a strategy of degendering, in favor of the development of policies to combat gender-based violence. With the new framing, structural problems could not be addressed directly but, by insisting on the multidimensional nature of the problem, the EP attempted to introduce elements of a rights frame alongside the dominant public health frame in order to attend to several interrelated problems (and solutions) within the policy issue.

As regards civil society actors, EWL and WAVE have used different strategies to put pressure on the EU institutions to maintain the original human rights content of the policy issue or to fill out the institutionalized frames in alternative ways.[5] Using strategies of gendering, these civil society actors try to counteract the discursive closure introduced by the dominant framing (public health), promoted by the institutional actors with the main decision-making power. The EWL, for instance, takes on a feminist framing, viewing the problem of violence as a structural one caused by gender inequality, male domination, and gender power asymmetries (see for instance EWL Position paper on the role of men and boys in achieving gender equality, 2004), or makes efforts to gender the public health frame (see for instance EWL indicators on policies against violence against women in relation to health, 2004). The civil society organizations agree on using the "women's rights as human rights" frame. Within this general trend, WAVE focuses on a human rights and justice frame with women as the main passive actor. Only rarely do any of the civil society actors make use of the public health frame because this framing of the problem does not allow for a gender inequality perspective. It articulates the problem as a matter of sickness, not of power imbalances and patriarchy. Furthermore, the civil society actors to a larger degree stick to the differentiations between public and private, highlighting the need for state intervention and legislation.

Strategic Framing in Resonance with the European Union Economic Agenda

The framing of gender-based violence as public health was also used strategically in another way, namely by accentuating its relationship to economic growth and development, which is central to the EU policy core. Health policies have been prioritized by the EU since the turn of the century, and the Community Action Programmes (1786/2002/EC and 1350/2007/EC) of DG for Health and Consumers reflect a tendency to define the public health problem as partly related to economic costs.[6] The second Community Action Programme (1350/2007/EC) relates health problems to the Lisbon strategy on growth and employment and specifically states that the public finances "are under pressure from rising health care and social security costs." The first Community Action Programme (1786/2002/EC) is more vague in its formulations regarding these aspects ("economic consequences of ill-health"). The Commission's White Paper, Together for Health: A Strategic Approach for the EU 2008–2013, (COM[2007]630) further specifies this framing, however, by explaining that "[h]ealth expenditure can be seen as an economic burden, but the real cost to society are the direct and indirect costs linked to ill health." Linking gender-based violence to public ill-health thus implies a strengthened focus on the economic costs of the problem. An important political objective in combating violence is to reduce public expenditure and improve economic prosperity. This spillover or interrelation between policy issues and framings can be detected for instance in the DAPHNE II program where the nature of the problem of violence is described by referring to "the serious immediate and long-term implications of violence for health, psychological and social development...and the high social and economic costs to society as a whole."[7] In this sense, the problem is not perceived as individual, but as something that affects overall economic growth as well as society's prosperity.

There is a tendency for gender equality issues to gain strength whenever they can be framed as an economic problem; the possibility of formulating policies within a given area in the EU is usually furthered in this way as the EU focus on economy and economic growth makes the gender equality argument more persuasive. This point is also made by one of my interviewees in relation to the public health framing of the issue of violence:

> In terms of what the Council is interested in... of course the argument that there is a social cost and an economic cost to the problem is a strong one, because the European Union is still predominantly an economic arrangement—the main area of focus is the economies of the countries—and social questions [are] the poor cousin still, of course, and there is... and there is not that much legislation on this side... so if you come up with economic arguments then that I think is something that this machinery here can understand... [if] you make the economic case strongly, it is much harder to argue against then... It's a good tactic, if you like, looking at it that way—at the EU level. (Council official, General Secretariat, interview May 2010)

The strategic framing of gender equality policies in economic terms that the interviewee is talking about is relevant both for the EU institutions themselves in their internal negotiation and for civil society actors when they set forward claims vis-à-vis the EU. Thus, the Commission points to the economic costs of gender-based violence and public ill-health in their proposal for the DAPHNE program, for instance, in order to push the decision through. The civil society actors, in their wish to influence policies, also go along with the economic argument even though they are skeptical about doing so:

> I mean we regard violence against women as a human rights violation and this is like the main perspective... Of course violence against women is a health issue, of course violence against women has costs to the society [but] this is a way of making the problem... raising awareness of the problem and regarding EU policy this is a way of trying to... get access to... to look at what is... within the legal framework of the European Union, where you can influence that... This is always the first thing, we say it is a human rights issue that costs a lot of money and that costs lives. And... and it pays off if you fund like... that is a way of argumentation we use, but I mean human rights issues, this is always like it is a human rights violation... So it is more this... more about the way how we argue. (WAVE representative, interview November 2008)

Civil society actors like EWL and WAVE do not abandon their own perspective on the problem of gender-based violence, but they do use the economical framing in order to gain more resonance within EU institutions focusing heavily on this realm. The interviewee quoted above emphasizes that the NGO does not modify their entire point of view for funding reasons but rather use the economic frame strategically in order to get funding and have their projects selected. The content of their claims and projects stays the same or is only slightly modified since they do consider multiple dimensions, as the quote shows. In other words, they take on board economic aspects of the problem along with their own reasoning (WAVE representative, interview November 2008).

Implications of Degendering: Framings of the Projects Selected for Funding Under the DAPHNE Program (1997–2005)

So far, several frames have been identified in the analysis of EU policy documents on gender-based violence. However, the question remains whether the increased attention in the texts to public health and economic and social costs of violence has any implications at the policy level. Empirically I now turn to the immediate implications of the policy framings in order to assess whether there is a spillover of frames from the binding policy documents to the selection of projects for EC funding under the DAPHNE program. The aim of including this perspective is to interpret the significance of the policy frames and their level of institutionalization. Thus, CFA, using just a few frame markers, was conducted on 412 projects selected for funding under the DAPHNE program from 1997 to 2005.

The EC implements the DAPHNE program by selecting projects for funding once the legal texts have been adopted. The DAPHNE unit of DG Justice sets annual priorities for this selection, and organizations undergo a "competitive review process" with the aim of being rewarded grants (Montoya 2008). Year by year, the number of organizations participating increases, as does the diversity of organizations and the transnational cooperation between them (ibid.). DAPHNE attributes action grants and operation grants; the EC does not want to create organizations that are highly dependent on the DAPHNE financing and therefore support is allocated to organizations that will be sustainable after the end of the project too. So, one of the evaluation criteria is the financial capacity of the organization. This leads to a focus on professionalization rather than capacity-building initiatives to strengthen civil society from below. In general, DAPHNE does not fund a lot of small NGOs because the process of documentation is very demanding. On the other hand, NGOs are only required a 20 percent selffunding under the DAPHNE program whereas other programs ask for 40 percent. However capacity-building activities and processes do occur: Montoya (2008) finds that EU contributes to the capacity building among domestic organizations through distribution of resources and facilitation of networking. In some countries this is supplementary to national measures or private sources of funding, in others the funding is the primary means of support.

The process of project selection implies interpreting the framings articulated in the key policy documents. This process can be more controversial than the actual policy-making process in itself. My findings suggest that the main policy articulation, that is, the one impacting the project proposals and selections, is precisely the one made by the EC when interpreting the decisions adopted on the DAPHNE program.[8] Thus, the EC can be attributed a significant interpretative power within the institutional context of EU policy making in this field, as its framings of the issue intervene between the adoption of the legal texts and the selection of projects.

Most DAPHNE projects are articulated under a frame, which can be described as *implicit gender inequality*; it has a multiple passive actor category in the sense that it covers the three main beneficiaries of the DAPHNE program, that is, children, young people, and women. A long list of intersectional categories is also mentioned, such as "migrant domestic workers," "women and girls with learning disabilities," or "women from disadvantaged urban areas." Gender equality is implicit and, most significantly, no actor category is mentioned as responsible for causing the problem. Another significant frame is *violence against children*; this frame combines "children" as passive actors with no mention of responsible actors, problem representations like "child abuse" and "violence against children," and children's rights as norm. The *structural gender inequality* frame described in chapter 4 is marginal among the project descriptions selected for funding under the DAPHNE program. The currently dominant frame in the EC policies on gender-based violence, namely the *public health* frame, is transversal in the sense that it runs through some of the project descriptions in combination with the other frames mentioned above, except structural gender inequality. It is, however, a rather weak frame as it is only rarely articulated as a fully fledged frame with several identifiable and characteristic frame markers. Projects where health concerns are considered to be an important part of the problem representation only amount to 4 percent of the total of projects selected for funding from 1997 to 2005 whereas health frame markers appear in 20 percent of the projects.

In general, the framing of the violence problem is very broad in the selection of projects for funding under the DAPHNE program, and it seems to cover an infinite number of violence forms. From the frame analysis it is clear that there is a prevalence of projects related to children and young people, which are not gendered,[9] and of projects concerning "gender-specific violence," that is, committed against women, rather than actual gendered violence with articulations of domination and unequal power relations. The public health frames are usually not gendered either. One of the implications of this is that most of the projects selected tend to be rather reactive in their prognostic approaches, that is, suggesting intermediate solutions to the problems instead of the more proactive, root cause related prognoses of the structural gender inequality frame. Goals such as strengthening the quality of the services provided or victim support measures are without a doubt necessary and valuable but, lacking the structural dimension, both diagnosis and prognosis are articulated without an eye on the possibility of eradicating the problem rather than just palliating it. Similarly, the public health frame with its focus on health-care services and targeting health-care professionals will provide a valuable, but only immediate alleviation of the problem, not a solution addressing the deeper gendered, structural dimensions of the problem.[10] The possibility of combining the two approaches—acting on the consequences and on the causes of the problem, financing projects that each addresses different dimensions of this—is furthermore limited by the marginal role attributed to projects characterized here within the structural gender inequality frame.

In theory, it is possible that projects have been framed strategically as public health in order to obtain funds but addressing, actually, structural gender dimensions of the problem of gender-based violence. However, this occurs only in one case where a project with a structural content was articulated as a project related to public health (2005-1-249-WYC).[11] Similarly, relatively few references are made in the projects to the economic costs and consequences of the problem of gender-based violence. When references are made, these appear in the problem articulation of domestic violence, where project descriptions explain why this is to be considered a problem.

Looking at the DAPHNE work programs, which are published yearly by the EC, along with two calls for proposals, and establish the priorities according to which projects will be selected for funding, there is a clear trend over the years from 2006 to 2010 toward a progressive degendering of the policy issue, a strong focus on violence against children, and a continued effort within the area of violent cultural traditions. Public health, human rights, and gender equality are all articulated as frames, and there is a broad take on the issue of violence. However, the dominant frame seems to be a kind of degendered mainstream similar to the one identified as implicit gender inequality in the projects selected for funding from 1997 to 2005.

In sum, the dominant frames identified in the DAPHNE projects dataset and the broad framing of violence as a public health issue allow for a large number of violence forms to be addressed through the program. Everything, that is, any kind of violence, fits. Certain priorities are set, however, and gender inequality as a structural reason underlying the problem of violence tends to disappear or become much less visible than when the issue was first introduced and institutionalized in the EU. Public health is a strategic framework, which only in a limited fashion spills over into the content of the projects selected for funding under the DAPHNE program. However, the gender inequality frame has been redefined or resemanticized from a radical, feminist articulation to a mainstream perception of a gender-specific topic without strong structural arguments. The focus is taken away from gender equality dimensions and structural concerns, as the structural gender inequality frame is marginal.

If the EU had finally decided on the women's rights as human rights framing of the problem of gender-based violence, the scope of the projects might have been just as broad but with more focus on structural dimensions. Nevertheless, I find that the implications of the dominant policy framings of the key documents of the DAPHNE program are more limited than what could be expected. The public health frame and the articulation of concerns regarding the social and economic costs of the problem of gender-based violence do not transcend significantly onto the content of the selected projects. The wide scope of the problem perception that is used when selecting projects can be attributed to the way in which the policy was framed and the strategic reasons for choosing one dominant frame (public health) over another (women's rights as human rights). Several framings are accommodated under the broad problem perception: This suggests that the initial framing of the problem, which is the one that is still partly underlining the EC interpretation (women's rights as human rights), and the one that was ultimately selected in order to satisfy member-state concerns (public health), coexist. The most significant implication of the interpretation of the DAPHNE program in the selection of projects is the lack of focus on gender inequality and the practical invisibility of structural dimensions in the framing and problem perception of the selection of projects. The result is a more mainstream version of the gender inequality frame, which is only implicitly present through weak frame markers. The public health framing of the policy documents to a certain extent neutralizes a potentially strong feminist problem perception, which would underline structural dimensions more.

Strategic Use of Ideas in the Process of Institutionalization of Frames

The analysis of EU policy developments within the field of gender-based violence sheds light on the interaction between context, ideas, and agency in EU policy-making processes. EU institutions and civil society organizations articulate strategic frames, related to processes of gendering and degendering, within the context of political and discursive opportunity structures, characterized by struggles over competences. This is not least due to the fact that a strong gendered understanding of the issue of violence against women prevails within the EU institutions despite the limitations related to the choice of legal basis for the DAPHNE program. The key actors may disagree on specific definitions and measures as well as the need for EU legislation within the field, but there is a consensus on the general objective and the broad gendered understanding of the problem.

Whether the problem is represented to be health or human rights violation, the institutionalization of the frame turns out to depend on other dimensions than ideas exclusively. The role of ideas in policies is significant in terms of creating policy change in the sense that ideas organized in specific frames limit or enhance the possibilities for political action and policy solutions. But the development of dominant frames depends to a large extent on agency and power, that is, who makes the framings change and how. As the case of the policies on gender-based violence shows, institutionalization of frames depends on the institutional context and especially the power and interests held by the institutionalized actors who, through framing strategies, engage in discursive struggles over hegemony.

Thus, the policy change was not just about ideas (as specific problem representation, for instance) but about the strategic use of ideas, whether aimed at ensuring the respect for the division of competences between the EU and its member states or with a view to reproducing specific policy agendas related to the content of the policies (i.e., violence against women as a gender equality issue). The contestation between the institutionalized actors centered mainly on the policy process (legislation or not) and less so on the policy content (inclusion of gender inequality as an underlying cause). The latter was primarily taken up by civil society actors, using (feminist) strategies of gendering. The EP tried to combine frames by adding a human rights perspective to the health frame. The aim was to be able to enhance the political action possible under the public health frame while accepting the closure imposed in terms of not harmonizing national legislation. The EP has appropriated itself of the public health frame in order to use it institutionally through simultaneous framing. The Parliament thus accepts degendering for strategic reasons in order to maximize its influence through the codecision procedure and, in this way, the EP is able to broaden the scope of the dominant framing. Similarly, the EC used its interpretative power and the broad definition of violence under the public health frame to maintain a wide scope in the selection of projects for funding. This complexity (i.e., the coexistence of competing frames within the same issue) reflects the level of contestation in the discursive field as well as the multidimensionality of the EU policy-making processes.

Strategic (De)Gendering

These findings call for a closer look at the mechanisms at play in processes of strategic (de)gendering. In relation to the adoption of EU policies on gender-based violence, processes of degendering occurred as a consequence of the lack of a clear legal basis for gender equality policies outside employment, the gender-blind definitions of violence when the issue was introduced on the policy agenda in general, and the way in which the public health frame narrowed down the gendered, structural content of the problem. Multiple discrimination policies cannot be said to result in processes of degendering in this case (as some may have feared; see chapter 2) though they may have had an effect in terms of the increased culturalization of framings within the policy area (see chapter 6). Rather, processes of degendering within the policy area of gender-based violence followed mainly from the reframing of the issue in terms of public health and economic costs as well as the struggle over competences.

Theoretically, the reasons for degendering vary; degendering happens out of ignorance (gender blindness), according to contrary policy agenda, and/or as strategic choice not to include gender explicitly. My argument for degendering being a strategic devise, on the one hand, and a matter of territorial defense, on the other, rather than a consequence of multiple discrimination, for example, relies on empirical arguments (the case of the DAPHNE program), theoretical arguments (contextualizing developments in a varied institutional context and depending on potentially gendered implementation) and methodological arguments (i.e., frames are simultaneous and have relative strength). Krizsán and Popa (forthcoming) argue that a gender neutral approach in policy making articulates a general perception of the problem, which does not challenge power relations and inequalities between women and men. This enhances the chances of inserting (gender equality) policy issues into a mainstream policy agenda but it also implies a risk of cooptation by other policy goals. On the other hand gender-neutral frames can also be used by feminists in implementation processes to regender the policy issues (ibid.). Concerning the gendered implementations of degendered policies, dimensions can slip in during the policy processes; the question is whether there are feminists located in the institutions to pick up the potential for gendering policies and develop it, using the texts agreed upon and the new opportunities they may, unwillingly or not, open.

Consequently, in policy-making, processes of degendering can be both positive and negative. This depends on the context in which they are embedded and, thus, the impact of the visibility or invisibility of gender concerns on the policy outcome is a matter of empirical scrutiny (Walby et al. 2009). The chances of furthering gender equality goals in EU policies may be enhanced by an explicit perception of gender inequality structures, but this is not necessarily the case. Sometimes the gender equality agenda is best advanced by modifying the frame strategically:

> Whenever you want to include a perspective, a component of whatever policy or group in society, to another policy, I think you need to understand first the language of the policy you want to influence. And you need to talk with the same words, using the same vocabulary. Because if you, if you only... talk from the women's perspective in feminist vocabulary, you are just aggressive and you just... you will never convince the one who don't want to be convinced. If you talk to men about economy, what they are losing by not having women... on board, for the diversity, the exchange of views, and also for conciliation of work and private life, because those men have also families and the younger men do wish to be more with their families than the

older ones. If you don't talk these words with them, they will not, never come to your ideas, they will just say 'okay, this is too feminist, too radical', and...it's always some kind of compromise...but when you really have to understand the perspective of the other, and try to use his, his or her perspective and try to say "okay, you think this but how can I convince you that part of my problem is a solution for you." (EC official, DG Employment, interview December 2007)

There is an obvious risk of cooptation of the gender equality goals, though, if these are reframed; again it depends on the specific developments in the empirical context. In the analysis of gender-based violence policies I found this to be only partly the case, as the gendered nature of the policy problem was kept intact whereas structural concerns diminished. A continued focus on the potentially degendered impact of the policies is, nevertheless, necessary and this is often left in the hands of civil society organizations putting pressure on the EU institutions.

Foreground and Background Frames

At a methodological level the findings of the DAPHNE case suggest a strengthened focus on frame nuances as well as on frame contextualization within institutional processes. To a certain extent, the public health frame is an example of a weak institutionalization as it is used as a vessel for strategic policy making (in order to pass legislation) but lacks transcending strength in terms of its influence on policy articulations within the area in general. It is a procedural rather than a normative frame, with a weak articulation (i.e., it has few significant frame markers). The invisibility of gender equality dimensions might suggest a conclusion in favor of the importance of institutions over ideas. However, and according to the theoretical implications of the gendered discursive institutionalism approach, I argue that institutions are the result of the (re)production of ideas and, as such, what matters is how ideas are institutionalized in specific contexts and settings.

In terms of institutionalizing the policy issue of gender-based violence, the DAPHNE program is and has been important as it gives the policies an element of continuity and keeps the issue on the EU agenda. The institutionalization of the problem perceptions related to gender-based violence was influenced by the constraints of the possible legal bases given the focus on division of competences in the 1990s and the 2000s and the skepticism with which member states perceive EU action in newly explored legal areas. Thus, the policy problem of gender-based violence was institutionalized formally as a public health issue, a framing that was nevertheless articulated with a large scope of action due to the EP and EC interpretation of the frame. This highlights the scope of agency and the possibilities of key actors to act within the institutional and discursive limits.

The framing is typical for a soft policy area where programs can be implemented, but legislation is out of the question. The underlying logic is to legitimate EU action, aiming at coordination, not harmonization, always respecting the principle of subsidiarity. This is a fine line, and the frames can be stretched, as conceptualized by Lombardo et al. (2009a), within these institutional limits as to what can be done and decided politically. There is a clear difference between the legal basis defended in the DAPHNE program and the framings articulated by the EC, the EP, and the Council, beyond the negotiations of this particular program. Soft policy documents with no binding measures can go further in terms of analyzing the causes of the problem in depth in the diagnosis or articulating comprehensive solutions in the prognosis. Even the Council presidencies focusing on the issue of gender-based violence tend to emphasize aspects of gender inequality in their policy documents. This does still not translate into policy output due to the legal and institutional constraints set by the division of competences between the EU and its member states, but it nevertheless shows the significance of the gendered understanding of the problem within the EU in general.

Thus, I argue that frames gain relative strength depending on whether or not they are institutionalized as foreground or as background. Simultaneous frames interact in the institutional setting: The public health frame, for instance, did not directly reduce the structural content of the gender equality frames. It modified and marginalized it, to a certain extent, but a completely gender-neutral framing of the policy issue of violence against women did not become dominant in the project selection under the DAPHNE program. There is still a strong internal gender equality framing of the issue of violence against women within the EU institutions, and the public health frame was not completely implemented as the main dominant norm at the EU level. Rather, it was used strategically in a setting of multiple discourses. Theoretically, Kulawik (2009) emphasizes that discourses must be treated systematically in order to address dominance. The systematic analysis of frames has shown how a focus on nuances contributes to the development of CFA as a methodological approach to policy-making processes. However, attention to nuances in framings, which will become salient when a detailed textual analysis of the policy documents is carried out, must be combined with a sensitive contextualization of both the policies and their framings. The latter can be achieved by emphasizing differences between EU institutions, the role of civil society actors, and, not least, strategic dimensions investigated through the use of elite interviews.

Furthermore the relations between different frames and their institutional context must be scrutinized. In the case of policies on gender-based violence, frames are embedded either in the institutional foreground or the institutional background. These terms are also used by Goffman (1974), and they resonate with the notions of public and hidden transcripts developed by Scott (1999). Even though the latter relates to a different framework (i.e., relations of domination and resistance among dominant and subordinated groups in society), his ideas are useful to reflect upon frame nuances in institutional contexts as well. Scott (ibid.) argues that discourses are articulated between dominant and dominated groups both publicly (public transcript) and privately (hidden transcript). The dominated or subordinated groups act in certain ways in public in order to please the dominant groups and use the discursive width in private to articulate resistances (see also García Agustín 2010). Similarly, Locher argues that "[n]orms can be in the forefront of social and political life or fade into the background" (2007, 79) (see also Finnemore and Sikkink 1998).

These theoretical arguments are easily translatable to the institutional context of policy making where strategic framing takes place in public (foreground) in relation to dominant discourses whereas the reproduction of marginal frames occurs in the discursive day-to-day practices as well as in soft policies (background). The space between the hidden and the public, the background and the foreground, is a site of constant discursive struggle. Framings can move from the background into the foreground, and vice versa, in the processes of institutionalization. Thus, I consider the differentiation between foreground and background useful to qualify the CFA. Frames will appear in the institutional foreground or the institutional background depending on the way in which they have been institutionalized.

Drawing again on the example of public health and structural gender equality as a dominant and a marginalized frame, respectively, I find that public health can be characterized as dominant in an official, formal sense, that is, related to foreground politics. It was institutionalized through a legislative policy process on the basis of member-state demands, predominantly. The structural gender equality framing remains strong in, at least, three ways: (1) it has been modified but not completely replaced by public health in the policy interpretation conducted by the EC through the selection of projects to be funded under the DAPHNE program; (2) it is continuously articulated and underlined as a still vibrant framing in the elite interviews conducted in relation to this research; and (3) the fact that health and gender-based violence issues are separated both in the new 2010–2015 strategy (COM[2010]491) of the Commission as well as in the previous Community Action Programmes is a sign of strong, gendered background frames within the field of violence against women. The dominant frame of the binding documents in the field, that is, the public health frame, did not spill over into the general policies on gender-based violence but was only applied to the DAPHNE program. The public health frame is, in other words, weakly institutionalized as a foreground frame. These findings speak to the theoretical argument that even though actors formulate frames, they cannot control them once they are articulated (see Orloff and Palier 2009). This applies both to dominant and marginal frames. In this regard, the interpretative power of the EC in the policy-making process is significant for the (continuous) institutionalization of specific frames.

In conclusion, structural gender equality is interpreted as a strong background frame, articulated, institutionalized, and reproduced by key EU actors in day-to-day discursive practices. However, the importance of having a legal text to refer to in terms of the discursive reproduction of the foreground frames should not be underestimated: The background frames that are institutionalized informally through discursive practices depend on the presence of specific actors, their commitment, as well as constant civil society lobbying to keep the framing on the agenda and reproduce it. The informal institutional resistance that keeps reproducing the background frame is not a given, and the risk of having the dominant frame spill over into the background is constant. The gender concerns in the empirical case used here to illustrate the methodological point do not reproduce themselves but must constantly be (re)articulated within the EU institutions. However, a background frame may also be (re)articulated and placed in the foreground if dominant, formal framings are challenged, for instance by civil society.

These findings call for increased attention toward the importance and complexity of simultaneous framings and their different scope of institutionalization. Differentiations between background and foreground frames can be made by paying attention to the nuances of the frames and the scope of their institutionalization in terms of strength and the dynamics of the policy processes whereby different frames are institutionalized simultaneously and interrelate in the institutional context. Thus, frames can be institutionalized both formally, through legally binding documents, for example (foreground), and informally through day-to-day discursive practices as well as soft policies (background). The frames furthermore interact in the sense that they may modify each other (in processes of stretching, for example, as conceptualized by Lombardo et al. 2009b; 2009c) or in terms of their relative strength, that is, background frames may be drawn into the foreground when a window of opportunity opens.

6

Problematizing the "Gendered Other": Integration, Violence, and Culturalization

The strategic use of framings and their institutionalization in the background or foreground of policies and structures (see chapters 4 and 5) are not the only ways in which (de)gendering has played a role in the development of EU policies on gender-based violence in recent years. Analyzing the ways in which these policies are framed vis-à-vis "migrant women" and "ethnic minority women," I argue that increased tendencies of culturalization, defined as an exclusionary form of intersectionality, are present at the EU level. This is, potentially, related to the risk of marginalizing and stigmatizing specific groups of people, especially when related to processes of community constructions around that which is interpreted as "European" versus the "foreign" or "non-European."

Intersectionality, defined as the interaction between different inequality creating categories, constituting specific forms of oppression or empowerment can be both exclusionary and inclusionary depending on the way in which it is used and articulated in political debate and policy making. However, in order to theorize the relation between processes of in/exclusion and the way in which different inequality categories are related in in/exclusionary terms, we must first turn to critical discourse analysis and its approach to identity constructions.

In/Exclusionary Intersectionality

A key element of identity constructions at the discursive level is through the use of the linguistic opposition between "us" and "them," or between the collectives of insiders and outsiders.

According to Wodak (2002; 2007), in-groups and out-groups are constructed discursively through the interlinkage between sameness and difference that determines who belongs and who does not belong to certain groups and communities. In other words, the way in which "we" is defined, and the elements that bind "us" together, excludes the "other," determining the characteristics of "them" through the discursive use of inclusionary and exclusionary mechanisms. In this way inclusion and exclusion become normality without the actors behind the practices explicitly acknowledging neither this intention nor its consequences. Relating these ideas, stemming from critical discourse analysis, to the ways in which different inequality categories intersect, we must realize how this interaction can occur in both inclusionary and exclusionary ways. This takes the intersectional analysis one step further: The positive or negative articulation of intersectionality becomes yet another dimension to the analysis of the ways in which the different inequality categories relate to each other, within the framework of discursive articulations and political strategies. This is in line with general discourse theory, where discursive strategies can be constructive, justificatory, transformative, and/or destructive, depending on the way in which they are articulated (Wodak 2002).

More specifically, inclusionary intersectionality focuses on the recognition of the interplay between different inequality creating categories and the potentially negative effects of this interplay. The normative objective is to further equality while acknowledging and respecting diversity (Christensen and Siim 2010). In terms of policy making, inclusionary intersectionality does not stigmatize certain groups, for instance by framing particular problem holders in a negative way (Roggeband and Verloo 2007). Exclusionary intersectionality, on the other hand, can be defined as the recognition and saliency of one kind of inequality at the expense of a negative accentuation of other categories. Inequalities, between ethnic majority and minority groups, for instance, are strengthened with the exclusionary consequences this may have in terms of constructing victims or marginalized (outsider) groups (Christensen and Siim 2010; Rolandsen Agustín 2009; Siim 2009). Denoting these same processes, Pringle (2006) refers to the idea of "abusing intersectionality." Exclusionary intersectionality focuses on the disadvantages of diversity in the interest of reaching equality aims; in other words, exclusionary intersectionality emphasizes the impossibility of reconciling diversity and equality, whereas inclusionary intersectionality perceives them as perfectly compatible (Mokre and Siim 2013).[1]

Ultimately, inclusionary intersectionality aims for the difficult balance between avoiding both to ignore differences and to overemphasize them, that is, integrating universalism with attention to differentiated positions and inequalities. When applied to the policy area of gender-based violence,

> an inclusionary discourse might frame violence against women in universal terms (widespread and pervasive) and in reference to gender equality, while also noting the different experiences and needs of particular groups of women...An exclusionary discourse will center on specific groups of women and particular forms of violence, deemphasizing or ignoring universal frames. (Montoya and Rolandsen Agustín forthcoming)

Culturalization can be understood as a specific form of exclusionary intersectionality whereby cultural differences are particularly overemphasized through exclusive references to culture, tradition, etc. as causes of gender-based violence. This runs parallel with identity constructions and the characterization of "us" versus "them" by underlining binary differentiations between insider and outsider groups of (non)belonging (Briceño 2004; Montoya and Rolandsen Agustín forthcoming). More specifically, in policy analysis we may detect processes of culturalization and exclusionary intersectionality when the diagnosis of the policy frame is articulated around a strong focus on culture with the simultaneous downplaying of any other trait of the groups of actors responsible for or affected by the problem. Furthermore, exclusionary culturalized frames are identified in particular when this focus in the diagnosis is combined with the absence of prognosis, that is, seeing culture as the main or exclusive cause of the problem without offering any solutions to this, thus making the entire policy frame rather deterministic.

One puzzle in this regard is whether the distinction between inclusionary and exclusionary intersectionality is equally relevant in relation to all inequality creating categories. We know that different inequality creating categories should not be considered equal in nature, that is, it is necessary to differentiate between them in terms of their substance (Verloo 2006). Similarly, the notions of inclusionary and exclusionary intersectionality should not be regarded as equally relevant for all types of intersections: They emanate from a particular empirical basis, namely that of the discursive interplay between gender and ethnicity, culture and religion. The notion of in/exclusionary intersectionality seems to be particularly relevant when addressing these exact categories and their intersections. This could be explained with reference to the (discursive) construction of national communities and spheres of belonging. In other words, it appears to be particularly pertinent to add this nuanced perspective on intersectionality in relation to discursive articulations of insider and outsider categories ("us"/"them") based on the categories of gender and ethnicity.

Empirically, the increased attention to diversity and difference in EU policies on gender-based violence, for example, is not in itself problematic. It only becomes problematic when the intersectional concerns are used in exclusionary rather than inclusionary ways. The way in which groups are named, for example by politicians and policy makers, tells us something about adequate visibility (in order to address particular problems) and stigmatization. Thus, I refer to the culturalization of policy frames as an increased attention to migrant women in policies on gender-based violence and the way in which a deterministic view on the relation between violence and culture is set forward in some EU policy texts. The framing of honor-based violence, for instance, depicts certain groups as inherently violent. This concerns especially immigrant men. In this way groups of migrants are stereotyped into specific cultural images and treated as internally homogeneous. These processes are the focus of the following analysis.

Collective Identity Constructions around European Values: Integration and Immigration Policies in a Gender Perspective

The increasing culturalization of the framing of gender-based violence is, to a certain extent, related to the multiple discrimination policies introduced on the EU agenda in the 1990s. They have resulted in a strengthened focus on particularly vulnerable groups within the policy area of gender-based violence. However, the emphasis in the framings on a deterministic relation between violence forms and culture or ethnicity also points to processes of discursive spillover between policy fields. The EU increasingly articulates a strong discourse around minority issues and immigration both at the EU and member-state levels. The culturalized framings within the area of gender-based violence draw on these general discourses and construct new problem representations within the policy area. As the findings presented below will show, the framing contributes to the construction of (exclusionary) identity categories, defining the symbolic frontiers between Europeans and non-Europeans. This resonates with Ferree's argument that: "Racializing and problematizing the immigrant family is an intersectional gender-and-race-based discursive strategy that builds a transnational European identity, but at the expense of non-Europeans, especially migrant women" (2012, 217). This "intersectional discursive strategy" at the expense of a minority group is what I refer to here as exclusionary intersectionality.

Policy analyses and interviews with key policy makers in the EU show that the introduction of culturalized forms of gender-based violence in EU policies is causally related with immigration. Since the mid-2000s this has translated into an increased attention to harmful traditional practices and female genital mutilation. This may partly be due to an actual detected increase in these forms of violence in the member states or it may be part of a political agenda and discourse related to the development of multicultural societies in Europe and increasing debates on immigration and integration, not least from Muslim countries. In the words of a Council official,

> the fact that Europe has been receiving immigration, well, it has made us confront much clearer, perhaps, issues like female genital mutilation, honor crimes, forced marriages. Issues, which we, perhaps, had overcome a little already... It is inevitable that, that we are seeing these phenomena in Europe now, first and foremost because we have immigration. (Council official, permanent representation, interview June 2010)

Above, I have argued that a shift in framings took place within the EU policies on gender-based violence as they went from being framed as a gender inequality and human rights issue to being dealt with within the framework of public health. Another significant shift in the EU frames on gender-based violence has been the shift from a public/private categorization of violence to one of culture/nonculture, particularly in relation to migration (see also Montoya and Rolandsen Agustín 2011). The shift from rights to culture can be interpreted as a shift from seeing migrants as citizens to seeing them as noncitizens, not identified with European values, with particular attention directed toward members of "culturally specific communities" or "ethnic minority groups." This confirms Ferree's characterization of EU intersectionality as constructed primarily around this binary distinction.

Overall, I find a tendency for migratory framings of gender-based violence in EU policies to move from a focus on securing rights for persecuted migrant women to a deterministic view on culture and violence, defining particular types of violence as belonging to specific cultures or ethnic groups. At the same time violence against majority women is never culturalized nor are majority groups stigmatized, through the construction of cultural stereotypes, in the same way as both (potential) victims and perpetrators from minority groups are.

In policy processes, nonviolence is articulated as a trait of Europeanness (Montoya and Rolandsen Agustín forthcoming). This draws the attention away from the gendered and structural dimensions of violence as a universal basis of all forms of gender-based violence. This is both related to inclusionary forms of intersectionality, whereby the specific situation of minority and migrant women are taken into account, as well as exclusionary forms, since these groups of women are often stigmatized (as victims) as are minority and migrant men (as perpetrators), characterized as particularly violent. I will now turn to the more detailed policy analysis of EU texts on gender-based violence in order to show how these mechanisms of culturalization and in/exclusionary intersectionality play out empirically in the development of the policy field.

Culturalization of Policy Frames within the Area of Gender-Based Violence

Across the EU institutions, we see tendencies toward increased culturalization of the area of gender-based violence. However, these processes occur in different ways; whereas the Council tends to focus on diagnosis and neglect prognostic elements, thereby culturalizing the area negatively by not attending to potential solutions, the Commission engages in culturalization processes by adding a strong focus on particular forms of violence ("honor-based violence," etc.) and deemphasizing other forms of violence among majority groups, making them less visible or urgent. Furthermore Commission policies tend to differentiate strongly between EU member states and non-EU member states in their conceptualization of different forms of violence and in this way depict nonculturalized forms of violence as almost already overcome within Europe. The case of the Parliament is more nuanced in the sense that trends of inclusionary framings mix with exclusionary forms, thereby making the potential culturalization of the area more complex (see also Montoya and Rolandsen Agustín forthcoming).

Inclusionary Framings of Gender-Based Violence

The early documents of the EP published in the 1980s focus largely on *securing rights for persecuted migrant women* when frames around violence and minorities are articulated. The report on Women's Rights (Doc. 1–829/80, 29.01.81), for example, articulates violence against migrant women in Europe as a problem due to the high economic and legal dependence (in terms of residence permit) of "foreign workers' wives and migrant women" on their husbands.[2] Migrant (working) women are described as "socially and culturally isolated" and their "poor record in equality" as well as the high level of unemployment among them are deplored (EP Resolution on the situation of women in Europe, OJ C 46, 20.02.84). The 1984 report of the Committee of Inquiry on the situation of women in Europe (Doc. 1–1229/83) directs particular attention to ethnic and sexual discrimination of second-generation immigrant girls (as women and as migrants) and the social, cultural, and linguistic isolation of elderly immigrant women. According to the report, the latter is related to the issue of violence:

> Most of these women accept total subordination to the man and even when they are ill-treated and beaten often do not rebel because in their isolated position even a violent husband is a point of reference to which they cling. In the majority of cases these women have no financial independence since they are housewives or have had unreliable and poorly paid jobs. (Doc. 1–1229/83)

The problem is articulated here as domestic violence, that is, occurring in the home, and it is not culturalized since it is perceived as the same kind of violence that female citizens of member states might be suffering. In other words, even though the quote generalizes the category of migrant women, the particular vulnerability of migrant women is not related to cultural traditions but to economic dependency and the migration situation.

In general, the 1984 report takes into account differences between women (citizens and noncitizens), but it also reproduces certain stereotypes (such as the assumption that immigrant women have never "known other than her role as mother and wife") while being, at the same time, comprehensive toward the particular problems of migrant women. Problems of gender equality are not perceived as cultural problems per se in the report but rather as universal structures of male dominance and a result of the immigration process and situation in itself:

> The forms of discrimination which lead to the ostracism of immigrant women are widespread and vary little from one country to another. They stem from the idea of women as subordinates, belonging to the lowest social strata, and as foreigners from the poorest countries with

different racial backgrounds...Discrimination within the family, on the other hand, is the result of the uneven rate of evolution between men and women. In most cases the man has emigrated ahead of the woman. (Doc. 1-1229/83, 05.01.84)

This is an example of an early EP articulation of intersectional ideas since the perception of gender inequality articulated here implies the intersection between gender, race, class, and citizenship status.

In the FEMM report on Violence against Women, this is articulated as a problem also for migrant women, but there is no diagnosis of it being particularly related to culture (A2-44/86; A2-004-86).[3] The report argues that dependency is a problem for these groups of women as it is for majority women, but the problem is exacerbated by the fact that they are in an immigrant situation, that is, not holding citizenship status in an EU member state. Thus, unequal gender relations and the problem of violence against women are characterized as universal since they exist on all levels and in all groups of society. In her analysis of the 1986 Resolution, Montoya (2013) moreover highlights that minority women were only perceived to be migrants, that is, the category of European nonmigrant minority women was ignored and no measures targeting this group were proposed. Moreover, Montoya emphasizes the fact that a particularly emotive language is used in the document when referring to the violence suffered by the group of migrant minority women (ibid.).

Thus, diagnostically economic dependency and lack of citizenship rights and legal protection in the context of migration processes are prevalent dimensions of these early reports and their framings of the problem of violence against (minority) women. The problem is seen as pervasive and related to structural gender inequality. Rather than ethnicity or culture, it is migration and citizenship status, that intersect with gender to create a particular version of the universal problem of gender inequality and gender discrimination through men's violence against women. In terms of prognosis, the strengthening of migrant women's rights and independence is dominant. This is particularly related to issuing individual residence permits, regardless of the husband's work situation. Thus, in the 1986 report and resolution (A2-44/86; A2-004-86) it is suggested that separate reception facilities for victims ("battered wives") coming from the group of minority women be set up, individual residence permits should be issued, and sexual abuse should be recognized as a legitimate ground for asylum.[4] The 1997 report and resolution on the EP Zero Tolerance Campaign (A4-0250/97; A4-0250/1997) treats the issue of ethnic minority and migrant women like the early EP documents: Special attention should be directed toward their particular problems as victims of violence, and immigration policies should provide for residence permits for persecuted women.

Exclusionary Framings of Gender-Based Violence

The universalist take on gender-based violence, seeing this as a pervasive problem affecting all groups of women (though articulating minority women as a "particularly vulnerable group" without going much into detail about this notion) gains strength throughout the 1990s. Thus the 1997 resolution and the 1999 report on establishing the DAPHNE program clearly lack attention to the idea of difference (Montoya and Rolandsen Agustín forthcoming). However in the 2000s, a shift takes place whereby an *increased focus on difference*, both in inclusionary and exclusionary ways, becomes apparent. By this time the EC has become more active in terms of policy development within the area of gender-based violence and it is not least in EC policies that we see this shift. As in the 1980s this is particularly related to immigration and immigrant women though the frames articulated differ significantly from the ones present in the early EP documents. Overall, the exclusionary intersectional framing of difference relates to negative perceptions of increased migration into Europe, especially by groups of Muslim immigrants, whereas the inclusionary framing can be seen as a reaction to antidiversity and even racist tendencies as well as to the exacerbated universalism prevalent in the policies of the 1990s (see also Montoya and Rolandsen Agustín forthcoming).

Thus, in the 2000s the articulation of gender-based violence as a policy problem in the EU documents is increasingly related to the issue of migration to the point where the cultural/noncultural forms of violence overshadow the debates on the public/private divide, which had been prevalent in the discussion on the conceptualizations of different forms of violence until then. The categorizations are by no means substituted with each other; rather, they coexist (through simultaneous framings), also in individual documents. However, the cultural/noncultural binary becomes the main distinction in the articulation of different forms of violence. This is both the case for EP policy documents and for the different phases of the DAPHNE program.

Concerning the latter, the shift toward a strengthened attention to immigration issues, female genital mutilation, and honor crimes is particularly visible in the third program where they are highlighted in the definition of violence (as "harmful traditional practices") (779/2007/EC). Similarly, in the recent Strategy for Equality between Women and Men (2010–2015) (COM[2010]491), female genital mutilation is singled out as a specific form of violence (together with trafficking).

One example of the culturalized framing can be found in the EP FEMM report on combating violence against women from 2005: "[W]hereas the types of violence affecting women can vary according to cultural tradition, ethnic origin, or social background; whereas female genital mutilation, so called crimes of honour and forced marriages are now a reality in the European Union as well" (A6–0404/2005). Attention is here drawn to a particular kind of violence that is associated with foreignness and being non-European. The attention is not problematic in itself; what is problematic is the exclusive focus on certain kinds of (culturalized) violence and not, for instance, migrant women victims of battering. In general, culture has a determining role in the problem perception articulated in the report (A6–0404/2005). Cultural tradition and ethnic origin are considered determining for the type of violence committed against migrant women, but there is hardly any mention of domestic violence committed against these same women, for instance (like in the early EP documents).

In prognostic terms, special programs for women from culturally specific communities and ethnic minorities are envisaged (A6–0404/2005): "The report devotes great attention to the worrying spread of honour killings and genital mutilation in the European Union. These are traditions that immigrants bring from countries where the balance of power between the sexes is even more skewed than it is in Europe" (Marianne Mikko, MEP, Socialist Group, EP debate 01.02.2006). The perception is quite deterministic in terms of the relation between culture and violence, and the migratory, cultural framing is related to a parallel framing of European values, creating a division between "us" and "them" (see also de los Reyes 2003), that is, the ones "bringing these kinds of violence to Europe." The cultural framings, in general, draw on a hegemonic discourse articulated from a Western perspective, which furthermore coincides with a territorial border-making process (i.e., the non-European is identified as cultural).

However, more inclusionary approaches to the prognosis of the problem are also found, for instance, in the 2006 EP Resolution on the current situation in combating violence against women and any future action, which recommends increased number of shelters and specialized training for experts dealing with honor crime victims as ways to address the forms of violence suffered by ethnic minority women (2004/2220[INI]). The resolution furthermore addresses the intersection between gender, migrant status, and family situation by calling on member states to provide "proper protection for immigrants, especially single mothers and their children, who often have inadequate means of defence or knowledge of available resources to counter domestic violence in Member States." This report is an example of how certain policy texts move beyond the mere diagnostic identification of culturalized forms of violence and takes the solving of the problems seriously by offering measures to combat the identified problems.

In general the EC puts increased emphasis on specific forms of violence, such as the "customary or traditional harmful attitudes and practices, including female mutilation, early and forced marriages and honour crimes," highlighted in the Roadmap for Equality between Women and Men (2006–2010) (COM[2006]92) as an urgent problem and more so than domestic violence, for instance, even though actual extent of the problems tells otherwise. Other policies, such as the Community Action program on equal opportunities for men and women 2001–2005 (COM[2000]335), show a more balanced approach to the problem as the document states that: "Particular attention needs to be paid to women who are subject to multiple discriminations (such as migrant women or women with disabilities, older women, women at risk of social exclusion, etc)" and suggests short-term residence permits for trafficking victims as a measure in this direction. The first three DAPHNE programs also underline the pervasiveness, and thus the universality, of the problem of violence. However the fourth DAPHNE program marks a shift by stating the following:

> Violence against women takes many forms ranging from domestic violence, which is prevalent at all levels of society, to harmful traditional practices associated with the exercise of physical violence against women, such as genital mutilation and honour-related crimes, which constitute a particular form of violence against women.

The increased focus on particular forms of violence, as part of a process of culturalization, is confirmed in an interview with an EC official, working on the DAPHNE program:

> I do think that over the years we have seen an increase both in the number of proposals we get for funding on migrant women and

in the number of proposals selected for funding. Every year in our annual work program we set a number of priorities on what kind of projects we would like to fund...recently, the past few years, for example, there has been increased attention on harmful traditional practices and female genital mutilation, which concern specific migrant groups that have particular practices such as honor killings, female genital mutilation and so on. (EC official, DG Justice, interview May 2010)

Culturalization, or exclusionary intersectionality related to culture, can be perceived as a problem because it relates gender-based violence exclusively to the culture of the "other," at the level of discourse; it stigmatizes and marginalizes particular minority groups; it ignores the structural, inequality dimensions of gender-based violence; it downplays the seriousness of majority or nonculturalized forms of violence such as battering by making it less visible; and it fails to address the pertinent issue of solutions to serious and real forms of violence suffered by vulnerable target groups. In terms of diagnosis and prognosis, culturalization also occurs in the form of intervention, which does not reach out to other areas, like the economy, but only relates to ethnicity, culture, race, etc.

Summing up, different forms of culturalization and culturalized framings of gender-based violence are found in the different EU policy texts, across time and across institutions. Intersectionality framings are mixed in the sense that inclusionary and exclusionary forms coexist, at times to an extent where the nuances between one and the other are hard to decipher. Nevertheless, the empirical findings presented here suggest a tendency toward increased appearances of exclusionary intersectionality framings of gender-based violence. The exclusionary framings are typically expressed through processes of culturalization. This occurs either through an almost exclusive focus on particular forms of violence, related to certain minority groups, the lack of prognosis when a relevant diagnosis is identified, and the articulation of a deterministic relation between culture and violence in particular policies.

SILENCES AND STIGMATIZATIONS

The general differentiation between domestic violence, which is increasingly downplayed and implicitly related only to the majority, and traditional or honor-related forms of violence, linked to minority groups and their specific cultures, contributes to processes of exclusionary intersectionality and othering of non-European identities.

It can be seen as a very limited and stereotyped way of attending to difference (see also Montoya and Rolandsen Agustín forthcoming). In this sense, de los Reyes (2003) argues that an opposition is made between traditional cultural patterns, pertaining to immigrant groups, and structural gender inequalities, which are universal or related to majority groups.

The cultural framing of the violence of "the others" is opposed to an almost invisible framing of the internal kinds of violence covered by the notion of domestic violence, for instance. The latter kind is never culturalized. This is an important silence within the policy issue: Cultural links or explanations are related to "honor crimes" but never to "battering," for example. The majority's forms of violence are often explained in terms of gendered power imbalances in these same documents, but this is not culturally articulated. Furthermore, the public/private differentiation increasingly disappears in relation to the cultural framing, that is, the distinction is only articulated in relation to nonculturally framed forms of violence.

The link that the documents create between particular kinds of violence and cultural minorities directs a needed attention to the specific problems related to female genital mutilation, for example, as a form of gender-based violence. However, the effect of the framing of these forms of violence as culturally or ethnically related, and the invisibility of other forms of violence as such, is that whole groups of migrants are stereotyped into a specific cultural image. The aim of establishing specific programs or initiatives for certain minority groups could be overshadowed by a disadvantageous effect of the cultural framing, that is, that of creating prejudice toward entire collectives, based on cultural assumptions. This leads to an overgeneralization, which is counterproductive to targeted political implementations in the sense that the cultural group in question can be seen as a completely homogeneous group characterized by tradition, underdevelopment, and irrationality.

One interviewee particularly sees the increased attention to issues such as female genital mutilation as linked to tendencies of prejudice in European societies and the EU political panorama:

> All groups are involved in combating violence against women but the conservative group does not want a directive on intimate partner violence...The conservative group wants a directive on violence against women which is only about female genital mutilation. I perceive that they want this because...In the Parliament now we know

that we have strong groups working with some sort of Islamophobia. If we then make a directive on violence against women and only take up female genital mutilation, then you have pointed out that it is them, it is these groups who have violence against women. And I think that is alarming because we have to look at intimate partner violence. (MEP, Green/Left Group, interview May 2010)

Phillips (2007) finds the whole notion of culture within multiculturalism problematic, precisely because it leads us to exaggerate the difference between cultures and cultural groups, thereby creating more cultural stereotypes than would otherwise be the case. Cultures tend to be viewed as internally homogeneous, and the individual perspective is overlooked. Usually, culture cannot explain the different forms of gender-based violence, Phillips argues. Furthermore, from any perspective of "us," minority groups tend to be viewed as more "cultural" (ibid.), as is the case with the framing of gender-based violence in the EU policy documents. Kantola (2010) warns about tendencies of "cultural blaming" whereby states blame violence on minority cultures, creating an inherent relationship between specific cultures and violence.

Kantola relates this tendency to a general shift at the national level that has increased the attention toward "tackling gender inequalities within minorities" (2010, 163). In the case of Sweden, Carbin (2010) finds that immigrant men are constructed in public and political discourses as inherently violent, and that violence in majority cultures is made invisible. A similar interpretation can be made of the EU case: The overall tendency is for an increased attention to cultural forms of violence, perceived as belonging to minority groups. The majority forms of violence are not culturalized and they are made more invisible through the emphasis on cultural forms, which tends to "normalize" other kinds of violence such as battering, for instance (Montoya and Rolandsen Agustín forthcoming). Through cultural framings, gender-based violence becomes a phenomenon related to foreign minority cultures exclusively (Carbin 2010). This tendency contributes to the othering and stigmatization of marginalized groups. It furthermore takes the attention away from the gendered, structural dimensions as a universal basis of all forms of gender-based violence (Montoya and Rolandsen Agustín forthcoming).

As regards the civil society actors, cultural framings are more seldom in the EWL texts when compared to the official EU institution documents. One important exception to this is the position paper

"The elimination of all forms of discrimination and violence against the girl child" (2007). In this document pornography is culturalized: "[In] current cultural processes...pornography slips into our everyday lives as an ever more universally accepted, often idealised, cultural element." Though pornography in itself is not considered to be form of violence, the EWL states in the document that "the way in which the image of girls is constructed in public space lowers her social value and promotes violence towards girls." This is one of the very few cases where the "insider" violence, that is, the kind of violence articulated as occurring in the European society, is related to a cultural framing through the linking of violence to pornography, which is depicted as cultural.

In sum, explicit mentioning of particular groups can be stigmatizing and exclusionary or inclusionary. This is an empirical and a contextual question. I agree with Walby, Armstrong, and Strid (2009) that intersectionality needs to be contextualized in the empirical reality of policy implementation and results in order to really assess potential stigmatization. The outcome of the policies should be scrutinized. In any case, visibility highlights the problem and cases of positive silencing may best refer to cases of advanced intersectional contexts (with a clear history of attending to intersectional relations, for example). The question is how policies can take into account difference and certain vulnerabilities without marginalizing specific groups and creating ethnocentric and deterministic understandings of violence and culture, for instance. There is a balance between a universal conception of women's rights and an intersectional understanding of women's positionality (focusing on structural inequality, not culture). Culturalization is a problem when culture becomes the only story, the lack of attention to other problem representations is apparent, and the focus is exclusively on particular groups without offering real solutions to their problems. Furthermore, when related to the construction of value communities and collective identities, culturalization contributes to processes of exclusion and othering in society (in this case at the transnational level) and it addresses minority and majority differences in negative ways.

Conclusions: Interrelating Gender Equality, Intersectionality, and Diversity at the Transnational Level

Analyzing the development of intersectionality at the European, transnational level implies looking at two parallel and interrelated processes of mobilization and institutionalization. Theoretically, I argue that in order to do so we must take into account the dimensions of ideas, agency, and context. These dimensions interact with each other as strategic policy frames are set forward in a context of particular political and discursive opportunity structures, which create dynamics of inclusion and exclusion within the European transnational framework of multilevel politics. Empirically the interrelation and interdependency are seen in the way in which claims-making efforts by transnational civil society actors are influenced by and simultaneously influence policy-making processes and policy developments in the EU institutions.

In this concluding chapter I will summarize the main theoretical contributions of the book as well as the key findings of the empirical analyses concerning the simultaneous and interrelated challenges of diversity and degendering. I synthesize the relation between gender equality, intersectionality, and diversity and, in addition, discuss the EU variant of transnational intersectionality. Furthermore, I point to another emergent challenge, namely that of conservative transnational women's organizations, in terms of their increased mobilization at the European level as well as the potential institutionalization of understandings of gender equality and women's interests that differ from the dominant discourses of the EU institutions.

Gender and Diversity in the European Union Variant of Transnational Intersectionality

The approach to intersectionality analysis in a transnational context, that has been developed both theoretically and empirically throughout the chapters of this book, focuses on the ways in which gender diversity, understood as the differences between women as well as between women and other social groups, is expressed and accommodated in civil society as well as in official EU institutions. Thus, it refers to claims, constituencies, and strategies in terms of the former, and policies and institutional structures regarding the latter. At the transnational, European level a contextualized, dynamic approach to intersectionality implies taking into account the interaction and mutual influence between EU institutions and transnational civil society organizations, the conditions of transnational mobilization, like the structures that facilitate or hinder mobilization, processes of inclusion and exclusion, civil society voices and their diverse access to policy-making processes in a multilevel polity, diversity of interests and actors, which lead to a focus on diverse understandings of gender equality, as well as minority and majority organizations defending women's rights, and the particular way in which intersectionality has been institutionalized in the EU.

The latter refers to the history of social and economic policies of the EU, which have influenced the institutionalization of both gender equality policies and intersectionality. According to Ferree (2008; 2009) the ideological combination of neoliberal economic policies and the European social model is a distinctive feature of this contextualization as is the citizen/noncitizen dichotomy that permeates conflicts, contestations, and policies, also in relation to gender equality as demonstrated by the empirical analyses carried out here (see chapters 3 and 6). Furthermore, I have argued how contestations over diverse understandings of gender equality and women's interests, the competition between different grounds of equality, which followed from the introduction of multiple discrimination policies in the EU, the previously privileged position of gender, as well as the emergence of minority organizations and diversity concerns in majority organizations in European civil society add to this particular institutionalization of intersectionality at the transnational level.

The saliency of different forms of collective claims making stemming from transnational civil society and diverse understandings of gender equality and women's interests in policy-making processes underlines the importance of analyzing in-depth the conflicts and contestations between different actors and frames. As argued throughout the book, ideas matter as do their strategic framings and here we must especially take into account the contextualization of frames and the way in which they interact with institutional structures and dominant discourses. This is relevant both when frames originate from civil society, seeking institutional resonance, and when they are institutionalized in the day-to-day practices of individual EU institutions, creating a differentiation between the background and the foreground.

The way in which CFA is perceived here sheds light on discursive struggles as well as the strategic use of ideas, thus emphasizing frame nuances, strategic agency, and the role of civil society actors. Furthermore, institutions are perceived to be in constant change as they are conceptualized as the (re)production of ideas and continuous discursive negotiations. This calls for an increased attention to the ways in which ideas are institutionalized in a specific context and, not least, the framing processes that keep playing out in the processes of institutionalization, beyond the mere agenda-setting and decision-making phases.

Gendered discursive institutionalism suggests that institutions are made up of ideas. This theoretical framework furthermore underlines that institutional changes occur in the context of political conflict, discursive contestations, and shifting alliances. The institutional (legal, political, and discursive) context as well as actor alliances interact with processes of policy frame articulation (see Kulawik 2009). Resistance is enacted through the challenging and renegotiation of meaning. The ideational dimensions constrain and enable policy change when alternative discourses and framings are set forward. However, the institutionalization of frames depends largely on agency and processes of in/exclusion. In other words, ideas interact with the institutional context within a transnational space of mobilization. Therefore, contextualization is a crucial dimension of the methodological and theoretical approach adopted here. I have argued that ideational dimensions play a determining role in policy making and policy change, alongside institutionalized and collective actors. The institutionalization of frames depends on the institutional and discursive context in which these processes take place as well as on key actors' strategic framing of ideas.

Overall, the findings show that ideas are used strategically by EU and civil society actors in order to advance policy claims and institutionalize policy framings. They are significant in the definitional struggles related to key notions such as "women's interests" and "gender equality," processes in which meaning is being constructed and reproduced intersubjectively. However, I also argue that a more dynamic perspective on ideas within institutional settings is necessary: While I suggest that the ideas behind claims-making efforts should fit the dominant institutional ideas in order to gain resonance, my analyses have also shown that even though dominant institutional ideas are not easy to change, they are not static, either. Rather, ideas are dynamic and diversified, frames differ between institutions, and therefore it is necessary to advance nuanced interpretations of these processes.

The dominant discourse in the EU institutions on diversity is multiple discrimination, as a (limited) form of intersectionality. Whereas intersectional articulations, viewing the interplay between inequality categories as interrelated and inseparable, is "embryonic" (Lombardo and Rolandsen Agustín 2012) and underdeveloped, multiple discrimination, and its additive approach to the interplay between several inequality categories and discrimination grounds, is widespread and takes on the status as official policy of the EU. A more elaborated approach to inequality grounds is generally lacking (as the specific interrelation between the different categories remains unarticulated in most cases), but multiple discrimination polices do offer possibilities in terms of advancing gender-and-diversity aims. The strengthened focus on the multiplicity of discrimination implies increased attention to diversified interests among different groups of women, for instance, thus moving away from a homogenizing view on women as a social category and the essentialization of their interests.

The shift from a strong gender focus to the diversity agenda, as expressed through multiple discrimination policies, holds advantages in terms of moving forward in equality issues. However, the particular institutionalization of intersectionality, in its EU multiple discrimination variant, emphasizes certain categories, such as gender-and-ethnicity as well as the citizen/noncitizen dichotomy as referred to above, and ignores others. The saliency of certain interrelated categories depends largely on the policy area in question: Whereas gender-and-ethnicity and gender-and-citizenship status are prevalent within the policy area of gender-based violence, where the focus on "ethnic minority and migrant women" is very strong, this is not necessarily the case in employment related policies, for instance. Gender-and-ethnicity and gender-and-citizenship status are, for instance, much less present in employment and labor market related policies as well as in policies on poverty and social exclusion, focusing instead on gender-and-age, for instance elderly women, or the situation of single mothers. These are intersections, which relate to the context of welfare and social services relevant to the policy areas in question (i.e., elderly and childcare as well as unemployment policies) (see Lombardo and Rolandsen Agustín 2012; Rolandsen Agustín and Siim forthcoming a). Other interrelated categories, such as gender-and-class, remain largely absent from EU policies. Class is, to a certain extent, euphemized as social exclusion in EU policies but in any case, multilevel politics come into play again, relegating concerns related to social politics and economic redistribution largely to the national level under member-state competence (ibid.).

The Dilemmas of Degendering and Diversity

Empirically I ask which processes of intersectionality we find, in practice, at the transnational level. Looking both at mobilization and institutionalization, this means that a bottom-up perspective, on the one hand, and a top-down perspective, on the other, is taken into account. In terms of mobilization I analyze the diversity of (intersecting) civil society voices, majority and minority organizations, and their interaction with EU institutions. Institutionalization, from a transnational perspective on intersectionality, calls for an analysis of the attention to different inequalities in policies, the interpretations of gender equality and women's interests, as well as processes of in/exclusion in policy making. Together, this means addressing the institutional setup, policies and policy making, as well as civil society mobilization and interaction with EU institutions. In other words, transnational intersectionality concerns both the diversity of women's collective mobilization (organizations and claims) as well as contestations over different policy meanings (interests and frames).

I address challenges related to diversity (chapters 2, 3, and 6), on the one hand, and degendering (chapters 4, 5, and 6), on the other. The challenge of diversity focuses on the particularities of the European transnational space of mobilization and EU policy making as well as the way in which European women's organizations have been affected by the challenge and responded to it. Highlighted here is the dimension of agency, understood both as EU institutions and civil society organizations, and their capacity to act within the European, transnational context. The challenge of degendering refers to the role of ideas and the institutionalization of frames in EU policy development within the area of gender-based violence, leading to a qualification of CFA as a method for conducting policy analyses.

The interaction between ideas, agency, and context results in strategic framings of gender equality policies and, in this case, of policies on gender-based violence. Struggles over frames as well as simultaneous articulations of different framings of the same policy issue reflect the ways in which ideas are used strategically in policy-making processes and in the institutionalization of policy issues over time. On the one hand, this occurred in relation to the DAPHNE program as the negotiation and adoption of the program was intertwined with disputes over the distribution of competences between the national and the transnational level in the multilevel structure of the EU. On the other hand, these dynamics enable a strategic use of degendered frames that can, potentially, be used for gender equality enhancing purposes at later stages of the implementation process, for instance. This is what is meant by the idea of feminist or gender equality concerned actors "picking up" degendered frames with the aim of advancing gender equality goals once legislation, for instance, has been passed.

As the analysis of the selection of projects under the DAPHNE program showed, the implications of the increased degendering of the policy area of violence against women over time were not necessarily the disappearance altogether of gendered content but rather a more strategic use of the opportunities and potential of the policy texts adopted. Thus, gendered understandings of the policy issue of violence against women did not disappear from the EU realm even though the DAPHNE program was formulated in increasingly gender-neutral terms. I refer here to the frames that are institutionalized through official policy texts as foreground frames, and the ones that are institutionalized in day-to-day practices as background frames. Their relative strength depends, largely, on the institutional context and, especially, the presence of gender equality conscious actors within this context as well as civil society pressure.

I also find tendencies toward degendering when intersectionality is used in exclusionary ways through the increased use of cultural explanations to violence and the simultaneous downplaying of structural perspectives on the problem, which would highlight gender inequality perspectives on violence against women. Here degendering may be strategic as culturalization connects the policy area of gender equality to that of immigration policies and the construction of Europe as a value community and the collective identity of European citizens. Gender is used as an instrumental category that contributes to the exclusionary use of intersectionality concerns, fomenting the difference between "us" and the "other" through the images of "migrant women" and "migrant men," and their association with less gender equal practices than what is expected (according to certain EU policy texts) in the European community. In other words, minority and majority differences are addressed negatively through the exclusionary use of intersectionality, with the risk of marginalizing and stigmatizing certain groups in society.

Civil society claims are adapted to the institutional agenda and its dominant discourses. Organizations use framing strategies to make their claims resonate with dominant EU discourses. The EU institutions, on their part, hold the power to include and exclude civil society actors from policy-making processes, thereby determining who are to be considered legitimate claims makers within the framework of each EU institutions. However, the findings of the analysis of gender-based violence policies also point to the need to nuance this argument as discourses are multiple and simultaneously articulated in the EU institutions. Thus, it is not straightforward to identify a single discourse to which the claims must adapt by way of their framing. Again, this suggests that CFA as a methodological approach could be qualified by paying increased attention to the differential strength and nature of the particular framings identified as dominant or marginal, articulated in the foreground or in the background of EU institutional practices.

I argue that the diversity challenge can be perceived as both an opportunity and a threat. The diversity frame is an opportunity for NGOs to address diverse constituencies more adequately. However, the diversity frame also implies a risk of marginalization whereby the attention to gender as an inequality creating category is blurred or disappears once other intersecting inequalities are taken into consideration (i.e., degendering). Similarly, the focus on the structural dimensions of gender inequality may be undermined by framing gender equality as women's individual, free choice. The latter may lead to political inaction or a failure to address the systemic causes of gender inequality. In policy making, I furthermore find potentially stigmatizing effects of the increased attention toward (ethnic) minority groups as gender-based violence is framed in cultural terms, and specific kinds of violence are depicted as inherent to certain ethnic groups. The diversity focus translates into stigmatization in some cases, thus undermining a potential focus on specific vulnerabilities at the intersection between gender and citizenship status, for example, in cases of domestic violence. At the same time, universal forms of violence are made invisible.

As regards the EU/civil society interaction, EU institutions and civil society organizations mutually influence each other. The EU preference for an integrated approach to multiple discrimination initially created competition between inequality grounds. With time, however, this has turned into new collaborations and alliances between different civil society organizations. The continued EC preference for interacting with one organization per inequality ground nevertheless creates a mismatch vis-à-vis the plurality of voices and organizations articulating demands in transnational civil society. In practice, I find a plurality of voices and a diversity of interests at the European transnational level, which reflect the heterogeneity of women as a group. Majority and minority women's organizations differ in terms of their constituencies, organizational structures, claims, and strategies when it comes to addressing diversity. Importantly there is a need in the minority organizations, primarily, to attend to both representation of their interests, in terms of differentiated needs, for instance, and recognition of their voices and identity.

The diversity of women's claims, at the transnational level, calls for a reconsideration of the balance between policy making efficiency and pluralism of demands. A representational logic, whereby umbrella NGOs with national member organizations speak on behalf of large constituencies, is considered by the EC for instance to be more important than deliberation, which might, ideally, foment the articulation and inclusion of diversified and plural demands. This is not least the case in an EU policy-making system characterized more by efficiency and lobby-group advocacy than deliberative processes and debates in the public sphere (see also Lang 2009). Early on, the EWL showed a legitimate concern that gender would lose out from the introduction of multiple discrimination policies, and only slowly did the organization start to consider the new legal framework as an opportunity to advance women's different interests. The majority organizations were caught in the dilemma between wanting to address different women's concerns and trying to avoid a diminished role of the gender dimension in the broad EU picture (see also Woodward 2006).

This summarizes the main dilemma of diversity in the transnational sphere: How can a certain unity of claims, which is needed in order to influence EU policies with a strong gender voice, be combined with the collective representation of several and diverse women constituencies? Cooperation and coalition strategies among transnational women's organizations seem to be one adequate measure as are more inclusive policy-making processes through which more attention is paid to the diversified interests of different organizational constituencies, and thereby different groups of women, in a manner that, ideally, is still feasible within the dynamics of EU institutional structures and practices.

New Challenges to Gender Equality Mobilization and Institutionalization

In line with the identified characteristics of transnational mobilization, where minority women increasingly mobilize at the European level, I find that new organizations are emerging in the European civil society sphere as well. They seek funding and institutional legitimacy through recognition as interlocutors of the EU institutions. The inclusion of actors in EU policy making and the consequent legitimization of collective civil society representatives are linked to discursive struggles over meaning and definitions of "women's interests" and "gender equality." These discursive contestations have proliferated in recent years in the context of the EU and the transnational civil society.

The transnational space of mobilization in particular is characterized by the impact of the development of EU policies in the field of equality and nondiscrimination and a diversification of groups and demands. In genereal, I find that established women's organizations as well as dominant gender equality discourses within the transnational space are challenged on different fronts. This regards umbrella organizations focusing on a different inequality ground that possibly have more to gain from a change in the legal and political framework, and minority organizations, defining themselves based on an intersectional constituency. Likewise, more traditionally oriented organizations challenge the gender equality ideas of the majority organizations.

Organizations with minority intersectional constituencies who were not satisfied with the level of representation in majority organizations and/or the ability to make their voices heard in the EU context started to mobilize at the transnational level. Similarly, organizations with views on women's role and interests differing ideologically from those of the EWL, the EC, and the socialist and liberal MEPs initiated lobbying activities and built alliances with conservative forces in the EP and the Council. Whereas these new organizations emphasize women's right to choose whether to stay at home or enter the labor market, the EWL, the EC, and the socialist and liberal MEPs advocate for women's labor market participation as a primary goal. The latter can be considered the dominant discourse on gender equality currently in the EU when linked to objectives of economic growth and competitiveness.

Common to these new kinds of mobilization is dissatisfaction with the existing representation of women's interests at the EU level and a perceived lack of pluralism. Women are heterogeneous as a group, and so is the articulation and definition of their interests. The well-established, majority women's organizations are perceived as representing mainly white, middle-class women who are active on the labor market. They are challenged by claims based on ethnicity, social status, and divergent ideological standpoints. To a certain extent, this can be interpreted as a development of the different waves of feminism whereby women came to be perceived as an internally heterogeneous, not homogeneous, group. Different women within this group are now claiming institutional recognition and voice at the European level, highlighting precisely the heterogeneous condition. In part, this is due to the strengthening of particular groups because of technological developments, which facilitate transnational mobilization, enhanced internationalization, and migration flows, as well as the enlargement of the EU. Furthermore, the diversity agenda, originally articulated in terms of social justice within social movements, has gained strength due to its relevance in relation to the labor market (challenges and advantages of a diverse labor force) and the business sector (added value of diversity policies for marketing purposes as well as diversity management issues) (Kantola 2010; Squires 2006; Woodward and Wiercx 2003).

This plurality in current European civil society is underlined by the strengthening of conservative women's organizations operating transnationally and challenging dominant EU gender equality understandings. This additional challenge concerns both mobilization, in terms of the inclusion of conservative organizations in EU policymaking processes, and institutionalization, in relation to different and hitherto marginalized understandings of gender equality. At the beginning of the 2000s, women who did not feel represented by the existing women's organizations at the European level due to ideological differences began to mobilize transnationally. So far, this has only been hinted at in the literature (Roth 2007; Thiel and Prügl 2009; Woodward 2007; Woodward and Wiercx 2003).

Conservative women's organizations are mobilizing on the European level around a more traditional understanding of gender roles and the primary promotion of women's right to choose to stay at home for example. This reflects a struggle between dominant discourses on gender equality as well as their contestations both within and outside the EU institutions. This is not least the case of the EP. Whereas the FEMM Committee is usually characterized as one of the more consensus oriented committees of the EP, research points to important differences in this regard between policy areas: Some political debates are clearly marked by divergence between left- and right-wing groups of the EP, such as sexual and reproductive health and rights (see Rolandsen Agustín 2012), others are characterized by a higher degree of convergence.

The latter is the case of the debate on gender quotas in politics and the corporate world, for example, where a growing favorable consensus has emerged over the years (Pristed Nielsen and Rolandsen Agustín 2013). The issue of gender quotas has gained salience at the transnational level because of a few best practice examples from the member state level. In this way, the EP and the FEMM Committee serve as transnational catalysts for discussing and promoting gender equality policies and making policy innovations. The EP debates and institutional structure offer certain windows of opportunity when issues that cannot be debated nationally, are brought to the EU agenda. Policy initiatives at the national level inspire EU level debates and offer member states the possibility to join a trend at the transnational level (ibid.). Thus, processes of contestation and consensus coexist in the debates of the FEMM Committee of the EP among left- and right-wing MEPs.

Conservative women's organizations at the European level have emerged and gained strength at the same time as conservative understandings of gender equality were advanced under the FEMM Committee presidency of MEP Anna Zaborska of the EPP group (2004–2009). However, interviewees also report that there has, historically, been a significant representation of conservative MEPs with a gender equality agenda inscribed within a more general consensus within the FEMM Committee, thus advancing feminist goals beyond party lines. These "committed" women may have increasingly disappeared and the FEMM Committee is no longer the feminist stronghold it used to be. Ideologically, dominant EU discourses are questioned through the emergence of alliances and the inclusion of new civil society actors with the aim of (re)defining "women's interests" and the understanding of "gender equality." Within the context of the FEMM Committee, the interpretation of women's interests is being negotiated and (re)defined and hitherto dominant notions of gender equality (within the institution) are being challenged, for instance by the legitimation and inclusion of new (conservative) civil society organizations (see Rolandsen Agustín 2012).

This is the case of New Women for Europe (NWFE). NWFE is a European umbrella organization focusing on family and prolife issues and defending the different life preferences of women. It refers to a "career oriented" and a "home centered" lifestyle, with family childcare as the norm. According to NWFE, policies should be adapted to "women's realities," that is, acknowledge the choice of women to stay at home to take care of their families. NWFE was founded because these interests were considered not to be sufficiently acknowledged in the panorama of civil society/EU relations: "I got in contact with several women and NGOs that wanted to have a voice in the European Parliament and they didn't feel that the organizations that were already existing represented them...we grew up very, very fast, because there was a lot of demand" (founder of NWFE, interview October 2010).

Through strategic alliances within the EP and the FEMM Committee, and to some extent with member-state representatives in the Council, the NWFE succeeded in contesting the privileged status of the EWL at the turn of the century. Especially during the FEMM Committee chairwomanship of Zaborska (2004–2009), the NWFE was given a role, which, to some, was disproportionate to its size and membership base (former representative of EWL, interview October 2010). The organization developed relations with MEPs of the Conservative Group due to the perceived gap in the representation of diverse interests of women in the European civil society panorama:

> We had grown very fast, and our views, I mean, kind of were very eagerly expected or wished for by the MEPs. We found very fast that they really wanted to listen to us, because they really wanted to have an alternative to what they were having. (founder of NWFE, interview October 2010)

The struggle over the definition of the meaning of gender equality in the EU was related to the struggle over the symbolic and political "ownership" of the FEMM Committee and the ways in which women's organizations and their interests were to be represented and included in EP policy processes:

> I have some of the colleagues in EPP who really opposed to the policies of the European Women's Lobby because they thought, they were convinced that the Women's Lobby does not act adequately, represent the positions of all the women, and there the door closes some

times for the European Women's Lobby...I think some of my more conservative colleagues do not really agree with the positions of the European Women's Lobby and therefore are trying to advocate the existence of other women's groups. (MEP, Socialist Group, interview December 2007)

The ideological struggle revolved both around value-based and religious issues as well as the women-as-carers and women-as-workers dichotomy (MEP, Socialist Group, interview January 2008). In practice, the "battle" was fought not least in relation to the EP budgetary debates on financing of women's organizations: In debates prior to the adoption of a new financial regulation in 2002 concerning subsidies for women's organizations, the definitional struggles over women's interests were combined with arguments over collective representation with the conservative MEPs defending the inclusion of a variety of organizations, in the name of "democratic pluralism," and the socialists supporting continued differential treatment of the EWL as the representative of the unity of women's movements in Europe.[1] Roughly, in these struggles over representation and different interpretations of gender equality and women's interests, the Socialist Group of the EP and EWL were opposed to Conservative Group and NWFE, where the latter tried to question and challenge the dominant gender equality discourse of the EU and the FEMM Committee in particular and were, in part, successful in doing so (see also Rolandsen Agustín 2012).

These ideological struggles over the meaning of gender equality and women's interests in the transnational civil society constitute yet another challenge for the well-established European women's organizations, in particular the EWL, and the dominant EU discourse on gender equality as well as EU institutional structures for interacting with civil society organizations. The challenge underlines the empirical plurality of civil society voices defending women's interests at the transnational level and it highlights the relevance of looking deeper into who represents women collectively in Europe and who is attributed voice in the EU institutions (see Rolandsen Agustín 2012). As was the case with the strategic degendering of policies on violence against women, much depends on the ways in which actors make use of the framings. As argued by Ferree (2009), EU policies hold a potential for feminist advocates in terms of using strategic framing of policies to advance gender equality goals. Even though the multilevel structure of the EU presents limits as to how far it is possible to take transnational intersectionality and, especially, make articulated policies and claims in relation to specific, identified intersections, such as gender-and-class, actors from within the EU institutions as well as those representing civil society organizations may choose to make efforts to advance in intersectionality concerns, also in relation to the more marginalized intersections, by highlighting and strengthening the attention toward specific categories. As shown in the analyses presented throughout the book, the interplay between ideas, agency, and context at the transnational level can result in new possibilities for exploring the "hidden" potential of strategically framed policies.

Appendix

List of Empirical Documents: European Union Policies on Multiple Discrimination and on Gender-Based Violence

EU institutions

No	Institution	Document type	Topic	Reference	Date
1	Council	Directive	On the implementation of the principle of equal treatment for men and women as regards access to employment, vocational training and promotion, and working conditions	76/207/EEC	09.02.1976
2	EP	Resolution	On the creation of an ad hoc committee on women's rights	—	26.10.1979
3	EP	Report	On women's rights (ad hoc committee)	Doc. 1-829/80	1980
4	EP	Terms of reference	For setting up committee of inquiry into the situation of women in Europe	—	1981
5	EP	Resolution	On the position of women in the European community	OJ C 50 (09.03.1981)	11.02.1981
6	EC	Communication to Council	A new community action program on the promotion of equal opportunities for women (1982–85)	COM(81)758	09.12.1981
7	EP	Resolution	On the community action program	—	12.05.1982
8	EP	Resolution	On the burning of brides in India	Doc. 1-538/83	07.07.1983
9	EP	Report	Into the situation of women in Europe (committee of inquiry)	Doc. 1-1229/831 A, B and C	05.01.1984
10	EP	Resolution	On the situation of women in Europe	OJ C 46 (20.02.84)	17.01.1984
11	EP	Resolution	On the sentencing of a pregnant woman to be stoned to death	Doc. 1-1561/83	16.03.1984
12	EC	Communication to Council	Equal opportunities for women. Medium-term community program (1986–90)	COM(85)801	19.12.1985
13	EP	FEMM Report	On violence against women	A2-44/86	20.05.1986
14	EP	Resolution	On violence against women	A2-0044-86	14.07.1986
15	EC	Communication to Council	Equal opportunities for women and men. The third medium-term community action program (1991–1995)	COM(90)449	06.11.1990

16	EP	Resolution	On the evaluation of the third community action program on equal opportunities for women and men (1991–1995) and proposals for the fourth community action program (1996–2000)	A4–0104/95	14.06.1995
17	EC	Proposal for a Council Decision	On the fourth medium-term community action program on equal opportunities for women and men (1996–2000)	COM(95)381	17.11.1995
18	Council	Decision	Concerning a medium-term community action program on equal opportunities for women and men (1996–2000)	95/593/EC	22.12.1995
19	EP	FEMM Report	On the need to establish an EU-wide campaign for zero tolerance of violence against women	A4–0250/97	16.07.1997
20	EP	Resolution	On the need to establish an EU-wide campaign for zero tolerance of violence against women	A4–0250/97	06.10.1997
21	EC	Proposal for a Council Decision	On a medium-term community action program on measures providing a community-wide support to member states' action relating to violence against children, young persons, and women (the DAPHNE program) (2000 to 2004)	COM/98/0335	09.07.1998
22	Council	Opinion of the Legal Service	Legal basis for the EC proposal to establish the DAPHNE program (2000–2004)	5369/99	18.01.1999
23	EP	Second report	On the report from the EC to the Council, the EP, the EESC, and the CoR on the state of women's health in the European community	A4–0029/1999	22.01.1999
24	Council	Outcome of proceedings	On proposal for a Council decision on a medium-term community action program on measures providing a community-wide support to member-state action in relation to violence against children, young persons, and women (the DAPHNE program) (2000–2004)	5610/99	01.02.1999

Continued

EU institutions Continued

No	Institution	Document type	Topic	Reference	Date
25	Council	Outcome of proceedings	On proposal for a Council decision on a medium-term community action program on measures providing a community-wide support to member-state action in relation to violence against children, young persons, and women (the DAPHNE program) (2000–2004)	5994/99	17.02.1999
26	EP	Debate	On violence against women, the DAPHNE program	—	08.03.1999
27	EP	Resolution	On violence against women and the DAPHNE program	B4–0233/99	10.03.1999
28	Council	Conference	Campaign for zero tolerance against violence towards women	—	29.03.1999
29	EP	FEMM Report	On the amended proposal for a EP and Council decision adopting a program of community action (the DAPHNE program) (2000–2004) on measures aimed to prevent violence against children, young persons, and women	A4–0188/99	31.03.1999
30	Council	Outcome of proceedings	On proposal for a Council decision of the EP and of the Council adopting a program of community action (the DAPHNE program) (2000–2004) on measures aimed to prevent violence against children, young persons, and women	7124/99	12.04.1999
31	EC	Communication on amended Proposal	For EP and Council decision adopting a programme of community action (the DAPHNE program) (2000–2004) on measures aimed to prevent and protect against violence against children, young persons, and women (presented by the EC pursuant to article 250 (2) of the EC treaty)	COM (1999) 244	11.05.1999
32	EP	Resolution	On violence against women and the DAPHNE program	B4–0233/99	21.06.1999
33	EC	Presentation, Commissioner Anita Gradin	On the Eurobarometer n° 51.0 on "Europeans and their view on domestic violence against women"	—	14.07.1999

34	EP	Legislative resolution	Embodying Parliament's opinion on the amended proposal for a EP and Council decision adopting a program of community action (the DAPHNE program) (2000–2004) on measures aimed to prevent violence against children, young persons, and women	COM(99) 0082	30.07.1999
35	Council	Common Position	Acting in accordance with the procedure referred to in article 251 of the treaty establishing the European community, with a view to adopting a decision of the EP and of the Council adopting a program of community action (the DAPHNE program) (2000 to 2003) on preventive measures to fight violence against children, young persons, and women	37/1999	13.09.1999
36	EC	Communication to the EP	Pursuant to the second subparagraph of article 251 (2) of the EC treaty on the common position of the Council on the proposal for a EP and Council decision adopting a program of community action (The DAPHNE program) (2000–2003) on preventive measures to fight violence against children, young persons, and women	SEC/99/1550	01.10.1999
37	EP Council	COD procedure	On decision 1999//EC of the EP and of the Council adopting a program on community action (the DAPHNE program) (2000–2003) on preventive measures to fight violence against children, young persons, and women	3627/1/99 REV 1	07.12.1999
38	EC	Opinion	Pursuant to article 251(2) (c) of the EC treaty, on the EP's amendments to the Council's common position regarding the proposal for a decision of the EP and of the Council adopting a program of community action (the DAPHNE program) (2000–2003) on preventive measures to fight violence against children, young persons, and women amending the proposal of the EC pursuant to article 250(2) of the EC treaty	COM(1999) 670	08.12.1999

Continued

EU institutions Continued

No	Institution	Document type	Topic	Reference	Date
39	EC	Brochure	Breaking the silence, European campaign zero tolerance of violence against women	—	2000
40	EP Council	Decision	Adopting a program of community action (the DAPHNE program) (2000–2003) on preventive measures to fight violence against children, young persons, and women	293/2000/EC	24.01.2000
41	EP	Speech, MEP Maj Britt Theorin	On violence against women zero tolerance campaign. Conference held in Portugal, in the context of the zero tolerance campaign	—	05.2000
42	EC	Speech, Commissioner Anna Diamantopoulou	Speak out against violence against women, closing of the international conference in Lisbon on violence against women	—	04.05.2000
43	EC	Communication to the EP, the Council, the EESC and the CoR	Proposal for a Council decision on the program relating to the community framework strategy on gender equality (2001–2005)	COM(2000)335	07.06.2000
44	Council	Directive	Implementing the principle of equal treatment between persons irrespective of racial or ethnic origin	2000/43/EC	29.06.2000
45	EP	Legislative resolution	On the common position established by the Council, with a view to the adoption of a EP and Council decision adopting a program of community action (DAPHNE program) (2000–2003) on preventive measures to fight violence against children, young persons, and women	9150/1/1999	07.07.2000
46	EC	White Paper	On governance	SEC(2000) 1547/7	11.10.2000
47	Council	Directive	Establishing a general framework for equal treatment in employment and occupation	2000/78/EC	27.11.2000

48	Council	Decision	Establishing a community action program to combat discrimination (2001 to 2006)	2000/750/EC	27.11.2000
49	Council	Decision	Establishing a programme relating to the community framework strategy on gender equality (2001–2005)	2001/51/EC	20.12.2000
50	EP	Resolution	On sexual violence against women, particularly Catholic nuns	—	05.04.2001
51	Council	Presidency conclusions	On violence against women	6994/02	2002
52	EC	Report to the EP and the Council	On the DAPHNE program (2000–2003)	COM(2002)169	22.04.2002
53	EC	Staff working paper	Annexes 1–6 to the report to the EP and the Council on the DAPHNE program (2000–2003)	SEC(2002) 3380	22.04.2002
54	EP Council	Decision	Adopting a program of community action in the field of public health (2003–2008)	1786/2002/EC	23.09.2002
55	EP Council	Directive	On the implementation of the principle of equal treatment for men and women as regards access to employment, vocational training and promotion, and working conditions	2002/73/EC	23.09.2002
56	EC	Communication to the EP	Pursuant to the second subparagraph of article 251 (2) of the EC treaty concerning the common position of the Council on the adoption of a decision establishing a second phase of Community action (2004–2008) to prevent and combat violence against children, young people, and women and to protect victims and groups at-risk (the DAPHNE II program)	SEC/2003/1371	2003
57	EC	Call for proposals	The DAPHNE program 2000–2003 preventive measures to fight violence against children, young people, and women	2002/C 280/10	2003

Continued

EU institutions Continued

No	Institution	Document type	Topic	Reference	Date
58	EP Council	Proposal for a decision	Establishing a second phase of a program of community action (2004–2008) to prevent violence against children, young people, and women and to protect victims and groups at-risk (the DAPHNE II program) (presented by the EC)	COM(2003) 54	04.02.2003
59	EC	Speech, Commissioner Anna Diamantopoulou	Tackling domestic violence and trafficking in human beings–the role of the EU, member states and civil society, meeting of EU experts on domestic violence and trafficking in women, Athens	—	30.05.2003
60	EP	FEMM Report	On the proposal for a EP and Council decision establishing a second phase of the DAPHNE program	A5–0280/2003	24.07.2003
61	EP Council	Amended proposal for a decision	Establishing a second phase of a program of community action (2004–2008) to prevent violence against children, young people, and women and to protect victims and groups at-risk (the DAPHNE II program) (presented by the EC pursuant to article 250 (2) of the EC treaty)	COM(2003) 616	15.10.2003
62	Council	Common position	With a view to adopting decision 2004/ … /EC of the EP and of the Council of … adopting a program of community action (2004–2008) to prevent and combat violence against children, young people, and women and to protect victims and groups at-risk (the DAPHNE II program)	5/2004	01.12.2003
63	Council	Presidency conclusions	On the ministerial conference Diversity and participation: the gender perspective	12644/04	2004
64	Council	Report on Presidency activities	Dublin conference on violence against women	9828/04	2004

65	Council	Draft Council conclusions	On sexual harassment at the workplace	15202/04	2004
66	EP	FEMM Recommendation	For second reading on the common position adopted by the Council with a view to adopting a EP and Council decision adopting a program of community action (2004–2008) to prevent and combat violence against children, young people, and women and to protect victims and groups at-risk (the DAPHNE II program)	13816/1/2003	17.03.2004
67	EP	Legislative resolution	On the proposal for a EP and Council decision, establishing a second phase of a program of community action (2004–2008) to prevent violence against children, young people, and women and to protect victims and groups at-risk (the DAPHNE II program)	COM(2003) 54	25.03.2004
68	EP Council	Decision	Adopting a program of community action (2004 to 2008) to prevent and combat violence against children, young people, and women and to protect victims and groups at-risk (DAPHNE II)	803/2004/EC	21.04.2004
69	EP Council	COD procedure	On decision No …/2004/ /EC of the EP and of the Council adopting a program on community action (2004–2008) to prevent and combat violence against children, young people, and women and to protect victims and groups at-risk (the DAPHNE II program)	3647/04	21.04.2004
70	EP	Legislative resolution	On the Council common position, with a view to the adoption of a EP and Council decision adopting a program of community action (2004–2008) to prevent and combat violence against children, young people, and women and to protect victims and groups at-risk (the DAPHNE II program)	13816/1/2003	28.04.2004
71	EC	Green Paper	Equality and nondiscrimination in an enlarged European Union	COM(2004)379	28.05.2004

Continued

EU institutions Continued

No	Institution	Document type	Topic	Reference	Date
72	EC	Speech, Director Luisella Pavan-Woolfe	Violence against women–European Union perspectives. Conference on myths and facts on violence against women, Copenhagen	—	25.11.2004
73	Council	Directive	Implementing the principle of equal treatment between men and women in the access to and supply of goods and services	2004/113/EC	13.12.2004
74	EC	Final report to the EP and the Council	On the DAPHNE program (2000–2003)	COM(2004) 824	22.12.2004
75	EC	Staff working paper	Annex to the report to the EP and the Council on the DAPHNE program (2000–2003)	SEC(2004) 1595	22.12.2004
76	EP	FEMM report	On the proposal for a decision of the EP and of the Council amending Council Decision 2001/51/EC establishing a program relating to the community framework strategy on gender equality and Decision No 848/2004/EC of the EP and of the Council establishing a community action program to promote organisations active at European level in the field of equality between men and women	A6–0132/2005	03.05.2005
77	EC	Communication to the Council, the EP, the EESC and the CoR	The EC's contribution to the period of reflection and beyond: plan-D for democracy, dialogue and debate	COM(2005) 494	13.10.2005
78	EP	FEMM report	On the current situation in combating violence against women and any future action	A6–0404/2005 2004/2220 (INI)	09.12.2005
79	EC	Call for proposals	For specific cofunded projects .The DAPHNE II program (2004–2008) to prevent and combat violence against children, young people, and women, and to protect victims and groups at-risk	2005/C 324/11	2006

80	EC	Call for proposals	The DAPHNE II program (2004–2008) to prevent and combat violence against children, young people, and women, and to protect victims and groups at-risk	2006–1	2006
81	Council	Draft Council conclusions	On men and gender equality	14845/06	2006
82	EP	Debate	On combating violence against women	—	01.02.2006
83	EC	Communication to the EP, the Council, the EESC and the CoR	A roadmap for equality between women and men (2006–2010)	COM(2006)92	01.03.2006
84	EP Council	Decision	Establishing the European year of equal opportunities for all—towards a just society	771/2006/EC	17.05.2006
85	EP	FEMM report	On the proposal for a decision of the EP and of the Council establishing for the period 2007–2013 the specific program "Fight against violence (DAPHNE) and drugs prevention and information" as part of the general programme "Fundamental rights and justice"	A6–0193/2006	19.05.2006
86	EP Council	Decision	Establishing a community program for employment and social solidarity (PROGRESS) (2007–2013)	1672/2006/EC	24.10.2006
87	EP	Resolution	On the current situation in combating violence against women and any future action	2004/2220 (INI)	24.11.2006
88	EC	Communication to the EP	On the common position concerning the common position adopted by the Council with a view to the adoption of a Decision of the EP and the Council establishing for the period 2007–2013 the specific program "Fight against violence (DAPHNE III)" as part of the general program "Fundamental rights and justice"	COM (2007) 0102	2007

Continued

EU institutions Continued

No	Institution	Document type	Topic	Reference	Date
89	EP Council	Decision	Establishing for the period 2007–2013 the specific program—fight against violence (DAPHNE III) as part of the general program—fundamental rights and justice	779/2007/EC	2007
90	EC	Call for proposals	Specific transnational projects. The DAPHNE III program (2007–2013) to prevent and combat violence against children, young people, and women and to protect victims and groups at-risk	JLS/DAP/2007–1	2007
91	EC	Call for proposals	The DAPHNE III program (2007–2013) to prevent and combat violence against children, young people, and women, and to protect victims and groups at-risk (Support to the activities of NGOs or other organisations through operating grants)	JLS/DAP/2007–2	2007
92	EC	Report	Tackling Multiple Discrimination: Practices, Policies and Laws	—	2007
93	EP	FEMM report	On a Roadmap for equality between women and men (2006–2010)	A6–0033/2007 2006/2132 (INI)	08.02.2007
94	Council	Common position	With a view to adopting decision No … / … /EC of the EP and of the Council of … establishing for the period 2007–2013 a specific programme to prevent and combat violence against children, young people, and women and to protect victims and groups at-risk (DAPHNE III program) as part of the general Program "Fundamental Rights and Justice"	4/2007	05.03.2007
95	EP	FEMM recommendation for second reading	On the Council common position for adopting a decision of the EP and of the Council establishing for the period 2007–2013 a specific programme to prevent and combat violence against children, young people, and women and to protect victims and groups at-risk (DAPHNE III program) as part of the general programme "Fundamental Rights and Justice"	A6–0147/2007	18.04.2007

96	EP Council	Decision	Establishing for the period 2007–2013 a specific programme to prevent and combat violence against children, young people, and women and to protect victims and groups at-risk (DAPHNE III program) as part of the general Program "Fundamental Rights and Justice"	779/2007/EC	20.06.2007
97	EP Council	COD procedure	On decision of the EP and of the Council establishing for the period 2007–2013 a specific program to prevent and combat violence against children, young people, and women and to protect victims and groups at-risk (DAPHNE III program) as part of the general programme "Fundamental rights and justice"	3626/07	20.06.2007
98	EP Council	Decision	Establishing a second program of community action in the field of health (2008–2013)	1350/2007/EC	23.10.2007
99	EC	White Paper	Together for health: A strategic approach for the EU 2008–2013	COM(2007)630	23.10.2007
100	Council	Presidency work programme	French presidency	—	2008
101	Council	EU guidelines	On violence against women and girls and combating all forms of discrimination against them	16175/08	2008
102	Council	Conclusions	On the review of the implementation by the member states and the EU institutions of the Beijing Platform for Action—the girl child	—	09.06.2008
103	EC	Report	The "For Diversity. Against Discrimination" information campaign. 5 years of raising awareness in the European Union	—	02.09.2008
104	Council	Conclusions	Gender equality: strengthening growth and employment—input to the post-2010 Lisbon Strategy	15488/09	10.11.2009
105	Council	Conclusions	On improving prevention to tackle violence against women and care to its victims within the scope of law enforcement	8310/10	04.2010

Continued

EU institutions Continued

No	Institution	Document type	Topic	Reference	Date
106	EC	Communication to the Council, the EP, the EESC and the CoR	Delivering an area of freedom, security and justice for Europe's citizens. Action Plan Implementing the Stockholm Programme	COM(2010)171	20.04.2010
107	EP	Declaration	Proposing the establishment of a European Year of Combating Violence against Women	0020/2010	09.2010
108	EC	Communication to the EP, the Council, the EESC and the CoR	Strategy for equality between women and men (2010–2015)	COM(2010)491	21.09.2010
109	EC	Staff working document	Background document accompanying the communication from the EC to the EP, the Council, the EESC and the CoR. Strategy for Equality between Women and Men 2010–2015	SEC/2010/1080	21.09.2010
110	EC	Staff working document	Actions to implement the Strategy for equality between Women and Men 2010–2015	SEC/2010/1079/2	21.09.2010
111	EP	Resolution	On priorities and outline of a new EU policy framework to fight violence against women	2010/2209 (INI)	05.04.2011
112	EP Council	Directive	On the European protection order	2011/99/EU	13.12.2011

Civil society organizations

No	Organization	Document type	Topic	Year
113	EWL	Charter of Principles	On Violence Against Women	—
114	EWL	Report	Towards a common European framework to monitor progress in combating violence against women	—
115	EWL	Report	Confronting the Fortress–black and migrant women in the European Union	1995
116	EWL	Report	Overcoming Discrimination. Selected strategies empowering black, ethnic minority and migrant women	1999
117	EWL	Study	On domestic violence: Unveiling the hidden data on domestic violence in the European Union	1999
118	WAVE	Recommendations	On Violence Against Women	1999
119	EWL	Position paper	EC's Package of proposals for the implementation of Article 13 of the Amsterdam Treaty	2000
120	EWL	Position paper	On integrating a gender dimension in the proposed measures to implement the anti-discrimination clause (art. 13 of the EC Treaty)	2000
121	WAVE	Training programme	On Prevention of Domestic Violence Against Women, European Survey, Good Practices Models	2000
122	EWL	Position paper	On the draft charter of fundamental rights of the EU	2000
123	WAVE	Fempower Magazine	On the theme of trafficking in women, No. 1	2001
124	EWL	Position paper	On strengthening women's rights in a multicultural Europe	2001
125	WAVE	Fempower Magazine	On the problems migrant women who are victims of (domestic) violence face, No. 4	2002

Continued

Civil society organizations   Continued

No	Organization	Document type	Topic	Year
126	EWL	Position paper	Shadow Directive on achieving equality of women and men outside the field of occupation and employment (European gender equality policies and legislation)	2002
127	EWL	Position paper	On integrating a gender perspective into the EU immigration policy	2004
128	EWL	Position paper	The role of men and boys in achieving gender equality	2004
129	EWL	Indicators	On policies against violence against women in relation to health	2004
130	EWL	Position paper	Women's sexual rights in Europe (Policy centre on violence against women)	2005
131	WAVE	Contribution	To the UN Commission on the Status of Women 2005–Beijing + 10 Review, Elimination of Violence against Women	2005
132	EWL	Position paper	Gender Equality Road Map for the European Community 2006–2010 presented by EWL (European gender equality policies and legislation)	2005
133	EWL	Project	Equal Rights, Equal Voices. Migrant Women in the European Union	2006
134	WAVE	Lobbying paper	On the CoE Campaign to combat violence against women, including domestic violence	2006
135	WAVE (CoE)	Blueprint	On the CoE Campaign to combat violence against women, including domestic violence	2006
136	EWL	Report	Reality check: when women's NGOs Map Policies and legislation on violence against women in Europe	2007
137	EWL	Position paper	In relation to the girl-child–The elimination of all forms of discrimination and violence against the girl child	2007

Notes

Introduction

1. As opposed to hard law (treaties and directives), soft law includes all policy documents of the EU, which have a nonbinding character, that is, no legal obligations are imposed on member states.
2. The idea of combining the two approaches was already proposed in 1974 by the feminist lawyer Eliane Vogel-Polsky who was a member of the EC Ad Hoc Group of Experts (Van der Vleuten 2007). Later on, the equal treatment approach was criticized for taking the rights of men as the standard for the development of gender equality policies. The positive action approach, on the other hand, focused on the specificity of women's experiences and needs.
3. In the scholarly literature of the field, gender mainstreaming is not thought to be used at its full potential in the EU institutions; it has been adopted quickly but it is being integrated into existing policies without challenging them. In practice, gender mainstreaming is used as an integrationist strategy, not an agenda setting, transformative one. Furthermore, measures of positive action are being abandoned as a consequence of the limited implementation of gender mainstreaming (Hafner-Burton and Pollack 2000; Lombardo 2005; Lombardo and Meier 2006; Verloo 2005a).
4. According to Van der Vleuten (2007), the EU gender equality policies are related to the main concerns of the time in which they were embedded: the 1950s focused on battles concerning equal pay, the 1970s were marked by high levels of unemployment, the 1990s saw an increased focus on competitiveness, and the 2000s accentuated multiple discrimination.
5. The antidiscrimination principles of the Amsterdam Treaty are covered by article 19 of the Lisbon Treaty. Article 10 of the latter envisages the mainstreaming of these principles into other policies of the EU.
6. See for instance the EC Green Paper "Equality and non-discrimination in an enlarged European Union" (COM[2004]379), the EC report "Tackling Multiple Discrimination. Practices, Policies and Laws" (2007), and the Council decision establishing a program relating to the community framework strategy on gender equality (2001–2005) (2001/51/EC).

7. Measures require unanimity in the Council and consultation of the EP.
8. There is a general agreement in the literature that the EU has played a significant role in advancing gender equality policies at the national level, despite specific cases of nonimplementation and member-state resistance. Van der Vleuten (2007) argues that member states have been forced to comply with transposition, despite its costs, because of a simultaneous pressure from the national and the supranational levels ("pincer mechanism"). However, the impact of EU gender equality policies on the national level is considered dissimilar and characterized by convergence, rather than harmonization (Liebert 2003; Lombardo 2003; 2004; Montoya 2013).
9. Throughout the book I use different terms to describe this phenomenon such as "heterogeneous," "diverse," "minority intersectional" constituencies, or membership: essentially this refers to the same phenomenon.
10. See however accounts of the results of the MAGEEQ and QUING projects (Krizsán and Popa forthcoming; Lombardo et al. 2009a; Verloo 2007).
11. The gender machinery, or what has been characterized as the "gender equality subsystem of the EU" (Lombardo 2003), includes the European Institute for Gender Equality (EIGE), Unit D1 on Gender Equality of the Directorate General Justice of the Commission (DG Justice), as well as the Committee on Women's Rights and Gender Equality (FEMM) of the European Parliament (EP) (Ahrens 2008; Fernández de Vega and Lombardo 2008; Kantola 2010; Squires 2010). In 2011 the Gender Equality Unit of the EC was moved from Directorate General Employment, Social Affairs and Equal Opportunities (DG Employment) to DG Justice (along with the rest of the Directorate on Equality). In the internal functioning of the Council and its General Secretariat, gender equality issues are especially dealt with in Directorate General G, Economic and Social Affairs and in various working parties, depending on the nature of the policy negotiated, for example the Working Party on Social Questions or the Working Party on Justice and Internal Affairs.
12. I consider ideas to be the "building blocks" of (policy) frames, which I perceive as specific representations of (policy) problems. I use the notion of "framing" to denote the practice or action of articulating frames (in policy processes, in this case).
13. I use the notion "discursive" here as a general expression for studying ideas and meaning making in policy processes whereas I consider frame analysis as a particular kind of discursive policy analysis. Frame analysis can, thus, be used as a specific methodological measure to identify broader discursive shifts and contestations in policy development.
14. Bacchi (2005) is critical toward the sociological frame theories because they tend to focus exclusively on the strategic shaping of frames (agency) instead of uncovering the underlying premises (structure). She argues that frames contain both an intentional element, making

it possible to use them strategically (collective action frames), and a cognitive element, which works on the unconscious level (interpretation frames).
15. The CFA approach has been developed in relation to the MAGEEQ (2003–2005) and the QUING (2006–2011) projects, both directed by Mieke Verloo and funded by the EC (Framework programs 5 and 6).
16. I include the three major EU institutions in the analysis, that is, the ones that are most directly involved in the policy-making processes (Council, Commission, Parliament). This means that the European Court of Justice, for instance, is excluded, despite its crucial role in terms of interpreting EU legislation (see for instance Hoskyns 1996). It is not directly a part of the key policy-making processes but rather an interpreter of these. The European Social and Economic Council is not included, either, even though it is the official voice of civil society organizations and social partners. I have chosen a different perspective on civil society interaction, which focuses on bilateral relations between the individual organizations and the EU in their formal and informal expressions. Here, I include only NGOs as civil society actors. This means that the European social partners, for instance, are not covered by the analysis: the social dialogue is a highly formalized process that differs considerably from the informal way in which NGOs and women's organizations are consulted in the EU.
17. All in all, 28 semistructured interviews have been conducted between 2007 and 2010: six interviews with officials from the EC (mainly DG Employment and DG Justice), six interviews with current and former members of the EP (FEMM Committee), eight interviews with officials from the Council of the EU (General Secretariat and member states' permanent representations), and eight interviews with leading representatives of transnational European women's organizations (European Women's Lobby [EWL], European Women Lawyers Association [EWLA], Women Against Violence Europe [WAVE], Black European Women's Council [BEWC], New Women for Europe [NWFE], Women Citizens of Europe Network/Red Ciudadanas de Europa [RCE], and Young Women from Minorities [WFM]). The interviews conducted can be characterized as both expert interviews and elite interviews: the interviewees are all experts within the field of interest of this book, that is, gender equality policies in the EU, and they are almost all part of the European elite, occupying jobs in the EU institutions or forming part of the leading groups of transnational, European organizations. Thus, they are covered by a definition of political elite interviewees as persons in "close proximity" to political power and policy making (Lilleker 2003).
18. The concept of power is used differently across the material; power is a plurifaceted and multidimensional term, and the empirical evidence analyzed here points to the relevance of different aspects of power. The EU institutions are characterized by their decision-making power, on

the one hand, and their institutional and discursive power to constitute legitimate claims makers (in civil society) and attribute voice and visibility (through inclusion and funding, for example), on the other. I interpret the power of civil society actors as discursive, deliberative and related to empowerment when actors mobilize, gain voice and are being recognized in the transnational political space. Thus, civil society actors gain power as a result of the strength of their ideas as well as their potential role as agents of social and political change. Civil society actors contribute to the democratic legitimacy of the political institutions through participatory (rather than representative) processes as well as lobbying efforts, and policy issues can easier be advanced institutionally if they count on civil society support and pressure.
19. The QUING project (Quality in Gender Equality+ Policies, 2006–2011) is financed under the EC's sixth Framework Programme and directed by Mieke Verloo.

1 Policy making, Institutionalization, and Collective Mobilization: A Model for Transnational Intersectional Analysis

1. Kantola combines the analysis of discourse, power, and gender through a methodological framework including feminist discourse analysis, comparative method, and institutional analysis (feminist comparative discourse analysis) in order to look at institutional constraints and opportunities, especially related to gender blindness and state feminism. She thereby addresses the discussions on structure and agency as well as change and continuity (2006). Here feminist discourse analysis is adopted in the institutional analysis but, contrary to Kantola, I do not apply these aspects to a comparative study of nation states. Kantola is aware of the influence of the suprastate level on national policies, but this is not the focus of her analysis (ibid.).
2. The main shortfalls of historical institutionalism as an individual approach are its tendency to explain continuity (by focusing on path dependency, for example) rather than change and its, at times, weak attention to the reasons why critical junctures emerge. Discursive institutionalism and gendered institutionalism contribute to counteracting these shortfalls theoretically.
3. Some authors refer to this approach as feminist institutionalism, others use the term gendered institutionalism. I prefer the latter because part of my empirical endeavor is precisely to determine what meaning is given to ideas like "gender equality," "feminism," and "women's interests" in the policy-making processes of the EU.
4. See also Krook and Mackay (2011) as well as Mackay (2011) for extended discussions on feminist institutionalism.

5. Again, I want to emphasize that there is a link between the new institutionalism approach and the question posed by Kantola (2006), on the one hand, and the theory on opportunity structures developed by Tarrow (1998), on the other.
6. According to Locher (2007), a constructivist focus is particularly relevant for the analysis of EU policy-making processes as these are usually informal and situated within a space of considerable communicative action and a high number of relevant actors.
7. If the Council rejects a proposal coming out of the consultation procedure, unanimity is required (Cini 2007).
8. Tarrow distinguishes internationalization from globalization, defining the latter as the "increased flows of trade, finance, and people across borders" (2005, 8). Transnational social movements can protest and mobilize against globalization as content whereas internationalization provides the framework of this mobilization (ibid.).
9. Academic debates on the concept of intersectionality abound. See for instance special issues of *European Journal of Women's Studies* 13(3) 2006, *Politics and Gender* 3(2) 2007, *International Feminist Journal of Politics* 11(4) 2009, and *Kvinder, køn og forskning* (Women, Gender and Research) 2/3 2006 and 2/3 2010.

2 Gender and Other Inequalities in the Institutionalization of Multiple Discrimination Policies

1. The 2004 EC Green Paper primarily focuses on the corporate strand of diversity, that is, the positive effects of diversity on companies' productivity and competitiveness.
2. See also the EC Green Paper "Equality and Non-Discrimination in an Enlarged European Union" (COM[2004]379).
3. On the international level, the process around the UN Beijing Platform for Action also resulted in increased mobilization.
4. According to Cichowski (2002), women's activism on the European transnational level and activists' participation in EU policy making were triggered by the debates around the equal pay provision of the Treaty of Rome (1957). Activists contributed to an interpretation of the legal act favoring social justice and gender equality goals even though the treaty article was originally aimed at counteracting uneven competition between member states within the common market.
5. The grounds of discrimination with their corresponding European umbrella organization are as follows: gender/EWL, age/European Older People's Platform, sexual orientation/International Lesbian and Gay Association, race/European Network Against Racism, and disability/European Disability Forum.

6. See the EC report "Tackling Multiple Discrimination. Practices, Policies and Laws" (2007).
7. See for instance the EC White Paper on governance (SEC[2000] 1547/7 final) and the EC Plan D for Democracy, Dialogue and Debate (COM[2005] 494 final).
8. "Wide consultation before proposing legislation" is a duty of the EC, according to Protocol no. 7 of the Amsterdam Treaty (europa.eu).
9. The latter merits special attention for being the most comprehensive study of the EWL to date. Strid (2009) argues that the "corporatist policymaking style of the European Commission" bases its legitimacy on organized interests and their representativeness. The EWL has adapted its structure and organizational form to the requisites of representativeness of the EC in order to gain funding and influence. In particular, the EWL has to be able to lobby on multiple levels in accordance with the decision-making structure of the EU, frame policies in a manner resonant with the EC objectives, and control the "interests aggregated" from member organizations. Strid demonstrates that the latter occurs through a "mechanism of moderation," which is "inherent in the process of adopting motions at the General Assembly," (2009, 251) and, thus, not imposed from above, that is, by the Brussels secretariat, as might be expected.
10. These analyses cover a number of methodological approaches of both quantitative and qualitative nature as well as a series of thematic dimensions such as network analysis of internet links between transnational women's organizations' websites (Pudrovska and Ferree 2004) and interviews and web-based data analysis of European women's networks practicing advocacy in relation to the gender mainstreaming strategy (Lang 2009), just to mention a few.

3 Minority Intersectional Constituencies and Women's Collective Mobilization at the European Level

1. There is, however, a parallel between the way in which I focus on the representation of minority women and their voice in politics and the theoretizations of Mohanty (2002), for example, within the realm of postcolonial feminism.
2. Exceptions are related to two different spheres of transnational activism: Whereas Woodward (2007) and Woodward and Wiercx (2003) mainly focus on large European umbrella organizations with a strong interaction with the EU institutions, Della Porta (2007) and Della Porta and Caiani (2007) address protest movements that do not engage in lobbying activities vis-à-vis the EU.
3. For analyses and theoretical debates on national women's movements, women's policy agencies and state feminism, see for example the research

conducted in relation to the RNGS project (Research Network on Gender Politics and the State).
4. Austria, Greece, the Netherlands, Ireland, Italy, Sweden, Switzerland, and United Kingdom.
5. See the EWL reports "Confronting the Fortress–Black and Migrant Women in the European Union" (1995), "Overcoming Discrimination. Selected Strategies Empowering Black, Ethnic Minority and Migrant Women" (1999), as well as the EWL Project "Equal Rights, Equal Voices. Migrant Women in the European Union" (2006).
6. For instance in the seminar "Incorporating Gender in Integration Policies: The Way Forward," celebrated the first of December 2008 in Brussels. The participating migrant women's associations were, among others, the African Women's Network, the Businesswomen Organisation of Lithuanian Ethnic Groups, the Immigrant Council of Ireland, the RESPECT network, and the European Network of Migrant Women.
7. Myria Vassiliadou is former secretary general of the EWL.
8. Other studies focus on how majority women's organizations address issues related to ethnic minority women at the national level as well as comparatively, resulting in "paternalism or paralysis" (Pristed Nielsen and Thun 2010), on how national women's organizations may use the European transnational level to gain leverage for their policy claims domestically, enabling or constraining their struggles for recognition (Hobson 2003; Hobson et al. 2007), or on the way in which women's organizations from Central and Eastern European countries experienced opportunities and constraints before and after the EU accession process (Roth 2007). In the latter case, the EU framework provided an opportunity to push national gender equality policies forward during the accession process whereas the time after the enlargement was considered more difficult because funding for women's NGOs at the EU level was not easy to obtain, and previously active foreign donors withdrew from Central and Eastern European countries (ibid.).
9. Women Against Violence Europe (WAVE) aims to combat violence against women and children, and promote women's and children's human rights. Even though the activities of the WAVE network (founded 1994) were initiated in relation to the World Conference on Women in Beijing in 1995, and as such emerged in the context of the UN rather than the EU, the network itself explains that the basic structure was not developed until 1997 when it was granted its first funding through the EC DAPHNE program.
10. Young Women from Minorities (WFM) aims to promote social integration of young minority women as well as overcome discrimination and exclusion. The WFM (founded 1995) emerged in the context of a youth campaign, in this case launched by the Council of Europe, titled "All Different–All Equal" through which the organization received funding for a pilot project and continued the work and the operation of the organization after the project and the campaign expired.

11. As a way to remedy this problem, the organization in question uses a rotation principle whereby the conferences are held in different countries each year. This also foments the participation of activists from the more marginal countries or regions as they will participate in the conferences due to the proximity of their location (WAVE representative, interview November 2008).
12. The two categories ("ethnic minority women" and "migrant women") are typically addressed together in the policy documents though they may differ considerably in terms of rights, demands, interests, and needs.
13. Yvette Jarvis is vice president of BEWC.
14. Some interviewees also underline the specialized field of their organization as unique and complementary to the broad perspective of the EWL, for example. Thus, specialized newsletters with advance information on key events (RCE representative, interview January 2008) or in-depth knowledge about legal issues and fundamental rights (EWLA representative, interview May 2010), for example, are highlighted.
15. Beatrice Achaleke is president of BEWC.

4 Gender-Based Violence and the Framing of Equality Policies

1. I use the terms "gender-based violence" and "violence against women" interchangeably when I refer to the general policies. The latter is the term most commonly used by the EU institutions.
2. Montoya (2008; 2013) analyses the EU accession process in particular and argues that it was seen as a political opportunity for national organizations to improve their capacity within the area of gender-based violence. The accession process combined legal transposition with softer measures such as social learning (Krizsán and Popa 2010), capacity building, and norm diffusion (Montoya 2008; 2013).
3. Furthermore, the transposition of EU directives at the member-state level worked as an opportunity structure for national advocates to influence interpretations and advance policies (Zippel 2004; 2006).
4. The public/private divide is related to state intervention or lack thereof: When defined as a private problem, states have no role to play in the area of gender-based violence whereas the contrary is the case with a definition focusing on the public nature of the problem. This is, to a certain extent, related to ideological positions regarding the normative role of the state as interventionist or not.
5. Directive 2002/73/EC of the EP and of the Council of 23 September 2002 amending Council Directive 76/207/EEC on the implementation of the principle of equal treatment for men and women as regards access to employment, vocational training and promotion, and working conditions.

6. Here a distinction is made between "output" as policy texts and discourses and "outcome" as the implementation of policies, that is, the material consequences.
 7. The expression "young persons" was employed in the first DAPHNE program whereas "young people" was used in the second and third. For reasons of clarity I will use the expression "young people" except when referring to specific document titles.
 8. In the fall 2007 I did a research stay at Complutense University (Madrid) where I worked with the Spanish QUING team, led by María Bustelo. Later, I was temporarily employed as a research assistant (2009) and a postdoctoral student (2011) on the project. I was particularly involved in the CFA of EU policies on gender-based violence together with the EU team (Emanuela Lombardo and Ana Fernández de Vega). The collaboration was developed through various research reports (Fernández de Vega, Lombardo and Rolandsen Agustín 2008a; 2008b; 2008c) and research seminars of the QUING project.
 9. Sensitizing questions can be for instance "who are the voices speaking in the text?," "what is represented as the problem?", and "which action is deemed necessary and why?."
10. The empirical material includes a wide range of document types, such as calls for proposals, common positions, communications, debates, decisions, declarations, directives, recommendations, reports, resolutions, opinions, presidency conclusions, proceedings, speeches, working documents, and green and white papers. See List of empirical documents.
11. In this particular policy tracing and in the general tracing and selection of the key policy documents within the policy area, different EU databases were used, that is, the EUR-LEX (database on EU law texts), the Public Register of the Council of the EU, the EP Register of Documents, the EP Legislative Observatory (with procedure files of policy processes), and the EP Archive and Documentation Centre (CARDOC).
12. The lack of a European social model can be interpreted as part of the explanation for the democratic crisis of the EU in general, with increasing citizen skepticism in the 2000s (as expressed, for example, in the treaty referendums in France and the Netherlands—Constitutional Treaty, 2005—as well as in Ireland—Lisbon Treaty, 2008).
13. Montoya (2013) focuses on EP policy documents in her classification and adds a separate analysis of the DAPHNE program. Thus, the last stage of the 2000s in Montoya's account is related to two resolutions adopted in the EP in 2006 and 2009 respectively.
14. The Committee on Women's Rights requested authorization to elaborate the report in December 1984, and the work was done throughout the following two years. The adopted resolution is identical to the text proposed in the report, but it also adds some new paragraphs. In general, the new elements take the recommendations further, for instance, in terms of data, financial aid, research, financial independence of

women, and the possibility of reporting cases of trafficking without being expelled from the country of residence.
15. The Parliamentary Assembly was established in 1958. In 1962 it changed its name to the EP. It was an appointed assembly (by the member states' national parliaments) until June 1979 when the first direct elections were held.
16. Nevertheless, the same interviewee also highlights the problematic relationship between the EU and the civil society organizations. Within the policy area of gender-based violence, the EU has funded many projects and the civil society has, to a certain extent, served as a service provider: "You could say as well [that the women's organizations] have been instrumentalized... because they've been sort of given the role to push forward a campaign... but I mean, it's a way to collaborate that's been quite effective" (EC official, BEPA, interview January 2008).
17. The EP FEMM Committee also issued an own initiative report on violence against women in 2005 (2004/2220[INI], 09.12.05). This report is framed in a feminist fashion as men's violence against women is explicitly stated as the main problem because it violates human rights and is based on men's superior position in relation to women. The gender power structures are a barrier to overcoming inequality and violence against women. The document addresses the economic dependency and the economic needs of women who are victims of violence. A multidimensional solution is suggested: Legal action should be combined with medical, social, and psychological measures in order to ensure prevention, protection, and support of victims, as well as training of professionals.
18. During the 1990s, the EC focused first and foremost on sexual harassment within the broader field of gender-based violence. The third medium-term Community Action Programme on Equal Opportunities for Women and Men (1991–1995) (COM[90]449) addressed the way in which sexual harassment affects the dignity of women and men at work, whereas the fourth Community Action Programme (1996–2000) (COM[95]381) broadened the scope to the fundamental right of women to both live and work in violence free environments. In the EC gender equality programs of the 2000s, violence against women is articulated under the heading "Promoting gender equality in civil life" (COM[2000]335). Domestic violence and trafficking are now the main areas of concern and they are perceived as a matter of women's human rights and structural gender inequalities, breaching the "fundamental right to life, safety, freedom, dignity and integrity" (COM[2006]92; COM[2010]491).
19. Policy actions are usually divided in prevention (gender equality for example), protection (human rights for example), support (public health for example) and prosecution (criminalization for example), and multidisciplinary solutions are preferred in progressive framings. This includes economic measures (economic independence as prevention or economic support for victims), labor market policies, and housing policies. The

history of combating gender-based violence is related to support and empowerment through the shelter movement. Only later did protection and prosecution for instance as well as state intervention emerge. One of the main issues now is the marketization of support services, that are being tendered out with potentially huge consequences for the NGOs and voluntary shelters.

20. See for instance the Spanish Presidency conclusions on violence against women (6994/02), the Dutch Presidency conclusions on the Ministerial Conference Diversity and participation: The gender perspective (12644/04), the Irish report on Presidency activities, Dublin Conference on violence against women (9828/04), the draft council conclusions on sexual harassment at the workplace (15202/04), draft Council conclusions on men and gender equality (14845/06), the Work program of the French Presidency (Autumn 2008), council conclusions on the review of the implementation by the member states and the EU institutions of the Beijing Platform for Action–the girl child (09.06.2008), and the EU guidelines on violence against women and girls and combating all forms of discrimination against them (16175/08).

21. Article 2 of the Treaty of the EU reads: "The Union is founded on the values of respect for human dignity, freedom, democracy, equality, the rule of law and respect for human rights, including the rights of persons belonging to minorities. These values are common to the member states in a society in which pluralism, non-discrimination, tolerance, justice, solidarity and equality between women and men prevail."

22. In terms of the latter, the conservative group of the EP wanted the directive to be about female genital mutilation instead of domestic violence broadly. The report was drafted by the chairwoman of the FEMM Committee, Eva-Britt Svensson of the leftist GUE/NGL, and the final text addresses the issue of violence broadly and from a multidimensional approach, which includes clear gender inequality and criminalization framings.

5 Transnational Policy Framings: (De)Gendering in the Context of Institutionalization

1. This issue is also touched upon in the 1986 report through the attached opinion of the committee on Legal Affairs and Citizens' Rights of the EP. It is noted that violence against women is covered by criminal law and, as such, falls under the competence of the member states. Community law cannot be used in this case because it does not provide for such measures as the community is mainly economic in nature. However, according to the opinion of the committee, the issue of violence against women could be interpreted more broadly and linked, as in the framing of the report, to sexual and economic dependence. Furthermore it is

argued that community law has already been extended, in some cases, to cover issues over which the community actually has no jurisdiction per se. In an effort to encounter a potential legal basis for community action within the field of violence against women, fundamental rights and the European Convention on Human Rights are mentioned as are the articles 100 and 235 of the EEC Treaty, which deal with the possibilities of harmonizing laws and, especially, authorizing community action where this is considered necessary in order to attain a community objective. It is, however, concluded that the social-policy provisions of the said treaty (articles 117–128) "offer the greatest scope for effective Community action to combat violence against women."

2. As of July 1, 2010, DG Justice was divided into two DGs: one for Home Affairs and one for Justice and Fundamental Rights. The DAPHNE program is situated in the latter.
3. The draft Council conclusions on gender equality originate in the Social Questions Working Party. The first DAPHNE project was negotiated by the Working Parties on Youth; on Social Questions; and on Public Health (3627/1/99 REV 1). In the second program, the Working Party on Justice Internal Affairs was added (3647/04), and finally the third program was negotiated solely by the Social Questions Working Party and the Justice Internal Affairs Working Party (3626/07).
4. The rules of qualified majority voting apply in the Council (see Introduction).
5. EWL and WAVE are the two most important NGOs within the field of gender-based violence at the European level. They both have a long history of activism, coordination, and lobbying in relation to gender-based violence. Institutionally, they have built strong structures to support the fight against violence. The EWL has set up a Centre on Violence against Women, which works to eliminate men's violence against women and furthermore manages the EWL European Observatory on Violence against Women, focusing on the improvement of policies within the area. WAVE, on the other hand, coordinates 91 Focal Points at the national level that collect and disseminate information on gender-based violence and work as contact points and information channels.
6. I want to underline the differentiation between the economic consequences (costs) and the economic causes (socioeconomic status) of public health problems. Both Community Action Programmes address the "socioeconomic health determinants," that is, the fact that persons with a lower socioeconomic status are more exposed to certain kinds of illnesses. The point I am getting at here does not relate to these concerns but to the costs of public ill-health in terms of hospital and medical care expenditures, for example.
7. Very similar formulations can be found both in the DAPHNE I and in the DAPHNE III programs.

8. The analysis builds on the descriptions of the projects selected in the period from 1997 to 2005. The project descriptions have been accessed through the DAPHNE toolkit website, which contains a database with all projects in the given period. On average, 46 projects were selected per year for grants of 12 to 24 months' duration. In 2004 and 2005, the average financing was between €100,000 and €200,000 (approximately $130.000-$260.000). The overall annual budget has been increased steadily, rising from €6.8 million ($8.8 million) in 2004 to €14.5 million ($18.8 million) in 2010.
9. There is only one case (2005-1-127-Y) where a project in the "bullying/violence in school" subframe is gendered; this is related to education in values of equality and respect in order to create positive relationship values in young people and avoid violence.
10. When treatment is suggested as a prognostic policy action or when training programs are directed toward health care professionals, for example, the scope of the measures depends on whether the ultimate target groups are victims or perpetrators. The measures are reactive if they address the victims, and they seem to convey an individualistic/pathological approach to the problem if targeted at perpetrators. In neither case do they address the root causes of the problem directly, like education, empowerment or awareness raising might, aiming at a change in attitudes and of the dominant social construction of (asymmetrical) gendered power relations.
11. The transversal public health frame is usually articulated more straightforwardly, like in the case of a project on the "health needs of women and adolescents who have been trafficked" (2002-082-WY). This project addresses the impact on health and well-being, which results from experiences of trafficking, and it deals only implicitly with gender equality dimensions.

6 Problematizing the "Gendered Other": Integration, Violence, and Culturalization

1. Based on the empirical results of the EUROSPHERE project, Mokre and Siim (2013) add to this a third distinction, namely ambiguous intersectionality, whereby diversity is seen as both furthering and hindering equality.
2. The report (Doc. 1-829/80, 29.01.81) states that provisions should be made to include wives in a European statute for foreign workers as a part of a Council framework for harmonizing policies on migration.
3. Culture is mentioned in the report but in relation to intergroup relations (host country population and minority groups), not intragroup dynamics.

4. The report (A2-44/86) furthermore states that women from minority groups should be able to deal only with female officers, if their "religious or cultural traditions do not permit them to meet and/or talk with men."

Conclusions

1. Until 2002, a single budget line for EU funds to women's organizations was earmarked for EWL. Around the turn of the century this was strongly criticized by conservative and right-wing MEPs as a way of monopolizing the voice of women, with the argument that one organization should not represent all European women. As a result the new Community Action Programme, which was adopted unanimously in the FEMM Committee, streamlined the financial requirements for organizations applying for funds with a common cofinancing rate of maximum 80 percent EU funding. Two types of budget lines with operating grants were envisaged: One for the EWL (though this was only mentioned in the annex) and one for other women's organizations, which had to go through a process of calls for proposals. A new multiannual framework program, the Community Programme for Employment and Social Solidarity (PROGRESS) (1672/2006/EC), was adopted in 2006 with a full harmonization of funding whereby calls for tenders apply in all cases and no particular organizations are mentioned in the policy text.

Bibliography

Achaleke, Beatrice. 2007. "The Dilemma of Black Women (interview)." *Equal Voices* 22:22–4.
Ahrens, Petra. 2008. "More Actors Butter no Parsnips: Gaining Insights into Gender Equality Programs of the European Union." Paper presented at the Fourth Pan-European Conference on EU Politics, University of Latvia, September 25–27.
———. 2010. "Mapping Gender Equality Policy Networks in the European Union." Paper presented at the ECPR Joint Sessions, Westfälische Wilhelms-Universität Münster, March 22–27.
Askola, Heli. 2007. "Violence against Women, Trafficking, and Migration in the European Union." *European Law Journal* 13(2):204–217.
Bacchi, Carol L. 1999. *Women, Policy and Politics: The Construction of Policy Problems*. London: Sage.
———. 2005. "Discourse, Discourse Everywhere: Subject 'Agency' in Feminist Discourse Methodology." *Nordic Journal of Women's Studies* 13(3):199–209.
———. 2009a. "The Issue of Intentionality in Frame Theory: The Need for Reflexive Framing." In *The Discursive Politics of Gender Equality: Stretching, Bending and Policymaking*, edited by Emanuela Lombardo, Petra Meier, and Mieke Verloo, 19–35. London: Routledge.
———. 2009b. *Analysing Policy: What's the Problem Represented to be?* Frenchs Forest: Pearson.
Balme, Richard, and Didier Chabanet. 2008. *European Governance and Democracy. Power and Protest in the EU*. Lanham: Rowman & Littlefield.
Beck, Ulrich. 2002. "The Cosmopolitan Society and Its Enemies." *Theory, Culture & Society* 19(1–2):17–44.
Béland, Daniel. 2009. "Gender, Ideational Analysis, and Social Policy." *Social Politics* 16(4):558–581.
Bell, Mark. 2002. *Anti-discrimination Law and the European Union*. Oxford: Oxford University Press.
Borchorst, Anette, and Monika Mokre. 2013. "The EU's Gender and Diversity Policies and the European Public Spheres." In *Negotiating Gender and Diversity in an Emergent European Public Sphere*, edited by Monika Mokre, and Birte Siim, 141–160. New York: Palgrave Macmillan.

Borchorst, Anette, and Mari Teigen. 2010. "Political Intersectionality. Tackling Inequalities in Public Policies in Scandinavia." *Kvinder, Køn & Forskning* 2–3:19–28.

Bretherton, Charlotte, and Liz Sperling. 1996. "Women's Networks and the European Union: Towards an Inclusive Approach?." *Journal of Common Market Studies* 34(4):487–508.

Briceño, Ybelice. 2004. "Inmigración, exclusión y construcción de la alteridad." In *Políticas de ciudadanía y sociedad civil en tiempos de globalización*, edited by Daniel Mato, 201–219. Caracas: FACES, Universidad Central de Venezuela.

Bygnes, Susanne. 2013. "'We Are in Complete Agreement': The Diversity Issue, Disagreement and Change in the European Women's Lobby." *Social Movement Studies* 12(2):199–213.

Carbin, Maria. 2010. *Mellan tystnad och tal. Flickor och hedersvåld i svensk offentlig politik*. Doctoral dissertation, University of Stockholm.

Christensen, Ann-Dorte, and Birte Siim. 2006. "Fra køn til diversitet- intersektionalitet i en dansk/nordisk kontekst." *Kvinder, Køn & Forskning* 2–3:32–42.

———. 2010. "Citizenship and Politics of Belonging–Inclusionary and Exclusionary Framings of Gender and Ethnicity." *Kvinder, Køn & Forskning* 2–3:8–17.

Christiansen, Thomas, Knud Erik Jørgensen, and Antje Wiener (eds). 1999. *The Social Construction of Europe*. London: Sage.

Cichowski, Rachel A. 2002. "'No Discrimination Whatsoever'. Women's Transnational Activism and the Evolution of EU Sex Equality Policy." In *Women's Activism and Globalization: Linking Local Struggles and Transnational Politics*, edited by Nancy A. Naples, and Manisha Desai, 220–238. New York: Routledge.

Cini, Michelle. 2007. *European Union Politics*. Oxford: Oxford University Press.

Collins, Evelyn. 1996. "European Union Sexual Harassment Policy." In *Sexual Politics and the European Union. The New Feminist Challenge*, edited by R. Amy Elman, 23–34. Providence: Berghahn Books.

Crenshaw, Kimberle W. 1991. "Mapping the Margins: Intersectionality, Identity Politics, and Violence against Women of Color." *Stanford Law Review* 43(6):1241–1299.

Cullen, Pauline. 2005. "Conflict and Cooperation within the Platform of European Social NGOs." In *Coalitions across Borders. Transnational Protest and the Neoliberal Order*, edited by Joe Bandy, and Jackie Smith, 71–94. Lanham: Rowman & Littlefield.

Cunningham, Susan. 1992. "The Development of Equal Opportunities Theory and Practice in the European Community." *Policy and Politics* 20(3):177–189.

De los Reyes, Paulina. 2003. *Patriarkala enklaver eller ingemansland? Våld, hot och kontroll mot unga kvinnor i Sverige*. Integrationsverkets skriftserie IV, Integrationsverket.

Della Porta, Donatella. 2007. "The Emergence of European Movements? Civil Society and the EU." CINEFOGO working paper no. 1.29.
Della Porta, Donatella, and Manuela Caiani. 2007. "Europeanization From Below? Social Movements and Europe." *Mobilization* 12(1):1–20.
Dombos, Tamás et al. 2009. "Critical Frame Analysis: A Comparative Methodology for the QUING Project." Paper presented at the ECPR First European Conference on Politics and Gender, Queen's University Belfast, January 21–23.
Dombos, Tamás, Anna Horváth, and Andrea Krizsán. 2007. "Where Did Gender Disappear? Anti-Discrimination Policy in the EU Accession Process in Hungary." In *Multiple Meanings of Gender Equality. A Critical Frame Analysis of Gender Policies in Europe*, edited by Mieke Verloo, 233–252. Budapest: Central European University Press.
Dostal, Jörg Michael. 2004. "Campaigning on Expertise: How the OECD Framed EU Welfare and Labour Market Policies—and Why Success Could Trigger Failure." *Journal of European Public Policy* 11(3):440–460.
Dryzek, John S. 2004. *Deliberative Democracy and Beyond: Liberals, Critics, Contestations.* Oxford: Oxford University Press.
———. 2005. *The Politics of the Earth: Environmental Discourses.* Oxford: Oxford University Press.
Duncan, Simon. 1996. "Obstacles to a Successful Equal Opportunities Policy in the European Union." *The European Journal of Women's Studies* 3(4):399–422.
Elgström, Ole. 2000. "Norm Negotiations: The Construction of New Norms Regarding Gender and Development in EU Foreign Aid Policy." *Journal of European Public Policy* 7(3):457–476.
Elman, R. Amy. 2007. *Sexual Equality in an Integrated Europe. Virtual Equality.* New York: Palgrave Macmillan.
Fernández de Vega, Ana, and Emanuela Lombardo. 2008. *QUING WHY Country Context Studies: The European Union.* Vienna: Institut für die Wissenschaften vom Menschen.
Fernández de Vega, Ana, Emanuela Lombardo, and Lise Rolandsen Agustín. 2008a. *QUING LARG Comparative Country Studies: The European Union.* Vienna: Institut für die Wissenschaften vom Menschen.
———. 2008b. *QUING STRIQ Intersectionality Report: The European Union.* Vienna: Institut für die Wissenschaften vom Menschen.
———. 2008c. *QUING LARG Country Report: The European Union.* Vienna: Institut für die Wissenschaften vom Menschen.
Ferree, Myra Marx. 2003. "Resonance and Radicalism: Feminist Framing in the Abortion Debates of the United States and Germany." *The American Journal of Sociology* 109(2):304–344.
———. 2008. "Framing Equality: The Politics of Race, Class, Gender in the US, Germany, and the Expanding European Union." In *The Gender Politics in the Expanding European Union: Mobilization, Inclusion, Exclusion*, edited by Silke Roth, 237–255. New York: Berghahn Publishers.

———. 2009. "Inequality, Intersectionality and the Politics of Discourse: Framing Feminist Alliances." In *The Discursive Politics of Gender Equality: Stretching, Bending and Policymaking*, edited by Emanuela Lombardo, Petra Meier, and Mieke Verloo, 86–104. London: Routledge.

———. 2012. *Varieties of Feminism. German Gender Politics in Global Perspective*. Stanford: Stanford University Press.

Ferree, Myra M., William A. Gamson, Jürgen Gerhards, and Dieter Rucht. 2002. *Shaping Abortion Discourse: democracy and the public sphere in Germany and the United States*. Cambridge: Cambridge University Press.

Ferree, Myra Marx, and David A. Merrill. 2000. "Hot Movements, Cold Cognition: Thinking about Social Movements in Gendered Frames." *Contemporary Sociology* 29(3):454–462.

Finnemore, Martha, and Kathryn Sikkink. 1998. "International Norm Dynamics and Political Change." *International Organization* 52(4):887–917.

Forest, Maxime. 2009. "Did Newcomers Make a Difference? Making Equality in the EU-27." Paper presented at the ECPR First European Conference on Politics and Gender, Queen's University Belfast, January 21–23.

García Agustín, Óscar. 2008. "Fronteras discursivas: Las políticas migratorias de inclusión y exclusión en la Unión Europea." *Discurso & Sociedad* 2:646–768.

———. 2010. *Discurso e institutionalización. Un enfoque sobre el cambio social y lingüístico*. Logroño: Universidad de la Rioja.

Goffman, Erving. 1974. *Frame Analysis. An Essay on the Organization of Experience*. Boston: Northeastern University Press.

Gregory, Jeanne. 2006. "Sexual Harassment: The Impact of EU Law in the Member States." In *Gender Policies in the European Union*, edited by Mariagrazia Rossilli, 75–92. New York: Peter Lang.

Grewal, Inderpal, and Caren Kaplan. 1994. *Scattered Hegemonies: Postmodernity and Transnational Feminist Practices*. Minneapolis: University of Minnesota Press.

———. 2000. "Postcolonial Studies and Transnational Feminist Practices." *Jouvert–A Journal of Postcolonial Studies* 5(1).

Hafner-Burton, Emilie, and Mark A. Pollack. 2000. "Mainstreaming Gender in the European Union." *Journal of European Public Policy* 7(3):432–56.

Hall, Peter A., and Rosemary Taylor. 1996. "Political Science and the Three New Institutionalisms." Paper presented as a public lecture during MPIFG Scientific Advisory Board Meeting, May.

Hancock, Ange-Marie. 2007. "When Multiplication Doesn't Equal Quick Addition: Examining Intersectionality as a Research Paradigm." *Perspectives on Politics* 5(1):63–79.

Hanmer, Jalna. 1996. "The Common Market of Violence." In *Sexual Politics and the European Union. The New Feminist Challenge*, edited by R. Amy Elman, 131–145. Providence: Berghahn Books.

Helfferich, Barbara, and Felix Kolb. 2001. "Multilevel Action Coordination in European Contentious Politics: The Case of the European Women's

Lobby." In *Contentious Europeans. Protest and Politics in an Emerging Policy*, edited by Douglas Imig, and Sidney Tarrow, 143–161. Lanham: Rowman and Littlefield.

Hjort, Katrin. 1997. *Diskurs – analyser af tekst og kontekst*. Frederiksberg: Samfundslitteratur.

Hobson, Barbara. 2003. "Recognition Struggles in Universalistic and Gender Distinctive Frames: Sweden and Ireland." In *Recognition Struggles and Social Movements: Contested Identities, Agency and Power*, edited by Barbara Hobson, 64–92. New York: Cambridge University Press.

Hobson, Barbara, Marcus Carson, and Rebecca Lawrence. 2007. "Recognition Struggles in Transnational Arenas: Negotiating Identities and Framing Citizenship." *Critical Review of International Social and Political Philosophy* 10(4):443–470.

Hooghe, Liesbet, and Gary Marks. 2001. *Multi-level Governance and European Integration*. Lanham: Rowman & Littlefield.

Hoskyns, Catherine. 1991. "The European Women's Lobby." *Feminist Review* 38:67–70.

———. 1996. *Integrating Gender: Women, Law and Politics in the European Union*. London: Verso.

Jarvis, Yvette. 2008. "Black Women Politics and Policy." Speech at the launch of the Black European Women's Council, Brussels, September 9.

Jenson, Jane, and Rianne Mahon. 1993. "Representing Solidarity: Class, Gender and the Crisis of Social Democratic Sweden." *New Left Review* 201:76–100.

Jørgensen, Marianne, and Louise Phillips. 2002. *Discourse Analysis as Theory and Method*. London: Sage.

Kantola, Johanna. 2006. *Feminists Theorize the State*. New York: Palgrave Macmillan.

———. 2010. *Gender and the European Union*. New York: Palgrave Macmillan.

Kantola, Johanna, and Kevät Nousiainen. 2009. "Institutionalising Intersectionality in Europe: Introducing the Theme." *International Feminist Journal of Politics* 11(4):459–477.

Kantola, Johanna, and Kevät Nousiainen. 2012. "The European Union: Initiator of a New European Anti-Discrimination Regime?." In *Institutionalising Intersectionality: The Changing Nature of European Equality Regimes*, edited by Andrea Krizsán, Hege Skjeie, and Judith Squires, 33–58 New York: Palgrave Macmillan.

Keck, Margaret E., and Kathryn Sikkink. 1998. *Activists beyond Borders. Advocacy Networks in International Politics*. Ithaca: Cornell University Press.

Kenny, Meryl. 2007. "Gender, Institutions and Power: A Critical Review." *Politics* 27(2):91–100.

Kenny, Meryl, and Fiona Mackay. 2009. "Already Doin' It for Ourselves? Skeptical Notes on Feminism and Institutionalism." *Politics & Gender* 5(2):271–280.

Khagram, Sanjeev, James V. Riker, and Kathryn Sikkink (eds). 2002. *Restructuring World Politics. Transnational Social Movements, Networks, and Norms.* Minneapolis: University of Minnesota Press.

Krizsán, Andrea, María Bustelo, Andromachi Hadjiyanni, and Fray Kamoutis. 2007. "Domestic Violence: A Public Matter." In *Multiple Meanings of Gender Equality. A Critical Frame Analysis of Gender Policies in Europe*, edited by Mieke Verloo, 141–186. Budapest: Central European University Press.

Krizsán, Andrea, Marjolein Paantjens, and Ilse van Lamoen. 2005. "Domestic Violence: Who's Problem?." *The Greek Review of Social Research* 117B:63–92.

Krizsán, Andrea, and Raluca Popa. 2008. "The Spillover Effects of Europeanization: EU Conditionality, Norm Diffusion and Strategic Discursive Action in Domestic Violence Policies in Central and Eastern Europe." Paper prepared for GARNET PhD School, Kassel, December.

———. 2010. "Europeanization in Making Policies against Domestic Violence in Central and Eastern Europe." *Social Politics* 17(3):379–406.

———. Forthcoming. "Frames in Contestations: Gendering Domestic Violence Policies in Five Central and Eastern European Countries." *Violence against Women.*

Krizsán, Andrea, and Mieke Verloo. 2006. *D9 Frame and Voice Analysis Methodology Manual* (QUING unpublished report). Vienna: Institut für die Wissenschaften vom Menschen.

———. 2007. *D10 Sampling Guidelines Manual* (QUING unpublished report). Vienna: Institut für die Wissenschaften vom Menschen.

Krook, Mona Lena, and Fiona Mackay. 2011. "Introduction: Gender, Politics, and Institutions." In *Gender, Politics and Institutions. Towards a Feminist Institutionalism*, edited by Mona Lena Krook and Fiona Mackay, 1–20. New York: Palgrave Macmillan.

Kulawik, Teresa. 2009. "Staking the Frame of a Feminist Discursive Institutionalism." *Politics & Gender* 5(2):262–271.

Laclau, Ernesto, and Chantal Mouffe. 1985. *Hegemony and Socialist Strategy. Towards a Radical Democratic Politics.* London: Verso.

Lang, Sabine. 2009. "Assessing Advocacy: European Transnational Women's Networks and Gender Mainstreaming." *Social Politics* 16(3):327–357.

Lazar, Michelle M. 2000. "Gender, Discourse and Semiotics: The Politics of Parenthood Representations." *Discourse and Society* 11(3):373–400.

——— (ed.). 2005. *Feminist Critical Discourse Analysis: Gender, Power and Ideology in Discourse.* New York: Palgrave Macmillan.

Liebert, Ulrike. 2003. "Between Diversity and Equality: Analysing Europeanisation." In *Gendering Europeanisation*, edited by Ulrike Liebert, 11–46. Brussels: PIE-Peter Lang.

———. 2007. "The European Citizenship Paradox: Renegotiating Equality and Diversity in the New Europe." *Critical Review of International Social and Political Philosophy* 10(4):417–441.

Lilleker, Darren G. 2003. "Interviewing the Political Elite: Navigating a Potential Minefield." *Politics* 23(3):207–214.
Locher, Birgit. 2007. *Trafficking Women in the European Union. Norms, Advocacy-Networks and Policy-Change*. Wiesbaden: VS Verlag Für Sozialwissenschaften.
Lombardo, Emanuela. 2003. "La europeización de la política española de igualdad de género." *Revista Española de Ciencia Política* 9:65–82.
———. 2004. "The Participation of Civil Society in the Debate on the Future of Europe: Rhetorical or Action Frames in the Discourse of the Convention." *Working papers of Universidad de Zaragoza* 3.
———. 2005. "Integrating or Setting the Agenda? Gender Mainstreaming in the European Constitution-Making Process." *Social Politics* 12(3):412–432.
Lombardo, Emanuela, and Petra Meier. 2006. "Gender Mainstreaming in the EU. Incorporating a Feminist Reading?" *European Journal of Women's Studies* 13(2):151–166.
———. 2007. "European Union Gender Policy Since Beijing. Shifting Concepts and Agendas." In *Multiple Meanings of Gender Equality. A Critical Frame Analysis of Gender Policies in Europe*, edited by Mieke Verloo, 51–75. Budapest: Central European University Press.
———. 2008. "Framing Gender Equality in the European Union Political Discourse." *Social Politics* 15(1):101–129.
———. 2009. "Stretching, Bending and Inconsistency in Policy Frames on Gender Equality: Discursive Windows of Opportunity?." In *The Discursive Politics of Gender Equality: Stretching, Bending and Policymaking*, edited by Emanuela Lombardo, Petra Meier, and Mieke Verloo, 138–152. London: Routledge.
Lombardo, Emanuela, Petra Meier, and Mieke Verloo (eds). 2009a. *The Discursive Politics of Gender Equality: Stretching, Bending and Policymaking*. London: Routledge.
———. 2009b. "Stretching and Bending Gender Equality: A Discursive Politics Approach." In *The Discursive Politics of Gender Equality: Stretching, Bending and Policymaking*, edited by Emanuela Lombardo, Petra Meier, and Mieke Verloo, 1–18. London: Routledge.
———. 2009c. "Conclusions: A Critical Understanding of the Discursive Politics of Gender Equality." In *The Discursive Politics of Gender Equality: Stretching, Bending and Policymaking*, edited by Emanuela Lombardo, Petra Meier, and Mieke Verloo, 186–203. London: Routledge.
Lombardo, Emanuela, and Lise Rolandsen Agustín. 2012. "Framing Gender Intersections in the European Union: What Implications for the Quality of Intersectionality in Policies?" *Social Politics* 19(4):482–512.
Lombardo, Emanuela, and Mieke Verloo. 2009. "Stretching Gender Equality to Other Inequalities: Political Intersectionality in European Gender Equality Policies." In *The Discursive Politics of Gender Equality: Stretching, Bending and Policymaking*, edited by Emanuela Lombardo, Petra Meier, and Mieke Verloo, 68–85. London: Routledge.

Mackay, Fiona. 2011. "Conclusion: Towards a Feminist Institutionalism?" In *Gender, Politics and Institutions. Towards a Feminist Institutionalism*, edited by Mona Lena Krook, and Fiona Mackay, 181–196. New York: Palgrave Macmillan.
Mackay, Fiona, and Petra Meier. 2003. "Institutionalism, Change and Gender-Relations: Towards a Feminist New Institutionalism?" Paper presented at the ECPR Joint Sessions, University of Edinburgh, March 28–April 3.
Mahon, Rianne. 2009. "The OECD's Discourse on the Reconciliation of Work and Family Life." *Global Social Policy* 9(2):183–204.
March, James, and Johan P. Olsen. 1989. *Rediscovering Institutions: The Organizational Basis of Politics*. New York: Free Press.
Marks, Gary, and Doug McAdam. 1999. "On the Relationship of Political Opportunities to the Form of Collective Action: The Case of the European Union." In *Social Movements in a Globalizing World*, edited by Donatella Della Porta, Hanspeter Kriesi, and Dieter Rucht, 97–111. New York: St. Martin's Press.
Mazey, Sonia. 2002. "Gender Mainstreaming in the EU: Delivering on an Agenda?" *Feminist Legal Studies* 10:227–240.
McAdam, Doug, John D. McCarthy, and Mayer N. Zald (eds). 1996. *Comparative Perspectives on Social Movements: Political Opportunities, Mobilizing Structures, and Cultural Framings*. Cambridge: Cambridge University Press.
McAdam, Doug, Sidney Tarrow, and Charles Tilly. 2001. *Dynamics of Contention*. Cambridge: Cambridge University Press.
Mendoza, Breny. 2002. "Transnational Feminisms in Question." *Feminist Theory* 3(3):295–314.
Mohanty, Chandra Talpade. 2002. "'Under Western Eyes' Revisited: Feminist Solidarity through Anticapitalist Struggles." *Signs* 28(2):499–535.
Mokre, Monika, and Birte Siim. 2013. "European Public Spheres and Intersectionality." In *Negotiating Gender and Diversity in an Emergent European Public Sphere*, edited by Monika Mokre, and Birte Siim, 43–60. New York: Palgrave Macmillan.
Montoya, Celeste. 2008. "The European Union, Capacity Building, and Transnational Networks: Combating Violence Against Women Through the Daphne Program." *International Organization* 62:359–372.
———. 2013. *From Global to Grassroots: The European Union, Transnational Advocacy, and Combating Violence Against Women*. Oxford: Oxford University Press.
Montoya, Celeste, and Lise Rolandsen Agustín. 2011. "The Othering of Domestic Violence: The EU and Cultural Framings of Violence against Women." Paper presented at the ECPR Second European Conference on Politics and Gender, Central European University, January 13–15.
———. Forthcoming. "The Othering of Domestic Violence: The EU and Cultural Framings of Violence against Women." *Social Politics*.
Naples, Nancy A. 2002. "The Challenges and Possibilities of Transnational Feminist Praxis." In *Women's Activism and Globalization: Linking Local*

Struggles and Transnational Politics, edited by Nancy A. Naples, and Manisha Desai, 267–281. New York: Routledge.

Nullmeier, Frank. 2006. "The Cognitive Turn in Public Policy Analysis." *GFORS Working Paper* 4, Bremen.

Orloff, Ann Shola, and Bruno Palier. 2009. "The Power of Gender Perspectives: Feminist Influence on Policy Paradigms, Social Science, and Social Politics." *Social Politics* 16(4):405–412.

Outshoorn, Joyce, and Johanna Kantola (eds). 2007. *Changing State Feminism*. Basingstoke: Palgrave Macmillan.

Paantjens, Marjolein. 2007. "EU Policies on Violence against Women. Contested Policy Areas and the Potential of a Governance Approach." In *Politics Beyond the State: Actors and Policies in Complex Institutional Settings*, edited by Kris Deschouwer, and M. Theo Jans, 235–250. Brussels: Brussels University Press.

Padamsee, Tasleem J. 2009. "Culture in Connection: Re-Contextualising Ideational Processes in the Analysis of Policy Development." *Social Politics* 16(4):413–445.

Payne, Rodger A. 2001. "Persuasion, Frames and Norm Construction." *European Journal of International Relations* 7(1):37–61.

Phillips, Anne. 1999. *Which Equalities Matter?* Cambridge: Polity Press.

———. 2007. *Multiculturalism without Culture*. Princeton: Princeton University Press.

Pringle, Keith. 2006. "En fallstudie av bruket os missbruket av intersektionalitet." In *Feministiske interventioner. Berättelser om och från en annan värld*, edited by Kerstin Sandall, and Diana Mulinari, 21–53. Stockholm: Atlas Akademi.

Pristed Nielsen, Helene. 2010. "A Common Cause? Anti-racist and gender equality activists in Europe." *EUROSPHERE Working Paper Series* 31.

———. 2013a. "Collaborating on Anti-Discrimination? Anti-Racist and Gender Equality Organisations in Europe." In *Negotiating Gender and Diversity in an Emergent European Public Sphere*, edited by Monika Mokre, and Birte Siim, 179–200. New York: Palgrave Macmillan.

———. 2013b. "Joint Purpose? Intersectionality in the Hands of Anti-racist and Gender Equality Activists in Europe." *Ethnicities* 13(3):276–294.

Pristed Nielsen, Helene, and Lise Rolandsen Agustín. 2013. "Women, Participation and the European Parliament." In *Negotiating Gender and Diversity in an Emergent European Public Sphere*, edited by Monika Mokre, and Birte Siim, 201–222. New York: Palgrave Macmillan.

Pristed Nielsen, Helene, and Cecilie Thun. 2010. "Inclusive Women's Organisations in Denmark and Norway?" *Kvinder, Køn & Forskning* 2–3:62–71.

Pudrovskab, Tetyana, and Myra Marx Ferree. 2004. "Global Activism in 'Virtual Space': The European Women's Lobby in the Network of Transnational Women's NGOs on the Web." *Social Politics* 11(1):117–143.

Rees, Teresa. 1998. *Mainstreaming Equality in the European Union: Education, Training and Labour Market Policies*. London: Routledge.

Richardson, Jeremy (ed.). 2006. *European Union: Power and Policy-Making*. Oxon: Routledge.
Roggeband, Conny, and Mieke Verloo. 2007. "Dutch Women Are Liberated, Migrant Women Are a Problem." *Social Policy and Administration* 41(3):271–288.
Rolandsen Agustín, Lise. 2008. "Civil Society Participation in EU Gender Policy-making: Framing Strategies and Institutional Constraints." *Parliamentary Affairs* 61(3):505–517.
———. 2009. "'It's All about the Women': Intertwining Discourses on Gender Equality, Ethno National Diversity and Identity Constructions among Danish Politicians." *EUROSPHERE Online Working Paper Series* 22.
———. 2010. "Diversity Claims-making in a Transnational Space of Mobilization. The Intersections of Gender and Ethnicity." *Kvinder, Køn & Forskning* 2–3:74–83.
———. 2012. "(Re)defining Women's Interests? Political Struggles over Women's Collective Representation in the Context of the European Parliament." *European Journal of Women's Studies* 19(1):23–40.
Rolandsen Agustín, Lise, and Silke Roth. 2011. "Minority Inclusion, Self Representation and Coalition-Building: The Participation of Minority Women in European Women's Networks." In *Transforming Gendered Well-Being in Europe: The Impact of Social Movements*, edited by Jean-Michel Bonvin, Mercè Renom, and Alison E. Woodward, 231–248. Ashgate, Aldershot.
Rolandsen Agustín, Lise, and Birte Siim. 2013. "Democracy, Diversity and Contestation: A Transnational European Perspective." In *The Democratic Predicament. Cultural Diversity in Europe and India*, edited by Jyotirmaya Tripathy and Sudarsan Padmanabhan, 115–140. New Delhi: Routledge India.
———. Forthcoming a. "Gender Diversities. Practising Intersectionality in the European Union." *Ethnicities*.
———. Forthcoming b. "Intersectionality, Diversity, and Gender Identity: National and European Belongings." In *Challenging identities. Individuals, collective, politics*, edited by Peter Madsen. New York: Routledge.
Roth, Silke. 2007. "Sisterhood and Solidarity? Women's Organizations in the Expanded European Union." *Social Politics* 14(4):460–487.
Ruzza, Carlo. 2004. *Europe and Civil Society: Movement Coalitions and European Governance*. Manchester: Manchester University Press.
———. 2011. "The International Protection Regime for Minorities, the Aftermath of the 2008 Financial Crisis and the EU: New Challenges for Non-State Actors." *International Journal on Minority and Group Rights* 18:219–234.
Schmidt, Vivien A. 2008. "Discursive Institutionalism: The Explanatory Power of Ideas and Discourse." *Annual Review of Political Science* 11:303–26.
———. 2011. "Reconciling Ideas and Institutions through Discursive Institutionalism." In *Ideas and Politics in Social Science Research*,

edited by Daniel Béland, and Robert Henry Cox, 47–64. Oxford: Oxford University Press.
Schmitter, Philippe. 2000. *How to Democratize the European Union…and Why Bother?* Lanham: Rowman & Littlefield.
Schwenken, Helen. 2009. "Migrant Women: Negotiating Rights and Recognition in the Political and Legal Framework of the European Union." In *Diversity in the European Union*, edited by Elisabeth Prügl, and Markus Thiel, 95–111. New York: Palgrave Macmillan.
Scott, James C. 1999. *Domination and the Arts of Resistance. Hidden Transcripts.* New Haven: Yale University Press.
Siim, Birte. 2009. "Citizenship, Diversity and Gender Equality: National Belongings and Intersections of Gender, Ethnicity and Religion." Paper presented at the ECPR Joint Sessions, University of Lisbon, April 14–19.
Snow, David A., E. Burke Rochford, Steven K. Worden, and Robert D. Benford. 1986. "Frame Alignment Processes, Micromobilization, and Movement Participation." *American Sociological Review* 51:464–481.
Soysal, Yasemin Nuhoglu. 2004. "Rights, Identity and Claims-Making." Paper presented at the Justice Across Cultures conference, Brandeis University, March 8.
Squires, Judith. 2006. "Diversity: A Politics of Difference or a Management Strategy?" Paper presented at the Research seminar on Intersectional Analysis, Aalborg University, January 18–20.
———. 2007. *The New Politics of Gender Equality.* Basingstoke: Palgrave Macmillan.
———. 2010. "Beyond Multiple Inequalities: Transversal Intersectionality, Diversity Mainstreaming and Participative Democracy." *Kvinder, Køn & Forskning* 2–3:85–93.
Stark, Evan. 2007. *Coercive Control: How Men Entrap Women in Personal Life.* Oxford: Oxford University Press.
Stephenson, Mary-Ann. 2005. "With Friends Like Anna Zaborska." *The Guardian* February 7.
Stratigaki, Maria. 2005. "Gender Mainstreaming vs Positive Action: An ongoing Conflict in EU Gender Equality Policy." *European Journal of Women's Studies* 12(2):165–86.
Strid, Sofia. 2009. *Gendered Interests in the European Union. The European Women's Lobby and the Organisation and Representation of Women's Interests.* Doctoral dissertation, Örebro University.
Tarrow, Sidney. 1998. *Power in Movement: Social Movements and Contentious Politics.* Cambridge: Cambridge University Press.
Tarrow, Sidney. 2005. *The New Transnational Activism.* Cambridge: Cambridge University Press.
Thiel, Markus, and Elisabeth Prügl. 2009. "Understanding Diversity in the European Integration Project." In *Diversity in the European Union*, edited by Elisabeth Prügl, and Markus Thiel, 3–19. New York: Palgrave Macmillan.

Van der Vleuten, Anna. 2007. *The Price of Gender Equality. Member States and Governance in the European Union*. Aldershot: Ashgate.
Vassiliadou, Myria. 2008. "EWL and BEWC, alliances for equal opportunities in Europe, from a feminist perspective." EWL contribution to the BEWC roundtable The Role of Black Women in an all inclusive Europe, challenges faced by Black European communities, Brussels, September 9.
Verloo, Mieke. 2001. "Another Velvet Revolution? Gender Mainstreaming and the Politics of Implementation." *IWM Working Paper* 5.
———. 2005a. "Displacement and Empowerment: Reflections on the Concept and Practice of the Council of Europe Approach to Gender Mainstreaming and Gender Equality." *Social Politics* 12(3):344–365.
———. 2005b. "Mainstreaming Gender Equality in Europe: A Critical Frame Analysis Approach." *The Greek Review of Social Research* 117B:11–34.
———. 2006. "Multiple Inequalities, Intersectionality and the European Union." *European Journal of Women's Studies* 13(3):211–228.
——— (ed.). 2007. *Multiple Meanings of Gender Equality. A Critical Frame Analysis of Gender Policies in Europe*. Budapest: Central European University Press.
Verloo, Mieke, Emanuela Lombardo, and María Bustelo. 2007. "Conclusions on Framing Gender Inequality as a Policy Problem in Europe." In *Multiple Meanings of Gender Equality. A Critical Frame Analysis of Gender Policies in Europe*, edited by Mieke Verloo, 281–301. Budapest: Central European University Press.
Walby, Sylvia. 2004. "The European Union and Gender Equality: Emergent Varieties of Gender Regime." *Social Politics* 11(1):4–29.
———. 2005. "Gender Mainstreaming: Productive Tensions in Theory and Practice." *Social Politics* 12(3):321–343.
———. 2009. *Globalization and Inequalities: Complexity and Contested Modernities*. London: Sage.
Walby, Sylvia, Jo Armstrong, and Sofia Strid. 2009. *D42 Conceptual Framework for Gender+ Equality Policies in a Multicultural Context* (QUING unpublished report). Vienna: Institut für die Wissenschaften vom Menschen.
Wijers, Marjan. 2006. "European Union Policies on Trafficking in Women." In *Gender Policies in the European Union*, edited by Mariagrazia Rossilli, 209–229. New York: Peter Lang.
Williams, Fiona. 2003. "Contesting 'Race' and Gender in the European Union: A Multi-layered Recognition Struggle for Voice and Visibility." In *Recognition Struggles and Social Movements. Contested Identities, Agency and Power*, edited by Barbara Hobson, 121–144. New York: Cambridge University Press.
Wodak, Ruth (ed.). 1997. *Gender and Discourse*. London: Sage.
Wodak, Ruth. 2002. "The Discourse-Historical Approach." In *Methods of Critical Discourse Analysis*, edited by Ruth Wodak, and Michael Meyer, 63–95. London: Sage.

———. 2007. "Discourses in European Union organizations: Aspects of Access, Participation and Exclusion." *Text & Talk* 27(5–6):655–680.
Wodak, Ruth, and Gilbert Weiss. 2005. "Analyzing European Union Discourses. Theories and Applications." In *A New Agenda in (Critical) Discourse Analysis*, edited by Ruth Wodak, and Paul Chilton, 121–136. Amsterdam: John Benjamins Publishing.
Woodward, Alison E. 2004. "Building Velvet Triangles: Gender and Informal Governance." In *Informal Governance in the European Union*, edited by Thomas Christiansen, and Simona Piattoni, 76–93. Cheltenham: Edward Elgar.
———. 2006. "Strained Bedfellows: Multi-level Interactions between Transnational Gender and Sexual Organizations in the European Union." Paper presented at the Sixth European Gender Research Conference, University of Lodz, August 31–September 3.
———. 2007. "Challenges for Intersectionality in the Transnational Organization of European Equality Movements: Forming Platforms and Maintaining Turf in Today's European Union." In *Gender Orders Unbound? Globalisation, Restructuring and Reciprocity*, edited by Ilse Lenz, Charlotte Illrich, and Barbara Fersch, 167–185. Leverkusen: Barbara Budrich Publishers.
———. 2008. "Too Late for Gender Mainstreaming? Taking Stock in Brussels." *Journal of European Social Policy* 18(3):289–302.
Woodward, Alison E., and Joke Wiercx. 2003. "Cross Dressing in the EU Lobby: Interactions between Transnational Gender and Sexuality Movements and the Future of Europe." Paper presented at the European Sociological Association Sixth Conference, Hanse Wissenschaftskolleg, September 25.
Young, Iris Marion. 2000. *Inclusion and Democracy*. Oxford: Oxford University Press.
Yuval-Davis, Nira. 2006. "Human/Women's Rights and Feminist Transversal Politics." In *Global Feminism. Transnational Women's Activism, Organising, and Human Rights*, edited by Myra Marx Ferree, and Aili Mari Tripp, 275–295. New York: New York University Press.
———. 2007. "Intersectionality, Citizenship and Contemporary Politics of Belonging." *Critical Review of International, Social and Political Philosophy* 10(4):561–574.
Zippel, Kathrin. 2004. "Transnational Advocacy Networks and Policy Cycles in the European Union: The Case of Sexual Harassment." *Social Politics* 11(1):57–85.
———. 2006. *The Politics of Sexual Harassment: A Comparative Study of the United States, the European Union and Germany*. Cambridge: Cambridge University Press.

Index

Achaleke, Beatrice, 194n15
advocacy coalitions, 19, 91, 93
agenda setting, 19, 28, 80, 82, 84, 93, 96, 99–100, 112, 159
Ahrens, Petra, 92
Amsterdam Treaty (1997), 120
   article 13, 2–3, 21, 49–50, 52, 55, 70, 89, 187n5
   article 152, 121, 126
   codecision and, 35
   Employment Framework Directive, 51
   gender mainstreaming and, 101
   Goods and Services Directive, 51
   Racial Equality Directive, 51
   Schwenken on, 71
Armstrong, Jo, 155

Bacchi, Carol L., 16, 103, 188n14
Beck, Ulrich, 47
Black European Women's Council (BEWC), 68–70, 73–4, 78–83, 189n17, 194n13, 194n15
boomerang patterns, 92
Bustelo, María, 195n8

Caiani, Manuela, 192n2
capacity building, 69, 92, 129–30, 194n2
Carbin, Maria, 154–9
Cichowski, Rachel A., 56, 191n4
citizenship, 46, 75–9, 82–4, 123, 145, 147–8, 158, 160, 162–3
claims making, 40, 47, 54–5, 63–7, 72–3, 76–9, 157
coalition building, 80, 83–4

codecision, 35–6, 90, 126, 134
Commission. *See* European Commission (EC)
Community Action Programme to Combat Discrimination, 51–2, 59
constructivist perspective, 12–13, 19, 32–3, 89, 94, 191n6
contextualization, 9–10, 13, 18–20, 25, 42, 45–8, 99, 135–8, 158–9
Council. *See* European Council
Critical Frame Analysis (CFA), 13, 16–19, 21, 27, 33, 97–100, 118, 129, 137–8, 159, 161, 163
Cullen, Pauline, 83
culturalization, 143–4, 146, 151–2, 155, 162

DAPHNE programs, 18, 89, 97, 99–100, 103, 105, 195n6, 198n2, 198n7
   culturalization and, 151–2
   degendering and, 135–7, 162
   first project of, 198n3
   funding of NGOs by, 130
   gender-based violence and, 136–7, 139, 149, 152
   history of, 110–15
   ideas and, 133–40
   legal basis for, 90, 117–40
   migrant women and, 149
   Montoya on, 195n13
   projects selected for grants, 118, 129–33, 199n8

DAPHNE programs—*Continued*
  public health framing and, 90,
    110–15, 117–21, 124–39
  WAVE and, 193n9
degendering, 4–6, 21–3, 39, 53,
    57–8, 97, 161–2, 169
  defined, 5–6
  human rights centered approach
    and, 123
  implications of, 129–33
  policies on gender-based violence
    and, 101
  strategic, 126, 134–6
Della Porta, Donatella, 192n2
democracy, 44–5, 55, 61, 81–2,
    189–90n18, 195n12
democratic pluralism, 169
Diamantopoulou, Anna, 110
Directorate General Employment,
  Social Affairs and Equal
  Opportunities (DG
  Employment), 53–4, 58, 62,
  85–6, 122–3, 188n11, 189n17
Directorate General Justice (DG
  Justice), 53, 121–3, 129,
  188n11, 189n17, 198n2
discourse analysis, 13–15, 19–20,
  141–2, 190n1
discourses, defined, 14–17, 27
diversity:
  institutionalization of, 25, 46
  intersectionality and, 21, 50–4, 57
  making room for, 6, 43–4
  mobilization and, 42–5, 50, 77,
    161, 166
domestic violence, 96–7, 101–3,
  110, 112, 114, 118, 131, 147,
  150–3, 163, 196n18, 197n22
Dostal, Jörg Michael, 28
Dryzek, John S., 27
Dutroux affair, 110

enlargement of EU, 3, 56, 101, 166,
  193n8
"Equality and Non-Discrimination
  in an Enlarged European
  Union" (EC Green Paper), 50,
  52, 58–9, 64, 70, 191n1
European Commission (EC), 11,
  164–5
  citizen participation and, 61
  codecision and, 35, 90
  culturalization and, 146, 151–2
  DAPHNE programs and, 89–90,
    110–15, 117–39
  DG Employment, 53–4, 58, 62,
    85–6, 122–3, 188n11, 189n17
  DG Justice, 53, 121–3, 129,
    188n11, 189n17, 198n2
  efficiency of (preference for one
    voice), 45, 50, 65, 72, 85–6
  exclusionary framings and, 149–52
  Gender Equality Unit, 123,
    188n11
  Green Paper on Equality and
    Nondiscrimination, 50, 52,
    58–9, 64, 70, 191n1
  integrated approach of, 41–2,
    52–3, 58–9, 64, 70
European Council:
  as closed institution, 66
  culturalization and, 146
  DAPHNE programs and, 90,
    105–6, 112–14, 117–25,
    128, 137
  decision making and voting
    procedures in, 34–6
European Disability Forum, 191n5
European Institute for Gender
  Equality (EIGE), 53, 188n11
European Network Against Racism
  (ENAR), 64, 191n5
European Network of Migrant
  Women (ENoMW), 81
European Older People's Platform,
  191n5
European Parliament (EP), 18, 50,
  54, 81, 84, 106, 117–18, 168,
  188n11
  civil society organizations and,
    61, 108
  as co-legislator with EC, 35

composition of, 3, 34, 82
DAPHNE program and, 90, 125–40
FEMM Committee of, 54, 102–3, 106–8, 125, 148, 150, 167–9, 188n11, 189n17, 196n17, 197n22, 200n1
gender-based violence and, 102–3, 105–10, 113–14, 124
inclusion of contestation within, 66
level of disagreement within, 102–3
Zero Tolerance campaign of, 103, 105–6, 109, 119, 148
European Social Forum, 47
European Truck Tour, 52
European Women Lawyers' Association (EWLA), 64, 85, 189n17
European Women's Lobby (EWL):
BEWC and, 80–3
cultural framings and, 154–5
ENoMW and, 81
ethnic minorities and, 70
feminism of, 62
founding and history of, 62, 198n5
funding of, 200n1
lobbying of, 47, 126, 129
membership of, 68–70
minority inclusion and, 59, 80, 86
mission of, 68
multiple discrimination and, 57, 60, 65, 70–2, 164
privileged position of, 11, 42, 84–5
European Year of Combating Violence against Women, 114
European Year of Equal Opportunities for All, 52, 73
European Year of Intercultural Dialogue, 69, 73

female genital mutilation, 96, 114, 145, 149–54, 197n22
feminist institutionalism, 190n3–4
feminist political analysis, 29–31
Fernández de Vega, Ana, 195n8
Ferree, Myra Marx:
on CFA, 19
on citizenship, 78, 158
on EU intersectionality, 9, 42, 45, 78, 145
on feminism of EWL, 62
on need for contextualization, 9, 45
on opportunity structures, 45–6
on resonance of frames, 16
on strategic framing, 169
frame analysis:
contextualization and, 18–20
criticism of, 188–9n14
defined, 2, 16, 188n13
discourse analysis and, 14–17
discursive opportunity structures and, 38
gendered institutionalism and, 29–32
history of, 12
ideas and, 10–11
power relations and, 15
See also Critical Frame Analysis (CFA); frames
frames:
defined, 12, 14
as distinguished from discourses, 14–17
foreground and background, 136–40
gender inequality, 22, 90, 98, 106–7, 109, 114–17, 124–7, 130–2, 138–9, 145, 148, 163
human rights, 22, 78, 90, 100–1, 109, 111–13, 117, 119–28, 132–4, 145
implicit gender inequality, 130–5
public health, 22, 90, 100–1, 109, 111, 113, 117–21, 124–39, 145, 199n11
See also Critical Frame Analysis (CFA); frame analysis
Fraser, Nancy, 30

gender mainstreaming, 1, 58, 101, 187n3, 192n10
gender inequality, frame of, 22, 90, 98, 106–7, 109, 114–15, 117, 124–7, 130–2, 138–9, 145, 148, 163
gender-based violence, 96, 98–9, 103, 146–9. *See also* DAPHNE programs; domestic violence
gendered discursive institutionalism, 19, 26, 29–33, 136, 159, 190n2
gendered "other," 6, 22, 141–56
globalization, 191n8
Goffman, Erving, 12, 138
Gradin, Anita, 110

Hancock, Ange-Marie, 85
hard law, 95, 187n1
hierarchy of (in)equalities, 21, 56–8, 60
Hobson, Barbara, 76
human trafficking. *See* trafficking

immigration, 22, 77–9, 81, 144–54
in/exclusion, 5–6, 15, 26–7, 30, 39, 65–6, 93–4, 159, 161
  intersectionality and, 21–2, 89, 141–6, 152–5
  legitimate claims makers and, 44, 63
  privileging of women's organizations and, 61
institutional advocacy, 45, 63
institutionalisms:
  discursive, 13, 25, 27, 190n2
  gendered discursive, 19, 26, 29–33, 136, 159, 190n2
  types of, 27–8
institutionalization:
  contextualized, 18
  of diversity, 25, 46
  of frames, 13, 18–19, 22, 32, 39, 117–18, 133, 136–9, 158–61
  of ideas, 25, 39, 46, 63, 91, 94

of intersectionality, 2, 5, 9–10, 21, 42–3, 50, 158–60
mobilization and, 6–9, 20–2, 47–8, 157, 161
of multiple discrimination, 49–50, 54
of power relations, 30, 40
International Lesbian and Gay Association (ILGA), 64, 191n5
International Relations, field of, 13
internationalization, 37, 166, 191n8
intersectionality:
  contextualizing, 9–10, 45–8
  defined, 8–10, 21, 41–2
  democracy and, 44–5
  as distinguished from multiple discrimination, 9
  diversity and, 21, 50–4, 57
  EU model of, 9, 22, 42, 45, 78, 145, 157–66
  in/exclusionary, 21–2, 89, 141–6, 152–5
  institutionalization of, 2, 5, 9–10, 21, 42–3, 50, 158–60
  mobilization and, 6–8, 43
intersectionality impact assessment, 86

Jarvis, Yvette, 194n13
Jenson, Jane, 63

Kantola, Johanna, 14, 25, 30, 34, 57, 85–6, 101, 112, 154, 190n1, 191n5
Keck, Margaret E., 91–2
Kenny, Meryl, 31–3
Krizsán, Andrea, 101, 135
Krook, Mona Lena, 190n14
Kulawik, Teresa, 30, 32, 38, 137

labor-market participation of women, 1–2, 11, 33, 46, 77
Laclau, Ernesto, 27
legitimate actors, 63

legitimate claims makers, 44–5, 63–6, 163, 189–90n18
Liebert, Ulrike, 34
Lisbon Treaty (2009), 36, 114, 187n5, 195n12
Locher, Birgit, 92–4, 109, 124–5, 138, 191n6
Lombardo, Emanuela, 85, 101, 137

Maastricht Treaty (1993), 35
Mackay, Fiona, 31–3
Mahon, Rianne, 63
Marks, Gary, 73
McAdam, Doug, 73
Meier, Petra, 101
mobilization, transnational:
　CFA and, 19
　constraints on, 67, 72–6, 79, 157–8
　diversity and, 42–5, 50, 77, 161, 166
　institutionalization and, 6–9, 20–2, 47–8, 157, 161
　opportunities for, 36, 45, 54–6
　selfmobilization, 84
　simultaneous national and global, 108
　transnational compared with national, 46–7
Mokre, Monika, 199n1
Montoya, Celeste, 92, 106, 130, 148, 194n2, 195n13
Mouffe, Chantal, 27
multiple discrimination:
　and Amsterdam Treaty, article 13, 21, 49
　culturalization and, 144
　defined, 2–3, 9, 40–1
　degendering and, 89
　EC's integrated approach to, 59, 64
　effects of, 70–2, 85, 101, 135, 144, 158
　EWL and, 57, 70–2, 60, 164

increased emphasis on, 4–6, 10, 160, 187n4
institutionalization of, 49–66
reaction to, 58–60

new institutionalism, 10, 26–33, 123, 191n5
New Women for Europe (NWFE), 168–9, 189n17
nongovernmental organizations (NGOs), 5, 100, 129–30, 168, 189n16, 197n19
　diversity frame and, 163–4
　EC and, 41–2, 59
　funding, 59, 90, 110, 129–30, 193n8
　managing vs. transcending differences, 83
　See also European Women's Lobby (EWL); Women Against Violence Europe (WAVE)
nonviolence as a trait of Europeanness, 146
norm diffusion, 91–3, 194n2
Nousiainen, Kevät, 85

opportunity structures, 25–6, 28, 40, 45, 48, 54–5, 73, 191n5, 194n3
　discursive, 11, 16, 33, 38–9, 46, 90, 133, 157
　political, 36–8, 91–4, 98–9
organizational discourse, 28–9

Parliament. *See* European Parliament (EP)
Phillips, Anne, 66, 154
policy actors, 34–5, 93
policy negotiation process, 120–1
power, use of the term, 189–90n18
power asymmetries, 22, 30, 32, 40, 126
Prügl, Elisabeth, 71
Pudrovska, Tetyana, 62

Quality in Gender Equality+ Policies (QUING) project, 19, 97–8, 188n9, 189n15, 190n19, 195n8

Reding, Viviane, 124
resonance, 2, 11, 16, 28, 63–6, 127–9, 159–60
Ruzza, Carlo, 3, 93

Schmidt, Vivien A., 27–9, 33–5
Schwenken, Helen, 71
Scott, James C., 138
selfrepresentation, 82–4
sensitizing questions, 97, 195n9
sexual harassment, 92, 96, 196n18, 197n20
Siim, Birte, 199n1
Sikkink, Kathryn, 91
social movements, 7, 12–13, 16, 36–7, 55, 91–3, 166, 191n8
Social Movement Studies, 13
soft law and policy, 1, 21, 90, 95, 100, 137–8, 140, 187n1
Soysal, Yasemin Nuhoglu, 76–7
Squires, Judith, 40, 43–4, 65
Strid, Sofia, 62, 95, 155, 192n9
structural gender inequality, 22, 90, 98, 106–7, 109, 114–15, 117, 124–7, 130–2, 138–9, 145, 148, 163

Tarrow, Sidney, 28, 36–7, 191n5, 191n8
Theorin, Maj Britt, 110
Thiel, Markus, 71
trafficking, 92–3, 96, 110, 150, 151, 195–6n14, 196n18, 199n11
transnationalism:
 activism 37, 55, 62, 66–8, 74, 192n2
 advocacy networks, 91–2
 norm diffusion, 91–3, 194n2
 political opportunity structures, 36–7. *See also* opportunity structures

space, 8, 19, 21, 25–6, 40, 43, 45–50, 54–5, 159, 161, 165
See also mobilization, transnational
Treaty of Rome (1957), 1, 17, 191n4

umbrella pattern, 92
United Nations (UN), 4, 67, 90, 96, 125, 193n9

Van der Vleuten, Anna, 187n4, 188n8
Vassiliadou, Myria, 193n7
velvet triangles, 91–2
Verloo, Mieke, 16–17, 85, 189n15, 190n19
violence against women.
 See gender-based violence
visa policies, 74–6
Vogel-Polsky, Eliane, 187n2

Walby, Sylvia, 95–6, 155
What's the Problem Represented to be (WPR), 16–17, 27
Wiercx, Joke, 55, 59, 192n2
Williams, Fiona, 70
Wodak, Ruth, 142
Women Against Violence Europe (WAVE), 75, 85, 126–9, 189n17, 193n9, 198n5
Woodward, Alison, 55–6, 59, 63, 192n2
World Health Organization (WHO), 125

Young, Iris, 44
Young Women from Minorities (WFM), 83–4, 189n17, 193n10
Yuval-Davis, Nira, 47

Zaborska, Anna, 167–8
Zero Tolerance of Violence against Women Campaign, 103, 105–6, 109, 119, 148
Zippel, Kathrin, 91–3, 95

Printed by Printforce, United Kingdom